# DRIVING HOLIDAYS
## IN THE HIMALAYAS

# Bhutan

*"Climb the mountains and get their good tidings....
The winds will blow their own freshness into you,
and the storms their energy, while cares will drop off
like autumn leaves".*

John Muir

*Author*
## Koko Singh
*Editor*
Annu Sharma
*Photo Editor*
Ipshita Barua
*Photographs*
Annu Sharma
Ipshita Barua
*Design*
Pranab Dutta

*Rupa & Co*

Published 2007 by

*Rupa & Co*

7/16, Ansari Road, Daryaganj,
New Delhi 110 002

Sales Centers:
Allahabad    Bangalore    Chandigarh
Chennai      Hyderabad    Jaipur
Kathmandu    Kolkata      Mumbai
Pune

Printed in India by
Gopsons Papers Ltd.
A-14, Sector 60, Noida

Design and pre-press:
Great Latitude, New Delhi, India
www.greatlatitude.com

Cover : Taktsang Monastery, Paro

**ACKNOWLEDGEMENTS**

We are extremely grateful for the
support provided by the Department
of Tourism in Bhutan. In particular for
the inputs from Director General Lhatu
Wangchuk and Chimmy Pem. We would
also like to thank the Department of
Tourism for making available to us
some photographs of historical figures
featured in their publication 'Icons of
Awakened Energy'.

Of course the book would not have
been finished if Tashi Payden Tshering
had not spent hours poring over the text
for accuracy. Also thanks to Nado and
Pem Zam for their help and entertaining
company during our visit.

Our first journey would not have been
possible without the generosity of Rajiv
and Malini Puri who lent us their brand
new Innova, in which we travelled all
the way from Siliguri, through Bhutan,
finishing our journey in Guwahati.

# CONTENTS

Punakha Dzong

**D**RIVING Holidays in the Himalayas is a series of books that endeavour to give the reader a glimpse of many exciting, exotic locales that can be easily accessed by road and hopes to provide enough insight to make your trip a comfortable and memorable one.

The books already published in this series have extensively explored regions within the Indian Himalayas — Ladakh, Zanskar, Himachal Pradesh, Uttarakhand and Sikkim.

True to the series, this book too focuses especially on travellers who are fond of driving, have their own wheels (two, four — or even hired will do!), and love the mountains. Given the time constraints of our lives today, each book is designed to cover a fair degree of terrain in a week to ten days. Although it does not aim to visit every place possible in a region, it certainly traverses a reasonable cross-section. It reflects the author's own preferences of historic and picturesque places to visit and also makes staying recommendations ■

# INTRODUCTION

BHUTAN is indeed an extraordinary country – a verdant paradise of just over 600,000 people; an enlightened Buddhist monarchy with one foot firmly set in its culturally rich past while the other seeks an appropriate future. Landlocked and geographically isolated, the country began to tentatively reach out into the twentieth century only recently with roads being built in the 1960s and TV, Internet introduced only in 1999. At the turn of the century, the total number of tourists who visited the country was just six thousand! No small wonder then that Bhutan is often referred to as the last Shangri La – the fictional valley that James Hilton conjured for us in his classic novel *Lost Horizons* in the 1930s. In the novel the task of the high lama was to ensure this valley remained well hidden, to protect its people and their culture and traditions from the corrupting influences of the modern world.

In the fictional lama's words:

"We may expect no mercy, but we may faintly hope for neglect. Here we shall stay with our books and our music and our meditations, covering the frail elegances of a dying age, and seeking such wisdom as men will need when their passions are all spent. We have a heritage to cherish and bequeath. Let us take what pleasure we may until that time comes."

Hilton obviously drew inspiration for his Shangri La from the Tibetan belief of 'beyuls'; hidden valleys scattered throughout the Himalayas and chosen by Guru Padmasambhava to remain havens of tranquility and serve as safe refuge for followers of Buddhism during times of turmoil and threatening calamities. There are several valleys in Bhutan that live in a time warp even today, ready for the time they will be called upon to act as the vaults for the culture of humanity. Indeed it is this strong sense of destiny that is imbued in the psyche of the nation – since its birth in the fifteenth century – that is responsible for the extremely wary and cautious stance it has adopted while engaging the global world of today.

The moot question is 'What does this mean for you, dear reader and potential visitor?' Further chapters in the book will provide you with an outline of the history and religion of Bhutan but nothing you read will compensate for the incredible experience of travelling in the country yourself. This is a land of superb vistas ranging from the alpine to the tropical and magnificent architecture that is epitomised in the dzongs (fortresses), which stretch across

Black Hat Dance

the country. Come prepared to meet and interact with a people who are dignified, extremely friendly, hospitable and disciplined; their religion and culture permeates every aspect of their life. Bhutan is ranked as one of the safest tourist destinations on our planet — it has an extremely low crime rate and people do not exhibit that irritating, invasive curiousity that you find in many other destinations.

The entire population is uniformly clad in their smart traditional attire. The national dress — 'gho' for men and the 'kira' for women — is almost de riguer during the daytime but jeans and skirts come out in the

evenings and nights. The capital Thimphu has a pretty active night life with a couple of discos open till the wee hours of the morning.

Bhutan is an orderly country, particularly when compared with its large unruly neighbour India, and

**Near Pele La**

if you follow the system (which is pretty easy to do), you can travel far and wide without any hassles. The national language is Dzongkha and, as our guide succintly put it, "the international language is English"! English is understood and spoken in most of the western region but a guide who interprets is useful in the central and eastern section. Good accommodation is available at the main tourist destinations but the local cuisine can get monotonous over a long stay.

This is a holy land with many tales of miracles and replete with myths and legends. Almost eighty percent of the population lives in villages and small hamlets, many located a few hours or even a day from the roadhead. They live off the land, following agrarian practices established many generations ago. Although Bhutan cannot be deemed a 'rich' country, the fourth King Jigme Singye Wangchuck introduced a unique philosophy of governance which seeks another kind of prosperity – a high Gross National Happiness (GNH), rather than following only the conventional GNP measure! If you are looking for a spectacular destination with a living culture that goes back centuries, head to this enthralling Land of the Thunder Dragon before it becomes just another beautiful place to visit! ■

# THE HIMALAYAS

THROUGH the ages, the Himalayas have been revered by millions of Indians as the abode of the gods. The early 'rishis' (sages), referred to them as "the expanse of the two arms of the Supreme Being", suggestive of the whole world being locked in the Himalayas' divine embrace.

Writing in the fifth century, Kalidas, the renowned poet, has an evocative but apt description:

*In the northern quarter is divine Himalayas,*
  *the lord of the Mountains,*
  *reaching from eastern to western Ocean,*
  *firm as a rod to measure the earth....*
  *There demigods rest in the shade of clouds,*
  *which spread like a girdle below the peaks, but when the rains disturb them,*
  *they fly to sunlit summits....*

It is here that Shiva, the great god of destruction, found solace after the death of his consort Sati, and atoned for almost destroying the world with his dance, the 'Tandava Nritya'. After wooing the bereaved Shiva for over a thousand years, Parvati, the daughter of the mountains succeeded in winning his love. The Himalayas are studded with temples dedicated to Shiva and Parvati, and every year devotees in untold numbers travel hundreds, if not thousands, of kilometers, to visit their 'abode'.

In the words of the *Skanda Purana*:

"As the sun dries the morning dew, so are the sins of man dissipated at the sight of the Himalaya".

The snow capped Himalayan mountain peaks, wreathed in silent dignity and with a timeless, meditative quality to their stillness, have always lured the spiritually inclined. The profusion of temples and monasteries that dot the landscape of this range stand mute witness to their quest to commune with a higher force. Though a majority of the population in the Himalayan region follows Hinduism, a little known fact is that the physical area under Buddhist influence is close to fifty percent of its area! There are few enclaves here where the Buddhist culture reigns supreme and besides Ladakh and Sikkim in India, there is Bhutan. This is the only independent Himalayan country where Buddhism is the state religion.

Geologically speaking, the Himalayas are the youngest mountain range in the world and are actually still growing – up to 0.8cm annually. Samples

Singyephu Temple —
a 'retreat' at Taktsang

# THE HIMALAYAS

Mt. Everest seen from the Druk Air flight

extracted from the slopes of Mt. Everest confirm that in the past millennia, what is today the world's highest and longest (East to West) mountain range was once part of a vast ocean bed and the 'Roof of the World', Tibet, was the sea bed of the ancient Sea of Tethys!!

Eighty million years ago, in the period when dinosaurs roamed the earth – the Jurassic Age – the earth's land mass split into two great continents, Laurasia in the northern hemisphere and Gondwanaland in the southern hemisphere. Later the land mass, that is the Indian subcontinent, broke away from Gondwanaland and floated across the Earth's surface till it ran into Asia! This

titanic geological collision between the hard volcanic rock of India and Asia's soft sedimentary crust resulted in the creation of all the Asian mountain ranges such as the Karakoram, Hindu Kush, Pamir, as also the Tien Shan and Kun Lun. This process took between five and seven million years and the fact that the Himalayas are at the front of the continental collision accounts for their dwarfing the other ranges and for their continued upward movement.

The Himalayas stretch 2500km from Nanga Parbat (Pakistan) in the West to Namche Barwa (Arunachal Pradesh, India), in the East. The range boasts fourteen peaks in excess of 26,200ft/8000m, including Mt. Everest which at 29,028ft/8850m is the highest mountain in the world. The highest peak in Bhutan is a lofty 24,000ft/7314m.

The Himalayan range is actually three almost parallel mountain systems. At the top lies the Great Himalayan Range with perennial snow peaks rising to heights in excess of 16,500ft/5000m, preceded by the Middle Himalayan Range of peaks averaging between 13,000-16,500ft/4000-5000m. The foothills, or the Lower Himalayan Range, are the ranges bordering the plains with mountains up to 8000ft/2500m in height and, regrettably, it is only in this third and lowest, layer of mountains that most of our driving journeys are confined!

The Himalayas are also the source of the three major river systems of the subcontinent – the Indus, the Ganges, and the Brahmaputra. All these originate from glaciers, and are joined by many tributaries. The rivers of Bhutan form part of the Brahmaputra River system ■

# GEOGRAPHY AND LOCATION

BHUTAN is a landlocked South Asian country, covering an area of around 39,000 sq.km. It stretches 300km from East to West, while the North-South axis is around 140km. On its boundaries to the East, West and South lie the Indian states of Arunachal Pradesh, Sikkim and West Bengal/Assam respectively while to the North lies Tibet's Chumbi valley, sandwiched between North Bhutan and Sikkim.

There is no definitive version of how the country got its name – the most common interpretration is that it is derived from Bhot-stan, the land of the Bhotias (in the ancient Indian language Sanskrit, people originally from Tibet were called 'bhotia'). This was later corrupted by the early British explorers to Bootan or Bhotan. Another theory suggests that the name evolved from Bhotanta ('end of Tibet') or from Bhu-uttan meaning 'highland'. In the Dzongkha language Bhutanese refer to their country as Druk Yul (Land of the Thunder Dragon) and themselves as Drukpas. According to legend, when Tsangpa Gyarey Yeshe Dorje was consecrating a monastery in Tibet, he heard loud claps of thunder which he believed was the druk (dragon) and so chose to call the monastery 'Druk'. The religious sect he founded was called Drukpa Kagyu – this became Bhutan's state

Punakha valley

# GEOGRAPHY AND LOCATION

Wash your sins away!

religion and the country was thus referred to as Druk Yul.

Other ancient names for Bhutan were Lho Jong Men Jong (The Southern Region of Medicinal Herbs) and Menjong Gyalkhab (Land of Medicinal Plants), as a tribute to their rich flora.

Topographically ascending from the South to the North, the land has often been likened to a staircase! It climbs from the plains and foothills which lie at a lowly 985ft/300m to the Himalayan peaks in the North that are as high as 22,960ft/7000m and more. Technically, Bhutan is in the central Himalayan region, bordered by the high Himalayas running West to East on the northern border. However, the land is further sub-divided by a series of mountain ranges that are 13,120 -16,400ft/4000–5000m high (like the Pele La range), and run North to South. These create a series of valleys, with formidable ridges separating them, and each valley is a veritable independent eco-system. They were linked to each other by mountain trails till a motorable road was completed in 1975 linking Paro in the West with Trashigang in the East – an extremely scenic 609km or so journey that allows you to traverse the country in three days. Called the East-West Highway, or the Lateral Road, this narrow but well surfaced mountain road takes many a twist and turn and some sharp ascents leading you over spectacular high passes (some over 9840ft/3000m), and through fascinating and dramatic landscape.

The country can be divided horizontally into four broad zones.

In the South are the 'duars' which are fertile plains lying between two rivers. The word 'duar' or 'dwar' is Sanskrit for entrance or gate. With an elevation of 100m, the region is almost flat and though originally a dense tropical jungle, it has now given way to paddy fields and tea gardens.

This first zone is only 15-30km deep and beyond it lies the second zone where the low foothills begin to rise. This is part of the terai region which extends from India, through Nepal, to Bhutan. With altitudes ranging between 985–3280ft/300-1000m this area is dominated by tropical jungles of broad-leaf evergreens, interspersed with some fertile terraced cultivation. There are also plantations of cardamom, oranges and bananas. Population is denser here and the border trading towns of Phuentsholing and Gelephu lie in this zone. The climate ranges from warm and humid to damp and misty in the hills.

Further North of this is an amazing matrix of broad valleys and densely forested hillsides with

# GEOGRAPHY AND LOCATION

**CHINA (Tibet)**

Terigang 7300
Tsendagang 7100
Masangang 7165
Jejegangphugang 7100
Table Mo 7100 (Zo
Gangchenta 6794
Gangla Karchung 6395
Thangza
Limithang
Geche
Chebesa
Bjichu Dramo
Gasa
Lingzhi
Mo Chu
Pho Chu
Jichu Drakye 6794
Rinchendzoe 5269
Jhomolhari 7326
Chuk
Jangothang
Tashigthang
Ta
Cheri
Maorothang
Zele La
Thimphu Chu
Tango
Dechenphu Gompa
Punakha Dzong
Taktsang Gompa
Kuruthang
Pele La
Drukyel Dzong
Paro Chu
THIMPHU
Lobesa
Samtengang
Gantey Gompa
Gom La
Dochu La
Wangdi-phodrang
Tsele La
Phobjika
Cher
Chele La
Paro
Simtokha Dzong
Chuzom
Dang Chu
Cho
Haa
Haa Chu
Dobji Dzong
Pangola Range
Bunakha
Takshey
Yaba
Amo Chu
Dagana
Gor
Sipsu
Dorokha
Chagzam
Chukha
Wang Chu
Damphu
Chengmari
Gedu
Dagapela
Samtse
Dala
Puna Tsang Chu
Sarpang
Phuentsholing
Sinchula
Kalikhola

**INDIA**

CHINA
(Tibet)

The external boundaries of Bhutan on this map have not been authenticated and may not be correct.

N
W E
S

a Gangri 7532 ▲

g)

Punsum

Lhobrak La

Kharchung La

Phomeje La

Chisangang Ri 6050 ▲

arthang

Me La

( Gokthong La

Tsochenchen

Kuri Chu

Singye Dzong

Kulong River

Melum La

INDIA

Gorsum

Lhuentse

Dong La

Trashiyangtse

Tang

Angar

Chorten Kora

rongsa

Jakar (Bumthang)

Membartso

Gortshom

Pemi

Kuenga Rabten

Ura

Thrumsing La

Gom Kora

Drametse

Radi

ang

Wiringla

Mongar

Trashigang

Merak

Zhemgang

Chamkar Chu

Nezaygang

Khaling

Nyere Ama Chu

Gonphu

Manas River

Wamrong

Mangde Chu

Dogar

Narphung La

Dhansiri River

ey

Pangkhar

Ngangla

Pemagatshel

Lodraigaon

elephu

Panbang

Dechhenling

Kawapani

Samrang

Lalai

Nganglam

Deothang

Manas

Samdrup Jongkhar

Bhangtar

**Mt. Jhomolhari and Jichu Drakye seen from the aircraft**

elevations ranging from 3280–11,480ft/1000–3500m. This Inner Himalayan temperate zone is the core of the country and most of the population resides here. The forests here are magical – thick with blue pine, conifer, oak, magnolia, maple, birch, rhododendron, willow, poplar, walnut and flowering dogwood. Depending on the elevation, the valleys support cultivation of crops such as maize, millet, barley, rice, wheat and

In the West lie the Great Himalayas which form the border and it is here that some of the highest peaks are located – Jhomolhari and Gieugang that are over 22,960ft/7000m, while Jichu Drakye and Gangchenta are in excess of 22,140ft/6750m. These high mountains are considered sacred, the abode of their deities, and most have not been scaled. Here too lie bewitchingly beautiful glacial lakes and alpine meadows covered in lovely wild flowers – anemone, primula, edelweiss, delphinium and the dwarf rhododendron.

Rare species like the snow leopard, musk deer and takin find their habitat in this area. There are four main valleys in the region – that of Haa at 8856ft/2700m, Paro at 7216ft/2200m, Thimphu at 7544ft/ 2300m, with Wangdiphodrang and Punakha at a lowly 4264ft/1300m joining to form a single long valley. Barring the Haa valley, where there is not much cultivation, western Bhutan is the granary of the country and is dominated by paddy fields and orchards. This is also the most prosperous section of the country and the wealth is reflected in their large houses, embellished with elaborate wood carving and intricate paintings. With the government exercising strict control over logging, these mountain slopes

buckwheat as well as cash crops of mushroom, asparagus, potato and cardamom. Fruits found here are apple, strawberry, mandarin orange and peach. There are, however, significant differences between the western, central and eastern parts of this zone.

# Geography and Location

are covered in a thick forest of conifers and decidious trees.

Crossing the Black Mountains via Pele La ('la' means 'mountain pass'), at 10,824ft/3300m, you enter central Bhutan. Its southern part, known as Khyeng, has a semi tropical climate and is covered with dense jungle while further in the North, the Trongsa valley has some area under terraced cultivation. To the East lie the four valleys (ranging from 8856 to 13,120ft/2700 to 4000m), that comprise the Bumthang region. The cultivation here is mainly buckwheat and the higher meadows are used for sheep and yak herding.

Heading eastwards you cross a high pass, Rodang La, 13,448ft/ 4100m and then descend sharply into eastern Bhutan which is considerably lower, warmer and drier than the central and western parts of the country. The southern section of this zone extends upto the Indian state of Assam and its fertile fields yield mainly maize.

The last major geographical zone is the northern region, lying above 11,480ft/3500m – that of the Greater Himalayas. Bhutan's highest peak, Jhomolhari (24,000ft/ 7314m) straddles the country's border with Tibet. The high altitude restricts cultivation to barley and root crops with the few inhabitants mainly engaged in yak herding.

A large part of this region stays covered with snow all year round and many of the giant massifs remain the abode of the gods, undisturbed by mere mortals trying to reach their summits!

Bhutan is a country traversed by many fast flowing streams and rivers which are called 'chu' and these drain into the duars. The Black Mountains which lie just beyond and above the capital Thimphu, form the main vertical watershed separating two river basins on either side and dividing the country into the western, central and eastern regions. Flowing southwards into India, these chu form four important tributaries of the mighty Brahmaputra which originates as the Tsangpo near Mt. Kailash (considered the center of the Universe by both Hindus and Buddhists). These rivers are liquid gold as their immense hydro-electric potential is being tapped and the power exported to India is Bhutan's major source of revenue. With their headwaters in the high mountains, or in adjoining Tibet, these rivers take on different names along their journey. Starting from the West, the Amo Chu flows from Tibet's Chumbi valley (which was part of the traditional trade route between India and Tibet), through the southwest corner of the country becoming the Torsa Chu

and exiting at the border town of Phuentsholing. The Thimphu Chu becomes the Wang Chu and during its turbulent descent powers the hydro-electric plants at Chukha and Tala, emerging in India as the Raidak River. Moving eastwards the Pho Chu and the Mo Chu converge near Punakha to form the Puna Tsang Chu. This drains the area between Dochu La and the Black Mountains, entering India as the Sankosh. Only the Manas retains its name – it is Bhutan's largest river. Since the central and eastern regions of the country receive heavy rainfall, this river system

**The Manas River**

drains around sixty-five percent of the country's precipitation. Of its three main tributaries, the Kuri Chu originates in Tibet, the Gomru Chu in the Indian state of Arunachal Pradesh while the Mangde Chu originates near Trongsa and joins the Manas Chu just before it enters India.

Since the central Himalayas bear the brunt of the monsoon, the rivers are large and powerful and have carved out broader valleys than those in neighbouring India and Nepal ■

# GETTING THERE

CONSIDERING Bhutan's relative remoteness and low profile in today's global world, one naturally assumes it would be difficult getting there. Fortunately, this is not at all true and you can approach the country both by air and by road.

Bhutan follows a policy of responsible tourism – they have carefully managed and controlled the growth of the tourist industry so that it does not adversely impact on either their distinct and deeply spiritual identity and cherished culture or damage their pristine and well-preserved environment. In keeping with the high benefit-low impact philosophy, efforts are being made to spread tourist-related and other development projects through the country rather than concentrating them only in a few spots (thereby spreading prosperity, discouraging rural migration and diluting environmental impact).

The first tourist entered the country only thirty-three years ago and even in 2006, the total number of non-Indian visitors was only 17,348. Foreign nationals who visit the country are required to pay a tariff of $200 per person per day in the high season (Mar-May, Sep-Nov) and $165 for the rest of the year. This possibly explains the limited number of visitors though

the charge does include stay, food, guide, transportation and permissions to travel and visit the various sites. However, this tariff is not applicable for citizens of India, Bangladesh and the Maldives.

(See box on 'Getting a visa' for additional details)

Bhutan waited till 1983 before it built an airport at Paro and the national airline, Royal Bhutan Airlines – more popularly known as Druk Air – is the only commercial airline using the airport. Paro airport (65km from the capital, Thimphu), is a stunningly picturesque terminal to fly into, past magnificent mountains into

Arriving at Paro

an emerald green valley dotted with beautiful traditional homes, monasteries and the distinctive dzongs. The airline has a fleet of four aircraft (two Airbus 319s and two BAe 146-100s), and flies to limited destinations. The most used entry points are New Delhi (India), Kathmandu (Nepal), and Bangkok (Thailand). Flights from Bangkok are routed either through Dhaka (Bangladesh) or Kolkata (India), depending on the day of the week.

Since strong gusty winds at Paro are a common feature after noon, all arrivals and departures are in the morning. Bhutan local time is half an hour ahead of India and six hours ahead of GMT (12 noon GMT corresponds to 6 pm Bhutan Standard Time).

**For strong legs only!**

For those in the mood for a little

# GETTING A VISA

Bhutan has a unique system for allowing you to enter the country. At first this may appear complicated but in fact it works pretty well!

Visas are arranged only by tour operators and the actual visa is issued when you arrive in the country — whether by road at Phuentsholing or by air at Paro. The fee is a nominal ($20) and is to be paid on the spot. You will also require two photographs. The visa is issued for the exact time you intend to stay in the country but if required can be extended, courtesy your tour operator.

The whole process takes around two weeks and what you need to get the show on the road is:

a) Decide on how long you intend to stay in Bhutan and draw up a rough itinerary.

b) Select a tour operator, discuss your plans with them before you firm up the itinerary and then let them set up the trip for you.

c) You will be required to make the entire payment in advance to the tour operator before the visa application can be processed. (Refunds, in the event of a cancellation, are difficult so it is best to cover that contingency through travel insurance.)

The tour operator submits your visa request (sans the passport — so don't worry!), to the Department of Tourism who verifies that your payments are in and then issues an approval letter. On the basis of this clearance, the tour operator now files a final visa application with the Ministry of Foreign Affairs and they usually take a week to process it before sending your operator a visa confirmation number. The last, and key element in the plot is Druk Air who will only issue you a ticket to Paro once they have the confirmation number! The deck is now clear but to save time on arrival at Paro airport, it's best to carry a faxed copy of the approval letter.

## FOR INDIAN TRAVELLERS

Indian citizens do not need to get a visa but are issued a fourteen day (extendable) permit at the entry point. This is only issued once you produce some form of identification — your voter card, driving license or better still a passport, along with at least three photographs. If you are entering at Phuentsholing you need to get your ID proof authenticated by the Indian authorities at Jaigaon and then proceed to the Bhutanese immigration office. (Authentication is not required if you use a passport). Allow a couple of hours for this process and another half hour to get the vehicle entry permit made.

Indians flying into Paro are required to carry their passports as identification.

more adventure, the land route is via the Indian city of Siliguri located in the eastern state of West Bengal. Siliguri is easily accessed from Delhi or Kolkata by daily flights or overnight trains. From here it is a 150km (2-3 hour) drive to the Indian border town of Jaigaon.

The road surface is rather good and there are enjoyable views of gently undulating hills and rich green tea gardens interspersed with paddy cultivation. The gateway, or 'dwar', to Bhutan on this route is Phuentsholing and Paro is a 160km (5-6 hour) drive — and this is where your Bhutanese odyssey begins!

Thimphu city bus

## TRAVEL WITHIN THE COUNTRY

There is no railway network in Bhutan so your only option is to travel this exotic land by road. The roads in the country are well surfaced but narrow – barely one and a half lane wide, and come with many a serpentine twist. There is a local bus service between

This air journey is possibly the most spectacular flight over mountainous terrain that an ordinary traveller can embark on (Delhi to Leh-Ladakh, is a close second!).

Aim for a window seat on the left hand side of the aircraft and enjoy a heart-stopping view of a succession of snowy peaks spread before you like cresting waves of a vast heavenly ocean! Shortly after take off, the majestic and peerless massif of Mt. Everest comes into view, followed in rapid succession by a continuous chain of snowcapped giants including Makalu (27,755ft/8462m), Nuptse (25,932ft/7906m), Lhotse (27,883ft/8501m) and Cho Oyu (26,742ft/8153m). A little later you can see the guardian deity of neighbouring Sikkim, mighty Kanchendzonga (28160ft/8585m). Then on the views of the peaks are more distant but while flying into Paro you should be able to the spot the beautiful snow clad Jhomolhari (24,000ft/7314m) and Jichu Drakye (22,924ft/6989m).

The sharp descent can be gut wrenching but as you enter the valley, prior to touching down, look for the magnificent Paro Dzong and the Taktsang Monastery perched on an imposing precipitious cliff.

major centers but the frequency is limited and the bus is invariably overcrowded. The most convenient option is to have your tour operator arrange a hired car with driver-cum-guide. You could also drive up from India in your own vehicle but would need the tour operator to arrange a guide to travel with you — an accompanying guide is almost mandatory and definitely a convenience vis a vis the language, the routes and of course handling permissions etc. Permits for travel to different regions in Bhutan can be obtained from the Department of Immigration, Thimphu and for select areas also from Phuentsholing.

Permissions are also required to visit most dzongs and gompas and these can easily be arranged by your tour operator or by visiting the Department of Culture, Thimphu. It is best to obtain permission to visit all the places in the area to avoid being disappointed if you add something en route.

Traffic in Bhutan is very organised and compared to India extremely civilised. A single toot on the horn will suffice to inform the vehicle in front of your intentions and rest assured he will give way ASAP. (The only exception may be the occasional Indian army truck that you encounter!) It is easy to identify the ownership of a vehicle

with Bhutanese number plates — BP is private, BG — government, BT — taxi, RBA is army, while BHT is for the royal family (overtaking not advised!).

An important point to note is that entry by road is only allowed through Phuentsholing. You can

Chele La — definitely worth a visit

exit at Samdrup Jongkhar, which lies at the south-eastern corner of the country, and make your way to Guwahati, the capital of the Indian state of Assam. Please check with your agent if this exit route is open before you make your plans. (Indians can enter from Samdrup Jongkhar and Gelephu too.)

Guwahati has convenient flights to Delhi/Kolkata as also rail connections. If you have a few days to spare you could take in the game sanctuaries of Manas (famous for its elephants), and Kaziranga where you can spot the one-horned rhino ■

# CLIMATE AND WHEN TO VISIT

CLIMATIC conditions vary vastly across the country. One can be in shorts and a T-shirt and within a few hours of travel need a warm parka! There are also large fluctuations in temperature even at the same destination or general area. Another peculiarity is that since each of the valleys is virtually an independant eco-

system, there is no such thing as a general weather forecast or even an accurate local one!

However, one can safely rule out having to face the kind of blistering heat the adjoining Indian plains experience. The maximum temperature in the extreme South of Bhutan usually does not go above 35°C at the peak of

**Snowfall above Thimphu in mid-March**

At the Paro Tsechu

summer (May/Jun) and remains a comfortable 15°C at the height of winter (Dec-Feb). Temperatures in the central valleys, where you would be spending most of your time, is much lower – the summer maximun does not exceed 30°C and nights are in the 15-20°C range. In winter the day temperature is around 15°C but at night it gets cold, with sub-zero conditions being the norm. Snowfall is rare but the surrounding mountains certainly receive a liberal dose. Within the central region, the eastern part with a lower average altitude, is warmer than its western section.

Bhutan experiences a reasonably heavy monsoon (Jun-Sep), particularly in the South where the average rainfall is around 350cm per year. In neighbouring India, New Delhi at 61cm is a poor cousin in this respect and even Mumbai at 230cm, pales in comparison. However, Cherrapunji in Meghalaya, the wettest place in the world, lies not too far to the East and receives 1100cm annually! During the monsoon the valleys are enveloped in magical swirling mists and the whole region is unimaginably lush green but you rarely catch a glimpse of the snow clad peaks. The low clouds, however, often impair visibility

## TEMPERATURES

| MONTHS | PARO Max–Min | | THIMPHU Max–Min | | PUNAKHA Max–Min | | WANGDI Max–Min | | TRONGSA Max–Min | | BUMTHANG Max–Min | | MONGAR Max–Min | | TRASHIGANG Max–Min | |
|--------|-----|-----|-----|-----|-----|-----|-----|-----|-----|-----|-----|-----|-----|-----|-----|-----|
| JAN | 7 | -8 | 12 | +3 | 18 | +7 | 15 | +7 | 11 | +1 | 8 | +1 | 20 | +10 | 15 | +4 |
| FEB | 13 | +3 | 17 | 0 | 19 | +7 | 21 | +7 | 14 | +1 | 13 | +1 | 25 | +10 | 17 | +5 |
| MAR | 14 | +2 | 14 | +5 | 24 | +8 | 23 | +9 | 15 | 0 | 16 | +5 | 27 | +9 | 18 | +5 |
| APR | 15 | +3 | 19 | +9 | 25 | +10 | 25 | +13 | 17 | +4 | 16 | +6 | 27 | +16 | 21 | +9 |
| MAY | 21 | +12 | 19 | +14 | 24 | +10 | 25 | +13 | 20 | +5 | 9 | +8 | 30 | +20 | 20 | +12 |
| JUN | 23 | +13 | 24 | +15 | 21 | +11 | 28 | +18 | 20 | +13 | 20 | +12 | 30 | +21 | 19 | +15 |
| JUL | 23 | +15 | 29 | +18 | 26 | +17 | 29 | +19 | 21 | +15 | 21 | +13 | 31 | +22 | 22 | +6 |
| AUG | 29 | +15 | 25 | +17 | 25 | +11 | 29 | +20 | 20 | +15 | 22 | +14 | 39 | +34 | 22 | +16 |
| SEP | 23 | +11 | 21 | +16 | 26 | +11 | 29 | +20 | 13 | +13 | 21 | +13 | 30 | +24 | 21 | +15 |
| OCT | 20 | +9 | 19 | +11 | 25 | +11 | 27 | +19 | 20 | +13 | 19 | +10 | 29 | +18 | 20 | +11 |
| NOV | 14 | +3 | 17 | +6 | 22 | +12 | 23 | +11 | 18 | +11 | 15 | +2 | 26 | +13 | 17 | +13 |
| DEC | 11 | +4 | 15 | 0 | 23 | +9 | 20 | +13 | 14 | +2 | 14 | +5 | 24 | +7 | 16 | +15 |

resulting in cancellation of flights. For road travellers, this season holds the threat of landslide-blocked roads. So, if you want to enjoy the monsoon magic, you should build in buffer days in your itinerary!

On the other hand the period Oct–Mar mostly offers azure skies, good snow views and minimal rainfall.

Based on generalised expectations of weather, Mar 1st–May 30th and Oct 1st–Dec 15th are the best times to visit Bhutan but for those who don't mind the cold, the period between Dec-Feb is the very best for spectacular snow views of the Greater Himalayas. Of the two mentioned above, the spring season offers the visitor an amazing display of rhododendrons, magnolias and many other flowering shrubs in full bloom. During Oct-Dec you will miss the profusion of colour but will be rewarded with virtually no haze to 'cloud' the horizon and superb views of the snow covered Himalayan peaks.

Another point to ponder while deciding the timing of your visit is whether you want to experience one of Bhutan's visually stunning and often soul stirring cultural/religious festivals – the tsechus. These festivals are spread through the year and for details see Festivals page 86 ■

A bountiful harvest

# THE ECONOMY

ALMOST eighty percent of Bhutan's population is engaged in agricultural activity and animal husbandry. Barring the fertile central valleys and the southern region bordering India, much of the land is too steep and thickly forested to allow large scale cultivation. Arable land accounts for under 10% of the total area but since it supports a population of only 125,000 families or so, the standard of living is adequate. Those located in the western region are quite prosperous when compared to their eastern brethren. The principal crops are maize, rice, wheat, buckwheat, barley and millet with vegetables, potatoes and fruits supplementing the cereal crops. Most households also raise poultry and cattle. Yaks are reared at higher altitudes.

Though most of the population is pastoral, the agricultural sector currently accounts for only about thirty-five percent of the country's Gross Domestic Product (GDP). Interestingly, it is not industry or the service sector that contribute to any significant extent to the rest of the GDP – the bulk of it is accounted for by the production and export of hydro-power to India. It is estimated that the total hydel potential of the country is 30,000MW of which under 5% is currently being tapped. There are two main projects, both located on the Wang Chu at Chukha and Tala. Bhutan's developmental plans give priority to its environment. As a result they seek to develop their hydro-electric power potential cautiously with small dams and this policy extends to their approach of controlled mining and quarrying as well as restricted felling of trees for wood.

Other contributors to the economy are the export of apples, canned fruits and juices, as also mushrooms to Japan. There is a limited export of wood products, lemon grass oil, as also calcium carbide and cement. A most unusual contributor to the economy is the export of postage stamps. Bhutan has produced a vast collection of exotic stamps – some made of silk or metal, others have 3-D images  and some are even mini phonograph records!

Tourism is the second biggest contributor to the national GDP even though its full potential is yet to be realised. The country has been conservative in opening up its borders to visitors and even today prefers to restrict numbers in an effort to protect their distinct culture and traditions. Following a unique philosophy of measuring the country's progress by its Gross National Happiness (GNH) – rather than GNP – Bhutan's goal is an equitable spread of prosperity rather than skewed development in an ad hoc manner, just for the sake of so called progress. With this principle being the cornerstone of nation building, priority is given to rural development, healthcare and education as well as creating job opportunities and spreading this growth fairly over all regions so as to discourage migration to urban centers. However, to pursue these policies Bhutan has sought foreign aid, particularly in the social sectors of education and health. This has been forthcoming in generous quantities from India and from the European Union and Japan as also the Asian Development Bank and World Bank.

**Stamps – a most unusual contributor to the economy!**

# The economy

The country's currency is the Ngultrum (Nu) which is officially pegged to the Indian Rupee and in mid-2007 a dollar would buy you 41 Nu. The acceptance of credit cards is extremely limited, so its best to come well stocked with good old TCs (traveller cheques).

A little mentioned and certainly not adequately measured component of the economy is the rural household industry, involving the manufacture of jewellery, wood sculptures, handmade paper, bamboo products and most important of all, fabrics which are woven at home. Weaving received a great impetus with the onset of relative economic stability from the mid-nineteenth century onwards and cloth was one of the forms of paying local taxes. In the past production was for personal consumption and sometimes bartered but now it is primarily an income-generating activity. Two types of looms are generally favoured – a horizontal frame with pedals and a fixed vertical frame with a backstrap (a waist loom). Every step of the weaving process is by hand and this accounts for the fact that textiles and their products are relatively expensive in the country. Weaving is mainly undertaken by women and is today more prevalent in central and eastern Bhutan ■

Returning from the fields in the Bumthang region

# FLORA AND FAUNA

Spring is in the air...
and in the trees!

B Y VIRTUE of its varied climatic zones spanning the tropical, temperate and alpine – combined with the monsoon effect in all three – Bhutan is home to an exotic mix of flora and fauna that few places on the earth can match. The amazing diversity you can spot in a single day cannot fail to stun the senses. The fact that more than seventy percent of the land is forest only makes things better! There are over five thousand species of plants that grow here, including six hundred types of orchids, forty-five different varieties of rhododendrons, three hundred species of medicinal plants and over four hundred types of mushrooms.

Although large tracts have been cleared for agriculture, the southern tropical region is home to forests of sal, sissu and semal trees. Providing colour to the lush cultivated fields is the Indian laburnum whose beautiful yellow flowers bloom in April/May complementing the reddish-orange flowers of the 'Flame of the Forest'. Ascending from here you encounter vast forests of glistening pine (chir) trees with their oil-rich needles and oval shaped cones. The wood of the tree is used for making furniture while its resin is the main ingredient in the manufacture of turpentine.

Entering the temperate zone

# FLORA AND FAUNA

## TAKIN

The takin was chosen as Bhutan's national animal not only on account of its unique — albeit strange — appearance but also due to the myth surrounding its origin. Legend has it that once when Lama Drukpa Kinley (referred to fondly as the 'Divine Madman' by an English traveller), was travelling he was asked by the gathering to demonstrate his magical prowess. He ignored the request and asked to be served a whole cow followed by a goat for lunch. He proceeded to demolish them with great relish right down to the bones. After a loud satisfied burp he placed the goat's head on the cow's bones and with a snap of his fingers commanded the beast to rise. The sceptics were silenced when this apparition not only rose but proceeded up the mountainside and began to graze!

This large animal, which can weigh upto 1000kg, came to be known as the takin and to date has defied the efforts of taxonomists and biologists to classify it. (A separate classification, 'budorcas taxicolor' had to be created!)

The grazing habits of the takin are unique and add to the mystery — in open spaces like alpine meadows they function as a herd but when they migrate to the forest they graze individually or in small groups.

at around 5904ft/1800m, the pine gives way to dense forests of birch, maple, oak, magnolia and laurel. At higher elevations (7872ft/2400m+), one finds the hemlock, walnut, birch, spruce and the national tree — the cypress. The fir forms the tree line along with the juniper and blue pine, with its five-needle grouping and thinner cones. The rhododendrons bloom spectacularly between March and May and entire hillsides are ablaze with the brilliant red flowers of

this stunning tree known as 'etho metho', in Dzongkha. This is also the season for the creamy white magnolia and heady-scented daphne from which paper is made.

Between the tree line and the snow line are alpine meadows dominated by Himalayan grasses, dwarf junipers and flowering herbs. In spring/summer these are carpeted with a profusion of alpine flowers such as edelweiss, many varieties of primulas and rhododendron shrubs. The monsoon brings with it a second, even more vibrant blooming of dwarf irises, anemones, swathes of lilac primulas, delpheniums and ranunculus. Bhutan's national flower is the elusive blue poppy which grows above the tree line at altitudes between 11,480 and 14,760ft (3500 and 4500m). It flowers only once during its lifetime of several years and after producing seeds, withers and dies. This, combined with its locale implies that few people ever see

Takins in the Thimphu mini zoo

# Flora and fauna

The magnolia blooming in April

one, thereby lending it a mysterious and elusive quality, almost at par with the rare snow leopard.

Bhutan's forests are populated with a hundred and sixty-five species of mammals and the most common of these are the Himalayan black bear, sloth bear and a variety of deer such as the sambar and barking deer while spotting the dimunitive musk deer is a rarity. The forests are home to the rhesus monkey and the black faced langur but more interestingly, Bhutan is the only known habitat of the golden langur. The existence of this shy small primate was only brought to the notice of the scientific community in the twentieth century and its distinctive feature is its golden coat. The Royal Manas National Park, on Bhutan's central-south border with India, is home to wild elephants, tigers, leopards, rhinoceros, gaur, wild boar, wild dogs and deer.

At the other end of the country, in the alpine region you find yaks, the rare blue sheep (bharal), the Himalayan tahir (a type of mountain goat) as well as the rare Tibetan gazelle (chiru), with the snow leopard in the background somewhere! Last but certainly not least is the national animal – the large awkward looking, somewhat ungainly but completely unique takin. The alpine meadows are its home in summer while the broadleaf forest is its winter base.

For birders Bhutan is a veritable paradise with around seven hundred species having been recorded. As a matter of fact while driving across the country you are likely to come across small groups of avid bird watchers wandering into the jungle armed with their binoculars and cameras! The vulnerable black-necked crane is the most famous migratory visitor. (See Gantey section page 190)

Some other migratory bird species seen here are ospreys, waders and a wide variety of ducks besides snow pigeons, rosefinches, accentors and various pheasants like the monal, satyr tragopan, khaleej and blood pheasant. You can also spot minivets, barbets, sunbirds, warblers, cuckoos and yuhinas. At high altitudes you can see the raven, Himalayan griffon and the lammergeier lazily riding the air currents in search of prey, the raven and Himalayan griffon. More commonly visible are the blue whistling thrush, chattering yellow-billed magpies, choughs and many other species.

Two books which would be of immense use for those who want to know more are *An introduction to Bird Watching in Bhutan* by Carol and Tim Inskipp and *Birds of Bhutan* by Salim Ali et al ■

# HISTORY AND PEOPLE

BASED on the evidence of stone implements found, it appears that this land was first inhabited as early as 2000 BC. In all probability these were nomadic herders who lived in the low-lying areas in winter and moved to the alpine meadows in summer – a practice that is still followed today!

There are no surviving records, oral or written, of this period and history per se can only be authenticated from the seventh century AD. The country's history is inextricably linked with its religious figures and the events and legends surrounding them. According to tradition, Bhutan's history started in the seventh century when the Tibetan king, Songsten Gampo, constructed its first two Buddhist temples – Kyichu in the Paro valley and Jambay in the Choekhor valley in Bumthang. Till this time, like other parts of the Himalayan region, the people here followed an animistic religion – in this case, Bon (or Ben cho).

In AD 746 the Indian ruler of Bumthang, Sindhu Gyab (Sindhu Raja), was at war with a rival king and lost his son in battle. In his distraught state he angered the region's chief deity who extracted his vital force, bringing him close to death. An enlightened tantric master was needed to save the king

and the great Buddhist teacher, Guru Padmasambhava, was invited. Using his supernatural powers, he succeeded in subduing the wrathful deity. The Guru brought peace to the region and converted the

Victory chortens at Dochu La

deity, king and even his rival to Buddhism. During his meditation the Guru (Rinpoche) left an imprint (jey) of his body (kur) on a rock that you can view and this is where Kurjey Lhakhang now stands.

He visited many parts of Tibet and Bhutan performing miracles, meditating in caves (that have now become popular pilgrimage centers since they are considered spiritually powerful sites), and persuading

Spinning yarns!

people to the Buddhist path. The form of Buddhism practiced in Bhutan assimilated many existing deities into its pantheon as also some animistic practices of nature worship.

Guru Rinpoche visited Tibet at the invitation of Trisong Detsen who sought his help in building the Samye Gompa. On its completion, a monk body was installed here and a new school of Buddhism introduced which led to the ascendancy of this religion in Tibet. He then returned to eastern Bhutan and at Gom Kora is a rock that bears an imprint of his body, head and hat. He also flew to Taktsang (above Paro in the West), on a flaming tigress, thereby giving this famous monastery the name 'Tiger's Nest'. He is believed to have spent time meditating in a cave in this cliff side.

In the ninth century the ruler of Tibet, Langdharma, banned Buddhism and many monks fled southwards taking refuge in Bhutan. Although Langdharma was subsequently killed and Buddhism reinstated, the turmoil continued into the seventeenth century and numerous monks and noblemen settled in Bhutan.

Events in Tibet in the twelfth century had a major bearing on the course of history in Bhutan – indeed the impact has lasted till the present day. Lama Tsangpa Gyarey Yeshe Dorje (1161-1211) was building a monastery in the town of Ralung, East of the famous gompa at Gyantse. During the consecration, there was a loud thundering sound which was popularly believed to be the voice of the dragon (Druk), expounding the great truths of Buddhism. The monastery was thus named Druk and the strain of Buddhism which later evolved out of his teachings was called Drukpa Kagyu. In the seventeenth century when Bhutan was united under this form of Buddhism, they gave the country the name Druk

Yul – Land of the Thunder Dragon, and the inhabitants were called the Drukpas. The language, which was closely akin to Tibetan, was Dzongkha.

In Tibet, the Gelugpa sect was gaining in power and influence, resulting in large scale migration of the other sects to Bhutan and Sikkim. Western Bhutan soon became the place of refuge for the followers of Drukpa Kagyu. Of the many lamas who migrated to Bhutan at this time, Gyalwa Lhanangpa founded the Lhapa Kagyu lineage and established a system of dzongs (forts), similar to those found in Tibet. However, none of these are extant and the dzongs that you see throughout Bhutan now were built during the Zhabdung's reign and subsequent to it. Later Lama Phajo Drukgom Shigpo, who was a close disciple of the founder of the Drukpa sect, took control of the monastery that Lhanangpa had set up at Tango (near Thimphu). He is credited with establishing the Bhutanese form of Buddhism by converting most of the populace to Drukpa Kagyu. During the fourteenth and fifteenth centuries, several other prominent lamas contributed to the development of the Drukpa Kagyu lineage – Lama Ngawang Chhogyel built the gompas (monasteries) at Paro, Pangri, Zampa and Hongtsho while Lama Drukpa Kinley established Chime Lhakhang near Punakha.

Bhutan continued to be fragmented with different regions following their own stream of religious belief and a conglomeration of small feudal lords holding sway in some regions. Two of the prominent religious sects that established a firm lasting hold in the country were that of the Drukpa Kagyu and Nyingma. All through this period there was an influx of Tibetan nobles searching for safer and greener pastures and they carved out small enclaves for themselves, mainly in central Bhutan. As in the case of many nations, the status at the beginning of the sixteenth century was that of several chieftains vying with each other for supremacy or greater power – or at least jostling for increased space. The stage was thus set for one of Bhutan's most charismatic and influential leaders – the Zhabdung Rinpoche (Ngawang Namgyal), to make his mark but this happened more by accident than by design!

Ngawang Namgyal (1594-1651), was a descendant of Tsangpa Gyarey, the founder of the Drukpa lineage at Ralung. At the age of twelve, he was recognised as the reincarnation of Pema Karpo, the prince abbot of the monastery. As he grew older, this recognition was challenged by the ruler of neighbouring Tsang province and his position became untenable at Ralung. At the age of twenty-three, the protective deity Mahakala (Yeshe Gompo), appeared to him in the form of a raven and directed him to move South through Laya into Bhutan. He travelled extensively in West Bhutan, teaching the Kagyu precepts while growing in political stature. Repelling Tibetan invasions, he established the dominance of the Drukpa Kagyu sect. He took the honorary title of Zhabdung ('at whose feet one submits') and sought to unify the region under the banner of Druk Yul, the Land of the Thunder Dragon.

A towering personality who ably led the country in all spheres – spiritual, cultural and military – he is regarded as the founder of the Bhutanese state.

He exercised power and controlled the penlops (governors) through a series of dzongs that he built across the country. The mighty dzong at Simtokha (near Thimphu) was his first symbol of authority and this was built with a major difference. Hitherto the Bhutanese dzong was designed for military purposes, to serve as an invincible fortress, but Simtokha did not only play a defensive role but

Zhabdung Ngawang Namgyal

**Musicians at the tsechu**

housed a state monk body as well
as administrators. This eclectic
combination of civil, military
and religious authority became
the model for all future dzongs
and continues to the present day.
However, it was certainly not
smooth sailing for the Zhabdung as
the rival Buddhist lineages formed
a coalition and attacked Simtokha
in 1629. They were defeated but

his old adversary, the desi of Tsang
province, joined hands with the
defeated followers, the 'Five Group
of Lamas', led by the Lhapa sect.
However, after various attacks were
repulsed the Tsang desi accepted
defeat in 1639 and acknowledged
Zhabdung Ngawang Namgyal as
the supreme authority in Bhutan.
The Zhabdung established close
ties with neighbouring Cooch
Behar and Nepal and secured from
the king of Ladakh administrative

control of a number of sites in western Tibet for meditation and worship. Tibet continued to be in turmoil with the Gelugpa (Yellow Hat) order working to establish absolute control. It was during this time, while the Tibetans were occupied with internal strife that he constructed a series of dzongs – those at Paro, Simtokha, Punakha and Trongsa are still standing! The 'Great Fifth' Dalai Lama attempted to curb Drukpa power and invaded the country but was beaten back with heavy losses. The Zhabdung's successes led to great popularity within the region and the large militia at his command gave him effective control of the country.

Whenever he was free from defending his adopted land, the Zhabdung worked to build systems that would outlive him and provide an identity and raison d'être for a nation to emerge. He was clear that while following Tibetan Buddhism, a separate religious and cultural identity was necessary. Being a revered scholar, he worked on codifying the Kagyu teachings and specifying traditions that would shape this identity. To him goes the credit of defining the national dress and creating the series of tsechus (festivals), designed to commemorate various events of Guru Padmasambhava's life. He also formalised a system of taxes

and laws to govern the relationship between the clergy and lay people. His crowning achievement was the administrative system he bequeathed – the Zhabdung was the spiritual ruler and his successors would be reincarnations. The political and administrative functions were to be handled by the desi (temporal head/secular ruler), who would be elected to the post. The institution of the Je Khempo (chief abbot/ecclesiastical head) was established to head the monastic order with the Zhabdung transcending these two offices of equal import. At that time the country was divided into three districts (Trongsa in the Center, Paro in the West and Dagna in the South), each governed by a penlop (provincial governor). The central government was set up at Punakha and at the district level, the penlops represented the central government while three officers, called dzongpens (lords of the dzongs), were appointed to look after the sub-districts of Punakha, Thimphu and Wangdiphodrang.

The strain of all this hard work eventually took its toll on Zhabdung Ngawang Namgyal and he went into retreat at Punakha Dzong in 1651, but the campaign to unite the country continued with the central and eastern regions falling in line by 1655.

The Zhabdung never emerged from his retreat and it is surmised that he passed away soon after withdrawing from the public eye. His death was only revealed in 1705 and in the interim four successive desis managed to consolidate the sweeping changes that had united the land. Announcing his death, the Je Khempo proclaimed that there would be three simultaneous reincarnations of the Zhabdung – representing his body, speech and mind – of which only the reincarnation of the mind would be the head of state. This complex system did not work as there were uncertainties regarding who his true incarnation was and when the incarnate was too young to rule, the desi was in control. Since his was an elected office with almost unlimited control, rivalry, factionalism and virtual civil war became the order of the day for the next two centuries. During this period although only six mind incarnations were identified, the high turnover of desis told the tale of instability and infighting – there were fifty-five desis and as many as twenty-two were assassinated or deposed.

In the early eighteenth century Bhutan helped its neighbouring state, Cooch Behar, rout an invading Mughal army. Subsequently they became so closely involved in the affairs of the state that they ordered the capture and punishment of those who had assassinated the king they had helped place on the throne. In 1772 the regent of Cooch Behar decided to seek the help of the British to regain control of the state and in a move that proved to be a political miscalculation the ruling desi invaded Cooch Behar, kidnapped the crown prince and queen and subsequently captured the king as well. This really stirred up a hornet's nest since the East India Company at this point of time was determined, by hook or by crook, to establish its hegemony over the subcontinent. Events in Cooch Behar brought the hitherto unknown land of Bhutan under the malevolent and acquisitive gaze of the Company. The British therefore decided to intervene but their help came at a steep price to Cooch Behar as they not only charged a monetary remuneration of Rs. 50,000 to drive out the Bhutanese forces but in true buccaneering fashion then forced the ruler of Cooch Behar to cede his entire kingdom to the Company. British troops also occupied parts of southern Bhutan till a treaty was signed in 1774 at the behest of the Panchen Lama from Tibet. This honoured the East India Company's territory and allowed them the right

Sir Ugyen Wangchuck,
the First King of Bhutan

to cut timber in Bhutan's forests.
Internal problems continued to
beset Bhutan but the region was too
insignificant for the British to pay
any heed to for the next fifty years.

In 1826 the British gained
control of Bhutan's southern
neighbour Assam resulting in a
conflict over the ownership of
the riverine plains (the duars),
which were identified as excellent
tea growing areas. Whereas the
Bengal duars had been annexed
by Bhutan in the late seventeenth
century they shared control over
the Assam duars, on a time-
share basis. With the take-over of
Assam, the Bhutanese now had
to deal with the British and this
led to much strife. Eventually
in 1840-41 the British wrested
control after agreeing to pay an
annual compensation of Rs.10,000.
Ostensibly the motive was to
restore peace and prosperity to this
tract of the country but the real
objective was revealed in a letter
from Colonel Jenkins, the governor
general's agent:

"Had we possession of the Dooars,
the Bhootan Government would
necessarily in a short time become
entirely dependant upon us, as
holding in our hands the source of
all their subsistence".

At this time the designated
Zhabdung was only eighteen years
old and it was the Council of

Ministers that handled the state's
affairs. This Council consisted of
the Paro and Trongsa penlops,
the various dzongpens and other
officials. There was a bitter battle
for supremacy being waged by the
two penlops but Jigme Namgyal
(1825-82), the Trongsa leader,

managed to secure the upper hand and for the first time, in over a century, was able to re-establish peace and control through central governance.

By the early 1860s the British were through the Afghan Wars and the Anglo-Sikh one. The uprising against their rule in India, dubbed the '1857 Mutiny', had also been dealt with and now the time was ripe to get back to unfinished business – taking complete control of the duars. In November 1864 Ashley Eden, the secretary of the government

Trashichhoe Dzong, Thimphu

of Bengal, was dispatched to meet the Bhutanese desi. Though it was made abundantly clear that he was not welcome at this particular juncture, Eden pressed on regardless and met with a somewhat indifferent and hostile reception. Miffed by this treatment, in a rather high-handed manner Eden presented the Council of Ministers with a draft of the yet-to-be-negotiated terms implying this was the final non-negotiable treaty. The terms were completely unacceptable and the Bhutanese presented a counter treaty which returned all the duars to Bhutan! Aware of their ire and considering himself under threat, Eden signed the Bhutanese treaty but appended his signature with the words 'under compulsion' – a clause that the Bhutanese did not understand. Though he was castigated for his inept conduct and the mission deemed a failure, the Empire lost little time in striking back! Forces were dispatched and despite fierce opposition by the penlop's army the British succeeded in annexing the Bengal duars and to add insult to injury forced Bhutan to sign the Treaty of Sinchula in November 1865 (this time actually 'under compulsion'), giving control of the duars to the British forever and allowing free trade between the countries.

Despite this setback Jigme Namgyal retained his power, becoming the 51st desi in 1870. In 1879 he appointed his seventeen year old son Ugyen Wangchuck as Paro penlop and three years later, after his death, this remarkable young man marched on Trongsa and Bumthang. In 1882 he was appointed penlop of Trongsa, while still retaining the post of penlop of Paro. He was able to further strengthen the alliances forged by his astute father and in 1885 emerged as the supreme authority and appointed his own nominee as the desi. To his credit Ugyen Wangchuck was a realist and despite the humiliations inflicted by the British decided the way forward was by constructive cooperation and not confrontation. The British were keen on cementing ties with Tibet and Ugyen Wangchuck offered to use the good relationship the Bhutanese enjoyed with the Tibetans to further this effort. He accompanied Col. Younghusband's expedition to Tibet in 1904 and assisted in the negotiations which resulted in a treaty signed between the British and the Tibetans. For these efforts he was awarded the title of Knight Commander of the Indian Empire and in 1906 was invited to Calcutta (now Kolkata) to attend the reception for the Prince of Wales.

In 1907 Sir Ugyen Wangchuck was unanimously elected hereditary ruler of the country by a conclave of Bhutan's chieftains, principal lamas, representatives of monks, civil servants and the people. He was crowned on 17th December 1907 and became the head of state – the Druk Gyalpo (Dragon King). This ended the dual system of government established by Zhabdung Nawang Namgyal but the three incarnations of the Zhabdung continued to be

**Laya women**

Dungtse
Lhakhang, Paro

recognised and greatly revered by the people. Despite the fact that the neighbouring kingdom of Sikkim had a British resident, Bhutan maintained its independent status – the 1910 Treaty of Punakha confirmed that the British would not interfere with the internal administration of the country but would guide them in the field of external relations. King Ugyen Wangchuck passed away in 1926 and was succeeded by Jigme Wangchuck, his twenty-four year old son who became the second hereditary king of the country.

In 1947 the British finally bid adieu to the subcontinent and the new Indian government, led by Prime Minister Jawaharlal Nehru, signed a treaty with Bhutan modelled on the lines of the 1910 treaty with the British and also returned 82 sq.km of the duars in the South-eastern part of the country. King Jigme Wangchuck died in 1952 and was succeeded by his son Jigme Dorji Wangchuck who had been educated in India and England. The reign of the earlier two kings was marked by stability and prosperity, albeit in almost total isolation from the ever changing and developing 'outside world'. It soon became evident that this policy would have to be amended – a point hammered home by the Chinese invasion of

Tibet in 1959 and their incursions into India three years later. It was obvious to the king that in order to preserve Bhutan's independence they would have to embrace and join the world community. Viewed as the architect of modern Bhutan, King Jigme Dorji Wangchuck embarked on a plan that sought progress, prosperity and happiness while retaining the deeply spiritual values and cultural traditions of his people. He embarked on this journey taking a series of calibrated steps, strengthening and creating institutions at home while efforts abroad led to the country joining the United Nations in 1971. His achievements at home include the creation of the National Assembly, formation of the army and police forces, establishing the high court and implementing the country's first five-year plan in 1961. He also drew up a twelve volume code of law, abolished serfdom and reorganised land holdings. While moving forward he continued to lay strong emphasis on preserving the country's strong cultural and religious heritage.

In 1972, after his untimely death at the young age of forty-four, he was succeeded by his sixteen year old son Jigme Singye Wangchuck who has built a remarkable superstructure on the foundations laid by his father. He developed a plan for economic self sufficiency and coined the term Gross National Happiness (as opposed to the boring conventional Gross National Product) as a true measure of well being! He is the architect of the country's policy of environmental conservation where ecological considerations have reigned supreme over commercial interests. (Remarkably, although the policy requires that a sixty percent forest cover be maintained, over seventy percent is forested today). It is this amazingly responsible approach to their environment that has led them to restrict mining, felling of trees, discourage mass tourism and go in for smaller, less destructive dam building.

There are four key tenets of governance – equitable social development, conservation and protection of the environment, strengthening and preserving the unique culture and heritage of the people and providing good governance with increased peoples' participation. Emphasis has been laid on rural development, the spread of health and education to even the remotest areas, launching livestock and agricultural development schemes and promoting handicrafts. Development projects are judiciously spread over the country

to help provide jobs and improve livelihood as well as to discourage migration to urban centers.

In the 1990s the porous border between Assam (India) and Bhutan led to separatist groups from India, such as the United Liberation Front of Assam (ULFA) and the Bodo Liberation Tiger Force, using Bhutan as a base for conducting raids on targets in Indian territory. Polite warnings to desist did not work and finally the king personally led the Royal Bhutanese Army in a surprise operation which eliminated these unwelcome transgressors in 2003. Though the insurgents were heavily armed the operation was virtually bloodless for the RBA and this victory has been commemorated by a spectacular series of 108 chortens built at the crest of the Dochu La above Thimphu.

King Jigme Singye Wangchuck, Bhutan's fourth king, has now executed an unprecedented first for a Bhutanese monarch – or for that matter, any monarch in his prime – he relinquished the throne in December 2006, handing over the reins to Crown Prince Jigme Khesar Namgyel Wangchuck who is now the fifth monarch and head of state. He will be an absolute ruler of Bhutan but only till 2008 when the National Assembly and other institutions are envisaged

His Majesty Jigme Singye Wangchuck, the Fourth King of Bhutan

to have a far greater role than at present. A draft constitution has been drawn up and is under active consideration. Once it is adopted, Bhutan will become a parliamentary democracy with a constitutional monarchy.

**A Trongsa native**

Under the current dispensation the head of state and government is assisted by the Royal Advisory Council which was established in 1965. The council performs the dual function of serving as the ruler's sounding board and also overseeing the implementation of policies approved by the

National Assembly. In addition there are ten Council of Ministers elected by the National Assembly, comprising the ministries of Home Affairs, Finance, Agriculture, Communication, Trade, Industry and Power, Health, Education, Works and Housing, Labour and Foreign Affairs. The Zhabdung's original administrative system was modified in the twentieth century. The country is now divided into twenty dzongkhags (districts), each headed by the dzongda (governors) with the more populous ones being divided into dungkhags (sub-districts). The administrative unit is a block comprising several villages.

The National Assembly meets twice a year and of its hundred and fifty members, hundred and five are elected by the people in their own villages. The king nominates thirty-five members (mainly senior civil servants), while the clergy elects ten members. The other legacy of the Zhabdung, that of the institution of the Je Khempo continues to this time. The current incumbent, Trulku Jigme Choeda, is the seventieth elected chief abbot and head of the monastic establishment, continuing an unbroken chain of succession dating back to 1637.

The legal code, both civil and criminal, has its basic tenets rooted in history but these were comprehensively updated in 2001.

A high court with eight judges was established in Thimphu in 1968. Each district has its own judge, but most disputes are handled at the village level by the gup (headman), or the chimis (elected representatives). Minor litigation is quite common but Bhutan is a relatively crime free country and the need for formal lawyers is yet to be felt! Of course an aggrieved person can make a final appeal to the king whose word is supreme.

## PEOPLE

People here can be classified into three distinct ethnic groups – the Scharchops (people of the East), are believed to be the earliest inhabitants of the land. They are of Indo-Mongoloid descent and speak their own language and although neither their place of origin nor the time of their migration is clear, they live in the eastern region of the country. The Ngalops are descendants of the stream of Tibetans who started migrating to this country from the ninth century onwards. They dominate the country West of the Black Mountains and 'ngalop' means 'first to rise' – not literally, but the first to convert to Buddhism and adopt the Dzongkha language. In the North–West corner of the country, forming part of Gasa district, there is a small community of around a thousand people who inhabit the region known as Laya. Bordering Tibet, the people here have retained their traditional dress, customs and dialect. The women keep their hair long and top it with a conical spiked bamboo hat held in place with a beaded band in the back. They wear long woollen skirts and a jacket and adorn themselves with silver jewellery.

The third group comprises those of Nepali descent who started settling in the southern part of the country only in late nineteenth century. They are known as the Lhotshampas and consist of Nepali speaking ethnic groups such as the Gurung, Rai and Chettris.

The Bhutanese are very religious and this is evidenced by the numerous dzongs and monasteries that dot the landscape. In addition, every home has its own prayer room or altar and generally celebrates an annual festival called 'chogu'. This is when prayers of thanksgiving are offered for the year past as well as for the future well being of the family. Their spiritual beliefs and strong community ties allow them to live in perfect harmony with their environment, bear the challenges of its remoteness with fortitude and yet retain the capacity to enjoy simple pleasures with enthusiasm.

Interestingly, Bhutanese women enjoy an equal position in society to the men folk. It is not uncommon for a man to move into the wife's family home or share in the household chores. Women often inherit property from their parents and traditionally the marriage ceremony is a private family affair. In some parts of Bhutan there is actually no formal ceremony and according to custom, the suitor spends the night with the girl and if he stays on to meet the family over breakfast, they are considered married. Polyandry is also prevalent in some parts. The Bhutanese are refreshingly open about earthly matters – wooden phalluses are used by the atsaras during festivals and hang from the roof of many homes or are painted near the front door as symbols of fertility.

Of all the rites of passage, funerals are treated as very significant as they don't just mark the passing of the soul but also the beginning of its journey to rebirth. Funeral rites last up to twenty-one days and can be very elaborate. Children who die before the age of seven are sometimes given a 'sky burial' (similar to the custom followed in Tibet), so they are consumed by, and become a part of, nature.

Festivals are eagerly awaited by all stratas of society – people turn up in their finery and many a match is made then ■

# RELIGION

CLOSE to seventy percent of the population follow the Buddhist faith while the balance follow Hindu beliefs synthesised with a generous dollop of Buddhism. Besides offering spectacular natural beauty and a pristine environment, Bhutan's landscape is studded with a profusion of majestic dzongs, beautiful gompas (monasteries) and chortens (stupas or pagodas) that are evidence of a living spiritual culture.

Bhutan's official religion is Drukpa Kagyu, a school of Mahayana Buddhism and in this

**The vase — one of the eight lucky symbols**

# RELIGION

book we briefly discuss Buddhism as well as its introduction to the country via Tibet. At the outset, apologies to those of the faith for whom this would appear to be perfunctory and shallow, but hopefully will be of some value to other travellers, as it was to the author whose knowledge initially was quite superficial!

**Looking to the future**

## BUDDHISM

Buddha was born as Siddhartha Gautam and we are giving only a brief sketch of his life since many of you are familiar with this historical father of Buddhism. He was born over 2000 years ago to the royal family of Lumbini, which is a part of present day Nepal. At the age of twenty-nine, he renounced his family and all trappings of his life as a prince.

Following a path of penance and sacrifice, he achieved Nirvana, or enlightenment, after meditating under a Bodhi (peepul) tree for six years. Over the next forty-five years his teachings and discourses provided the foundation of Buddhism which is, strictly speaking, less a religion and more a philosophy with a code of morality. According to these beliefs, asceticism and renunciation of material life do not necessarily lead to enlightenment. This can only be achieved after recognising and accepting the Four Noble Truths, the core tenet of Buddhist philosophy. According to these Truths, all life is suffering arising from our sensual desires and the illusion that they are important. Suffering can only end when this realisation is fully accepted and this, in turn, can only be achieved by following the prescribed Eight-Fold Path. This path is that of right thought, right speech, right action, right way of life, right effort, right awareness, right intention and right concentration. This path leads to the extinguishing of desires and eventually to a state of Nirvana, having been through a process of rebirths where your action in each life determines the next life. This is 'karma' which is not simply fate but the path which leads you through the cycle of birth and death till you finally escape from the world of suffering. All human beings have the potential and the power to follow the path.

After the death of Gautam Buddha, referred to as Maha Parinirvana, the first Great Council of Disciples was held by Mahakasyapa in the kingdom of Magadh (India), to record, clarify and consolidate the teachings of Buddha. This council lead to the Theravada Teachings (doctrine of elders), that focus primarily on meditation and concentration – the eighth of the Eight Fold Path. As a result, this doctrine centered on a monastic life in which almost all the time was spent in meditation.

Buddhism developed rapidly in India under the patronage of King Ashoka in the third century BC and as his empire was vast, so was the spread of Buddhism. His children Mahindra and Sanghamitra are said to have carried the word of Buddhism to Sri Lanka. Missions were sent forth to other lands as well to spread the teachings of Buddha.

However, by the first century AD, the limitations of Buddhism's appeal (based on the individual working to achieve Nirvana, 'prati moksha', through meditation and the exclusion of a normal family life), were evident. A schism developed within the ranks of the followers with the objective of re-formulating the teachings of Buddhism to include and accommodate people from all walks of life and not only those who had renounced family life and become 'monks'. This 'new Buddhism' was

**Rock painting of Guru Padmasambhava en route to Tango Monastery**

called Mahayana Buddhism – the Greater Vehicle or literally, the Greater Ox Cart, since it would accommodate believers from all walks of life. Theravada, which was the mainstream Buddhism till now, was then, somewhat superciliously, referred to as Hinayana Buddhism – the Lesser Vehicle.

Mahayana Buddhism can be compared to the Protestant

reformers of sixteenth century Europe, where there is no claim for the creation of a new religion but rather 'recovery' of its original form. The Mahayanists claim that their canon of scriptures represented 'the final, refined teachings of Buddha', which had hitherto been extended only to the most faithful followers. Regardless of the controversy over its origins,

the Mahayana doctrine represents a significant departure in the philosophy with the objective of extending religious authority to a greater number of people, rather than a concentration in the hands of a few.

The most important changes were: The Theravada goal of attainment of Buddhahood was in practice intimidating and seemingly unachievable. Hence Mahayanists tried to make Buddhism a more esoteric religion by introducing two grades of attainment below the level of Buddhahood. One is the Pratyeka-Buddha, or one who has awakened to the truth but keeps it a secret and the other the Arhant-Buddha or 'worthy-one', who has realised the truth by learning it from others. The Arhant is the goal for all believers – he hears the truth, comes to realise it as truth and then passes into Nirvana.

Another major innovation was the idea of boddhisattava (being of wisdom), who lived many lives before attaining Buddhahood. Before Buddha entered his final life as Siddhartha Gautam, he had spent many lives working towards Buddhahood. In these previous lives, he was a 'buddha-in-waiting' or boddhisattava, who performed incredible acts of compassion and generosity towards his fellow human beings. Boddhisattavas do

not want to evolve into a state of Buddhahood till they have freed all humanity from its suffering. Mahayana Buddhism also went against the original belief that there would be only one Buddha and that no more would follow – their belief suggests that Buddha has prophesied the coming of the future Buddha – who should currently be passing through one of the many cycles of life as the 'Maitreya or Jampa' (Future Buddha). There is also a possibility of more than one Maitreya – if you're on the right track it could be someone you know, or even yourself!

Lastly, Mahayana Buddhism 'converted' Buddhism from a philosophy to a religion. Theravada Buddhism believes that Buddha was a historical person who, after his death, ceased to exist. The Mahayanists developed the doctrine of the Three Bodies or Trikaya. As per this, the Buddha was not a human being but a manifestation of a universal spiritual being which had three bodies:

– when on earth as Siddhartha Gautam, it was the Body of Magical Transformation, 'Nirmanakaya'.

– this form emanated from the Body of Bliss, 'Sambhogakaya'. Located in heaven, this is the ruling and governing god of the Universe. This Body of Bliss has many forms and the one ruling our world is Amitava who lives in 'Sukhavati', the Land of Pure Bliss, a paradise located in the western heavens.

– The Body of Bliss in turn emanates from the Body of Essence, 'Dharmakaya', which is the underlying rule and principle of the Universe. This is akin to a universal soul and Nirvana the transcendent journey to it.

Today Mahayana Buddhism is prevalent in Tibet, Bhutan, Ladakh, Japan, China and Vietnam while Theravada Buddhism prevails in Myanmar, Thailand, Cambodia and Sri Lanka.

## BUDDHISM IN BHUTAN

Bhutan came under the Buddhist influence via Tibet. Apparently this was foretold by the chief protagonist of the Vajrayana teachings of Buddhism – Guru (Rinpoche) Padmasambhava – when he travelled through Bhutan en route to Samye (Tibet) in the eighth century AD. Armed with his dorje (vajra/thunderbolt), he ensured the completion of Samye Gompa and introduced Nyingma Buddhism to the region. The name 'Vajrayana' is believed to have derived from this and the vajra is regarded as an important symbol. Evolving from Mahayana traditions, the Vajrayana belief focuses on existential problems and stresses on meditative processes under the direct guidance of a recognised teacher. This is often referred to as Tantric or Mystic Buddhism, has a collection of texts called tantras and besides yogic meditation uses mantras (phrases) and mudras (gestures). Tantric Buddhism combines male and female energies and one such deity is the Kalchakra – meditation and rituals called the Kalchakra Puja are conducted towards this deity and his consort Viswamata, for attaining Nirvana.

Amalgamating the ancient shamanistic Bon religion prevalent in Tibet with Vajrayana teachings, the Nyingma (Red Hats) tradition was established by Guru Padmasambhava. During his travel, Guru Padmasambhava is believed to have scattered many terma (hidden treasures) which are texts or religious objects that are meant to be found over time to help the spiritual progress of followers. These terma can be discovered and identified only by enlightened tantric lamas called tertons. A large number of these terma have been found in

**Offerings at a mani wall**

# RELIGION

## RELIGIOUS ETIQUETTE

Wearing shorts while visiting a dzong or gompa is not allowed and shoes should be removed before entering a lhakhang (prayer hall). The 'right' way of circumventing a chorten or gompa is from left to right i.e. in a clockwise direction. Monks who act as your guides do not expect any remuneration but contributions can be left in a donation box provided for the purpose.

Monasteries have rules regarding photography and in the interest of preserving these irreplaceable works of art, it is important to follow the regulations and refrain from touching the murals and other religious objects on display. The visitor is expected to respect and maintain the sanctity and tranquillity of the environment.

For Bhutanese citizens it is mandatory for both men and women to wear a ceremonial scarf when they visit a dzong or attend an official function. The men wear a three meter scarf, the kabney, which is draped over their left shoulder and knotted on the opposite side. The colour indicates the person's rank; white for private citizens, red for senior officials and saffron yellow for the King and Je Khempo — with many shades in between. Ladies wear a shorter scarf with fringed ends called the rachu and this is just draped over the left shoulder.

East Bhutan. Pema Lingpa, the best known terton, constructed several monasteries in the Bumthang region. (see page 198).

The Red Hats later split into three main strands: the original Nyingma; the Kagyu inspired by Gurus Naropa and Marpa; the Sakya inspired by the Indian yogi Virupa. The Drukpa Kagyu lineage was established at Ralung Monastery in Tibet and brought to Bhutan by Lama Phajo Drukgom

Shigpo and in the seventeenth century established as the official state religion by the Zhabdung Ngawang Namgyal. It follows the tantric tradition and recommends solitary meditation. Every home boasts a choesham (altar), usually bearing statues of the great trio: Sakyamuni, Guru Rinpoche and Zhabdung Rinpoche. 'Kagyu' means whispered communication and emphasises oral teachings from master to pupil besides yogic practices of breathing and postures. The Nyingma and its sub-group, the Kagyu, do not require monks to be celibate.

In Tibet the many divisions in the Red Hat sect resulted in the Gelugpa (Yellow Hat) sect becoming the dominant force from the sixteenth century onwards. Clashes between the two led to the Red Hats crossing into Bhutan and Sikkim ■

**Step by step, wheel by wheel**

# RELIGION

## BODDHISATTAVAS

Boddhisattavas are beings who have attained enlightenment, but refusing to accept Nirvana choose to reincarnate so they can help release sentient beings caught in the cycle of suffering and rebirth. The boddhisattava will not accept the reward of Nirvana till all beings have been led to enlightenment.

Some of the most revered boddhisattavas are:

### ▶▶ MAITREYA

(Jampa in Tibetan), is the 'Buddha of the Future'. It is believed he will reappear on earth to restore the purity of the dharma, to deliver all sentient beings to enlightenment by revealing all that is hidden by ignorance and time. He is one boddhisattava whose believers and devotees span both the Hinayana and Mahayana sects. He will be the last of five Buddhas to gain supreme enlightenment in this aeon. He is shown holding the stalk of a lotus in his hand and is depicted either sitting or standing.

### ▶▶ AVALOKITESWARA

(Gazing down Lord), embodies the compassion of all the Buddhas (karuna), and is regarded as the guardian of the country. The Dalai Lama and the Karmapa are considered living manifestations of Avalokiteswara. He is from the Lotus family and a family protector along with Manjusri and Vajrapani. His colouring symbolises passionate concern for beings and he is depicted either sitting in full lotus position or standing. He is shown with two, four or a thousand arms, being all-encompassing.

### ▶▶ PADMASAMBHAVA

(Guru Rinpoche), was a renowned tantric saint from northern India who brought Buddhism to Tibet. He is shown seated on a lotus, wearing a red cap and with his legs crossed. In his right hand he holds the vajra (thunderbolt) while the left rests on his lap.

### ▸▸ VAJRAPANI

He is a wrathful boddhisattava and is one of the three protectors of the family, with Avalokiteswara and Manjusri. He fights a spiritual battle against forces of ignorance, craving and the samsara. He is depicted as a blue tantric figure with a flamed halo and wearing a garland of skulls and a wreath of snakes.

### ▸▸ MANJUSRI

(Prince of Wisdom) is a family protector, along with Avalokiteswara and Vajrapani. He represents wisdom, intelligence and confers mastery of dharma. Second only to Avalokiteswara, he is a very popular boddhisattava and is shown holding the sword of truth in his right hand to cut through ignorance while the left hand is held out, palm forward, in the teaching mudra.

### ▸▸ GREEN TARA

She is the 'Boddhisattava of Compassion', gentle, heartfelt and born from the tears of Avalokiteswara. She protects and guides believers on the path of enlightenment and is often referred to as the Swift One due to her immediate response to prayers. She is the Wisdom Consort of Transcendental Buddha Amogasiddhi. She is portrayed with her left leg resting on the right thigh while the right leg steps forward gracefully in front of her. Her left hand is held in front of her heart, in the 'mudra of granting refuge' while the right hand rests on her knee in the 'mudra of generosity'.

### ▸▸ WHITE TARA

She is the Mother of all Buddhas and belongs to the Lotus family of Amitava. She energises those who visualise her to follow the spiritual path they have set out on. She is associated with health, strength and longevity and is shown sitting on a lotus and with seven eyes — the normal pair plus one in the center of the forehead in the 'third-eye' position and eyes on the palms of her hands and the soles of her feet.

## THE WHEEL OF LIFE

The Wheel (Mandala) is a depiction of existence, with all its conditions and circumstances that is called samsara or sangsara – the unsatisfactory cycle of life, death and rebirth that can continue endlessly unless we work to change the situation. The Lord of Death, Yama, is depicted biting into the wheel and holding it firmly, implying that if the right path is not followed destruction will result.

The Hub contains the three poisons — lust or desire symbolised by the cock, aversion or hatred depicted by the snake, and the pig representing delusion or ignorance.

The Middle Ring, divided into six segments depicts the realms where all sentient beings are reborn.

Heaven is the divine realm and residence of Devas or Gods, who are born here by virtue of the good karma of meritorious deeds and charitable actions in previous lives. However, since enlightenment has not been attained they must continue on the Noble Path, or risk leaving the realm after exhausting their good karma.

The Human realm is one of trial for humanity with good and evil influences co-existing.

The realm of Beasts is where those who have been cruel and have followed animal like instincts have been relegated to.

Hell is the darkest realm where those who harboured intense hatred are now tortured by scorching heat and icy cold.

Hungry Ghosts is the realm of those who are extremely selfish and even after death are consumed by desire—here they are in a constant state of hunger and thirst.

The Asuras is the realm of powerful entities who harbour hate and jealousy—they are anti-gods who are constantly at war. Having embarked on the Noble Path they failed to follow it completely and while attaining great power, their anger and envy deny them entrance to heaven while other merits keep them out of hell.

In each of the realms there is a Buddha in a different colour to guide one onto the Noble Path.

The Outermost Ring depicts the twelve karma formations or the links of interdependence. Enlightenment can only be attained by freeing oneself from all these formations.

Craving · Clinging · Becoming · Feeling · Rebirth · Contact · Heaven · Asuras · Humans · Three Poisons · Old Age & Death · Six Senses · Beasts · Hungry Ghosts · Name & Form · Hell · Ignorance · Consciousness · Acts of Volition

**Tangkha depicting the Wheel of Life in the 400-year-old Tawang Monastery, Arunachal**

# RELIGION

## CHORTENS

In ancient times chortens, (Tibetan for stupas), were built as relic holders, but are now mainly built in honour of the Living Buddhas or boddhisattavas. Chortens are shaped to symbolise the five elements of nature: Earth, Water, Fire, Air and Ether – which is the medium that the body converts to after death. The rectangular base represents the earth. The next, somewhat circular one, being water, the conical section symbolises fire, topped by a crescent representing air, with the oval right at the top being ether.

## PRAYER FLAGS AND PRAYER WHEELS

Chortens are usually surrounded by prayer flags and prayer wheels. The flags are often white in colour, representing purity of thought and are supposed to carry the prayers of the faithful on the wings of wind.

Made of strips of cloth in oblong, rectangular or triangular shape, with holy inscriptions and lucky signs printed on them, these prayer flags are of four types. Those for luck are long narrow and oblong shaped victory banners and have a substantial amount of text on them, whereas others bear the symbol of the Dorje (Thunderbolt). The 'Wind Horse' flags depict a horse with a jewel on its back.

Prayer flags are an integral part of the landscape – on hilltops, trees and buildings.

Prayer wheels have holy mantras inscribed on them and rotating them brings a feeling of peace and tranquillity besides good luck. So go ahead and give those wheels a spin or buy your own personal handheld prayer wheel like those frequently seen in the hands of monks and other devotees. These are usually found in shops conveniently located near most gompas.

**Chendebji Chorten, Bhutan**

# EIGHT LUCKY SYMBOLS

Decorating gompas as well as various items of religious use, and others of tourist interest, you will notice eight symbols. These signs of the Buddhist faith symbolise the Eight Fold Path and are used as signs for good luck.

### GOLDEN FISH
Represents the eyes of Buddha who, like the fish, could see through muddy waters. The pair represents the interdependence of the female and male.

### PARASOL
Symbolises preservation and protection from harmful forces and negative energies.

### VASE
Repository of fulfilment, long life, good health and prosperity.

### ENDLESS KNOT
Represents Eternity and Unity – also called 'Mystic Dragon'.

### LOTUS
Despite having its roots in dirt, the bloom is beautiful and represents purity of mind and body.

### DHARMA WHEEL
Symbolises liberation from death and rebirth.

### VICTORY BANNER
Triumph and victory of good over evil, as also over ignorance.

### CONCH
Spread of dharma and awakening of sentient beings from their state of ignorance.

## GURU PADMASAMBHAVA

Guru Padmasambhava, the Lotus Born, is popularly known as Guru Rinpoche (Precious Teacher) and is renowned as the second Buddha in the Himalayan region. His coming was predicted by the historical Buddha (Sakyamuni). Talking of his birth, the Rinpoche is reported to have said, "Some people believe that I revealed myself upon the pollen bed of a lotus in the Dhanakosha Lake in the country of Urgyen; some people believe I was born as Prince of Urgyen and others believe that I came in the flash of a thunderbolt to the Nainchak hilltop. There are many distinct beliefs held by different individuals and peoples, for I have appeared in many forms.

However, twenty-four years after the Parinirvana of the Buddha Sakyamuni, the Adibuddha of Boundless Light, Amitava, conceived the Thought of Enlightenment in the form of the Great Compassionate One, Avalokiteswara, and from the heart of the Great Compassionate One, I, Padma, the Lotus Born Guru, was emanated as the syllable 'HRI'. I came like rain throughout the world in innumerable billions of forms to those who were ready to receive me. The actions of the Enlightened Ones are incomprehensible! Who is to define or measure them!"

The tale now shifts to the remote mountain kingdom of Sahar in India (presently known as Mandi) where Mandarava, the daughter of Raja Arshadhar, much to her father's chagrin refused to marry any of the numerous suitors wooing her. One night Lord Buddha appeared in her dream and asked her to come to a grassy knoll nearby to receive instructions. The next day she went to the designated spot, accompanied by her attendants. To their great amazement Guru Padmasambhava emerged from the end of a rainbow. The maidens were mesmerised by his presence and returned regularly, spending their days listening to his discourse on the Vajrayana teachings and Mandarava soon emerged as the star pupil. However, news that his daughter was keeping 'strange company' soon reached the king and he dispatched his courtiers to check. When they confirmed the story the king flew into a rage, had Padmasambhava arrested and restricted the princess to the castle. To eliminate the menace, Padmasambhava was set afire on a pyre on the very same grassy knoll. Observers saw an eight year old boy seated on a lotus surrounded by rainbows formed above the flames. The fire raged for seven days till a lake appeared and Padmasambhava's lotus throne rose out of the waters with the great teacher completely unharmed — this lake at Rewalsar became a holy destination for pilgrims. The king realised his folly and begged the guru to become the spiritual teacher of Sahar. He graciously acceded to this request and became known as Guru Chimi Pema-Pungni (The Immortal Lotus Born Teacher). The princess became one of the guru's closest disciples and later one of his two main consorts, accompanying him on his further travels.

Guru Padmasambhava is, however, best known as the founder of Tibetan Buddhism and according to one version it is from Rewalsar that he embarked on his epic journey to Tibet. Around AD 750, the Tibetan King Trisong Detsen wanted to make Buddhism the state religion and tried to establish a monastery at Samye. Both the aristocracy and the practitioners of the traditional Bon religion were opposed to this move. The construction of the gompa was plagued by a succession of earthquakes which were attributed to the malicious machinations of the local demons. Though the Buddhist teachers were superior to the Bonpo priests in doctorinal debate, they were no match when it came to 'magic'. The famed Indian teacher Shankarakshita, who was helping the king, asked him to invite Guru Padmasambhava to help in the task of subduing and converting these very skilful negative forces. Armed with his dorje (thunderbolt), Padmasambhava succeeded in silencing the detractors of Buddhism, even converting many of them to help spread the religion in Tibet. He introduced the Nyingma form of Buddhism and was instrumental in establishing a body of monks at the Samye Gompa which went on to become the principal center of learning in the region. The Tibetan Queen Dakini Yeshe Tsogyal became his second consort and it is from Tibet that he made his final ascent into the heavens.

In Bhutan he was responsible for introducing the Buddhist faith first in the Bumthang region and then spreading it to the rest of the country. During a second visit he meditated at several spots including Gom Kora in the East and Taktsang in the West. Guru Padmasambhava is depicted in eight different manifestations derived from different stages in his life. These range from the fearsome, when he was challenging and subduing the forces of evil to the most common representation as a great and enlightened teacher.

# FESTIVALS

THERE are numerous festivals celebrated in Bhutan – both secular and religious ones. Of the former, the most important is the National Day which commemorates the consolidation of the country and establishment of monarchy on 17th December 1907. The King's birthday, Coronation Day and the various New Year celebrations (a different one for each region or community), are other secular festivals.

The most popular religious festival is the tsechu which honours the memory of Guru Padmasambhava by depicting key episodes or great deeds from his life. These usually take place on the tenth day of the particular month in the Bhutanese calendar.

The tradition of the Bhutanese tsechu was established by Zhabdung Ngawang Namgyal in the sixteenth century and many of the dances and ceremonies performed today are attributed to him or Pema Lingpa. The festival lasts between three to five days and is celebrated in all the major dzongs in the country at varying times of the year (details are given in the festival calendar).

The religious dances are called chhams and are performed by monks as well as lay people, with the dances remaining the same but the order of performance varying

The 'band' at the Paro tsechu

# FESTIVALS

An atsara on the editor's lap!

from place to place. The tsechu is a religious festival and it is believed that by attending it a person gains merit. It also serves as the largest annual social gathering for the area, with people decked up in all their finery coming to join in the celebration of good over evil, hoping that all their unanswered wishes and prayers would be considered.

Besides the dancers and musicians, a key character at the tsechu is the atsara. These are clowns who wear dramatically expressive masks with big red noses and are an indispensable element in the otherwise solemn and sometimes tedious ceremony.

Their exaggerated gestures and irreverant jokes provide comic relief when the audience gets restive and only they are allowed to confront the monks and 'mock' the religion (without any malicious intent). They are actually treated with great respect as they are believed to be representatives of the ancient acharyas — the Sanskrit word for religious teachers.

While indulging in their antics the atsaras also help in maintaining order, and it is normal for both locals as well as tourists who get close to them to reward them with a nominal two/five Nu for their efforts! During the interval between chhams women in gorgeous traditional attire sing and perform classical dances.

Some tsechus end or begin with the unfurling of a huge embroidered tangkha depicting Guru Padmasambhava and his eight manifestations. Such a tangkha which is worshipped, is called a thongdrel (liberation on sight) and it is believed that simply by viewing it some are delivered from the cycle of reincarnation or their sins of this lifetime are washed away.

At some tsechus there is the custom of the wang — a collective verbal blessing given by a high priest followed by the distribution of coloured sacred threads which the devotees tie around their necks as evidence of the blessing.

Some important dzongs celebrate another annual festival (besides the tsechu), called a dromchoe which generally include dances to Yeshe Gompo (Mahakala) or Palden Lhamo — the protective Drukpa deities. If you are planning to attend a tsechu the detailed interpretation as also the sequence of the chhams on the various days can be obtained through your tour operator.

Our recommendation is that if you haven't been to a tsechu, plan your trip so that you can experience this unique event ◼

# FESTIVALS

## CHHAMS

Chhams are the core event of monastic festivals. These highly choreographed sacred dance dramas are performed by masked lamas to the accompaniment of the monastic orchestra. The central theme is inevitably the depiction of the triumph of good forces over evil. The lamas are dressed in rich brocade robes but it is the masks they wear that make these festivals unique. Some are fierce and scary, others benign and pleasant. They represent various divinities from the Buddhist pantheon. The fearsome masks are actually the boddhisattavas in their wrathful, tantric form. Most festivals are spread over three days — the first day starting with special prayers in front of the main guardian deities (Nyep), to ward off evil spirits from disrupting the festival. The mystic dances are performed at fixed times on both days and the hand gestures (mudras), have specific meanings associated with the rites. Music is provided by the twelve-foot long copper and brass horns, the melodious brass cymbals and the resonant drums and the atmosphere is one of great solemnity with an all-pervading spiritual ambience.

Some of the more important chhams that are performed at the tsechu are: 'The Dance of the Four Stags' which is a protective dance that marks the subduing of the God of the Winds by Guru Padmasambhava who then takes the god's stag as his mount. The dancers wear a horned deer mask in this chham.

'Dance of the Heroes' proclaims the glory of Buddhism and depicts Pema Lingpa's arrival in Guru Padmasambhava's heaven — Zangto Pelri — an endless mandala of rainbow hues. Although unmasked, the performers wear a crown and carry a small drum and a ball.

'Dance of the Stag and the Hounds' represents the conversion to Buddhism of a hunter, Gonpo Dorji, by Milarepa. This instructive chham is long and more like a play or dance drama and usually is enacted in two parts, each marking the end of day at the tsechu.

'Dance of the Drums from Drametse' is a very popular chham and was composed by a saint from eastern Bhutan who, by the strength of his magical powers, visited Zangto Pelri and the dance depicts his vision of this heaven and the victory of the gods over demons. Dancers wear animal masks and carry a big drum.

'Dance of the Black Hats' is a powerful purification rite which used to be performed by the Zhabdung. The dancers are spectacularly clad in colourful brocade and large hats and represent tantrics who cut down the demons and take possession of the earth. They protect it by dancing in the thunderbolt step, pounding the earth in a mandala formation. This ground-purifying chham is often performed before dzongs, chortens and temples are built.

'*Dance of the Twenty-One Black Hats with Drums*' signifies the triumph of Buddhism and the religion is represented by the beating of great drums.

'*Dance of the Lords of the Cremation Grounds*' carries tantric symbolism with skull clad dancers guarding the eight cremation grounds located at the edges of a cosmic diagram.

'*Dance of the Judgment of the Dead*' is an instructive chham that is divided into two parts. It deals with the travails of the after life when the dead are brought before the God of the Dead. There is a scale to weigh their good deeds against evil ones and each case is argued by both a god and demon (that are believed to live in each being), before a judgment is made.

'*Dance of the Eight Manifestations of Guru Padmasambhava*' is a glory dance that shows the eight aspects under which the Rinpoche manifested at various occasions over time. He is accompanied by his two consorts — Mandarava, the lady of wisdom, to the right and

Yeshe Tsogyal, goddess of knowledge (believed to be an incarnation of the Indian goddess Saraswati), to the left.

Other chhams performed are the *Lute Dance* which celebrates the founding and spread of the Drukpa school, *Dance of the Noblemen and the Ladies* show events in the life of King Nozong and carries some comic — and even lewd — touches. *Dance of Gingdong Tsholing* depicts the glorious heaven Zangto Pelri.

# FESTIVALS

| FESTIVAL | PLACE | 2007 | 2008 |
|---|---|---|---|
| Punakha Dromchoe | Punakha | Feb 21 - 25 | Feb 11 - 15 |
| Chorten Kora | Trashiyangtse | Mar 3 - 19 | Feb 21 - Mar 7 |
| Gom Kora | Trashigang | Mar 26 - 28 | Mar 14 - 16 |
| Paro Tsechu | Paro | Mar 31 - Apr 2 | Mar 17 - 21 |
| Chukha Tsechu | Chukha | Mar 31 - Apr 2 | Mar 19 - 21 |
| Ura Yakchoe | Bumthang | Apr 27 - May 1 | Apr 16 - 20 |
| Nimalung Tsechu | Bumthang | Jun 23 - 25 | Jul 10 - 12 |
| Kurjey Tsechu | Bumthang | Jun 25 | Jul 12 |
| Thimphu Drupchen | Thimphu | Sep 16 - 20 | Oct 4 - 8 |
| Wangdi Tsechu | Wangdiphodrang | Sep 20 - 22 | Oct 7 - 9 |
| Thimphu Tsechu | Thimphu | Sep 21 - 23 | Oct 9 - 11 |
| Tamshingphala Choepa | Bumthang | Sep 21 - 23 | Oct 8 - 10 |
| Tangbi Mani | Bumthang | Sep 25 - 27 | Oct 13 - 15 |
| Jambay Lhakhang Drup | Bumthang | Oct 25 - 29 | Nov 12 - 16 |
| Praker Duchhoed | Bumthang | Oct 26 - 28 | Nov 13 - 15 |
| Mongar Tsechu | Mongar | Nov 16 - 19 | Dec 4 - 7 |
| Pemagatsel Tsechu | Pemagatsel | Nov 16 - 19 | Dec 4 - 7 |
| Trashigang Tsechu | Trashigang | Nov 17 - 20 | Dec 5 - 8 |
| Nalakhar Tsechu | Bumthang | Nov 24 - 26 | Dec 12 - 14 |
| Trongsa Tsechu | Trongsa | Dec 18 - 20 | Jan 5 - 7 (2009) |
| Lhuentse Tsechu | Lhuentse | Dec 18 - 20 | Jan 5 - 7 (2009) |

*Tsechu dates are tentative and should be reconfirmed.*

# THE HOLIDAY

*f*rom now on, the author takes the steering
wheel and leads you through a most scenic
and spectacular land, with an itinerary
that unfolds over the next pages...

# TRAVEL PLAN

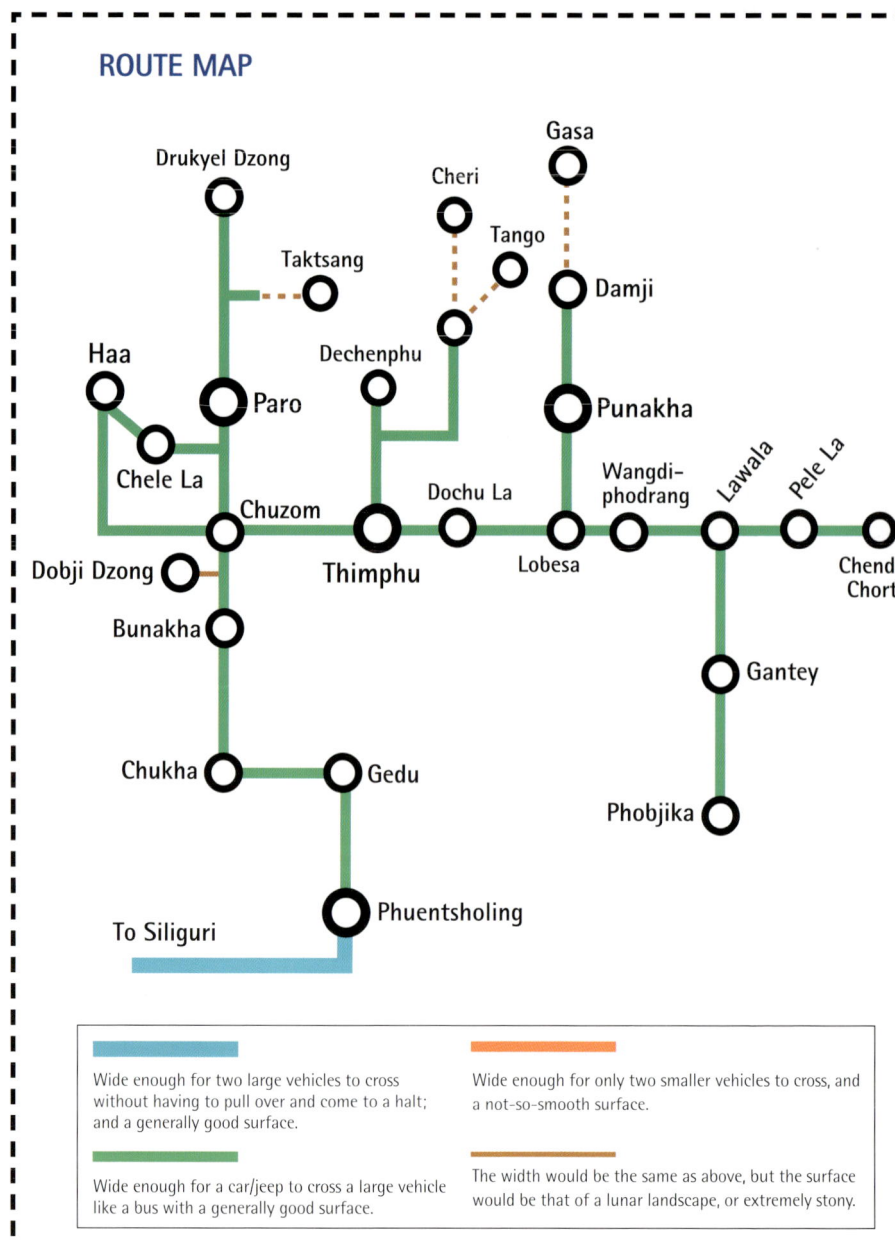

## ROUTE MAP

Gasa

Cheri

Drukyel Dzong

Tango

Damji

Taktsang

Haa

Dechenphu

Paro

Punakha

Chele La

Wangdi-
phodrang

Lawala

Pele La

Chuzom

Dochu La

Dobji Dzong

Thimphu

Lobesa

Chende
Chorte

Bunakha

Gantey

Chukha

Gedu

Phobjika

To Siliguri

Phuentsholing

| | |
|---|---|
| Wide enough for two large vehicles to cross without having to pull over and come to a halt; and a generally good surface. | Wide enough for only two smaller vehicles to cross, and a not-so-smooth surface. |
| Wide enough for a car/jeep to cross a large vehicle like a bus with a generally good surface. | The width would be the same as above, but the surface would be that of a lunar landscape, or extremely stony. |

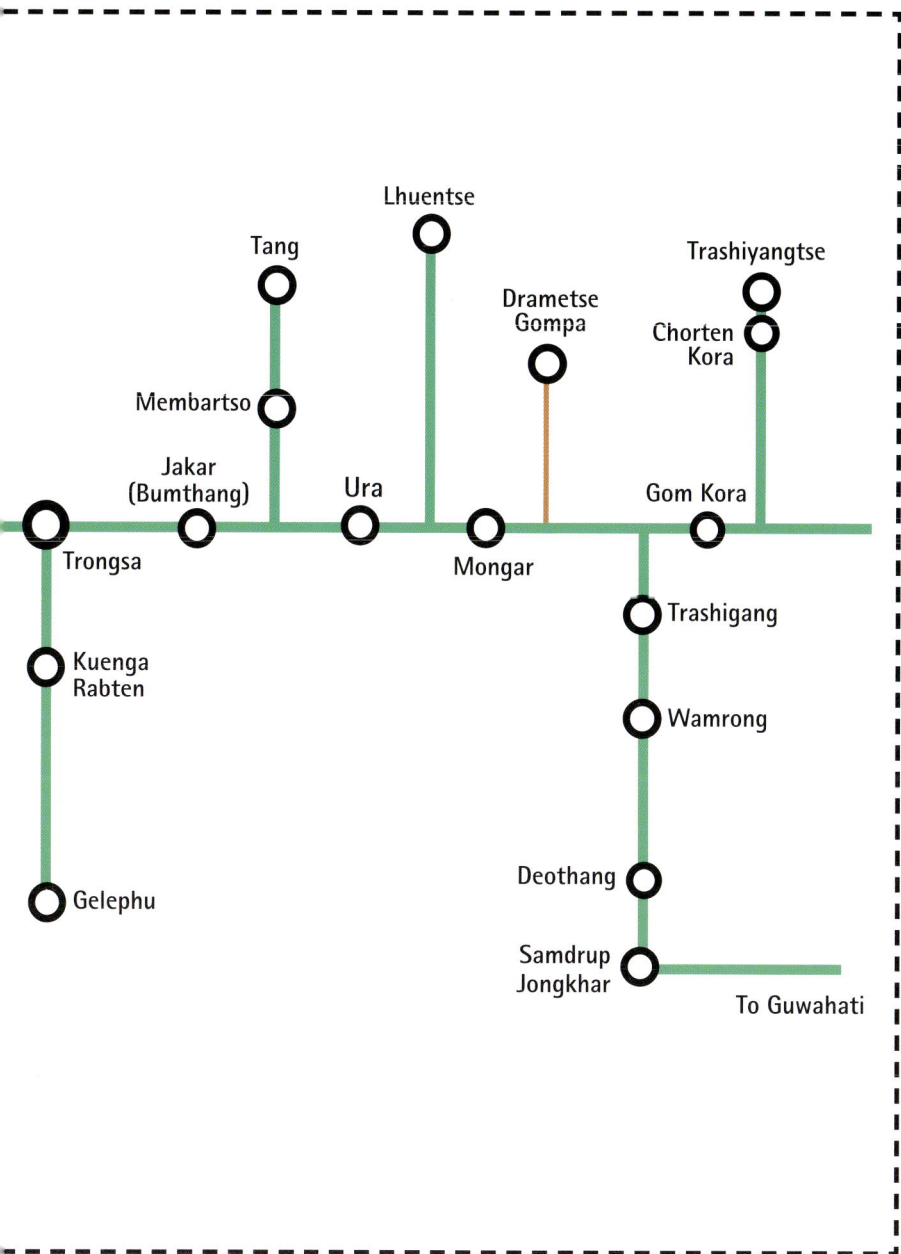

Lhuentse

Tang

Trashiyangtse

Drametse
Gompa

Chorten
Kora

Membartso

Jakar
(Bumthang)

Ura

Gom Kora

Trongsa

Mongar

Kuenga
Rabten

Trashigang

Wamrong

Deothang

Gelephu

Samdrup
Jongkhar

To Guwahati

### DAY 1
▶▶ **From Siliguri to Paro via Phuentsholing**

Drukyel Dzong — Paro — Chuzom — Thimphu — Dochu La — Dobji Dzong — Bunakha — Chukha — Dantak Canteen — Gedu — Phuentsholing — Jaigaon — Coronation Bridge — Binaguri — Dalgaon — Siliguri

You will get a good breakfast at Phuentsholing and can stop for a cup of tea at a dhaba en route.

| | | | |
|---|---|---|---|
| Siliguri-Sevoke | 20km | Bunakha-Chuzom | 37km |
| Sevoke-Phuentsholing | 128km | Chuzom-Paro | 24km |
| Phuentsholing-Gedu | 44km | Chuzom-Thimphu | 31km |
| Gedu-Bunakha | 57km | | |

Since you're probably rearing to hit the road and start an exciting holiday, you wouldn't mind making a reasonably early start! The Indian border town, Jaigaon, is around 2.5 hours away and if you leave Siliguri by 6 am you should be at the Bhutanese Immigration Office as it opens for business (remember Bhutan is thirty minutes ahead of IST).

Exiting Siliguri you drive through a pleasant forest on the road to Sevoke till you reach Coronation Bridge, 20km away. Crossing it, you turn left towards Binaguri which is 77km

Tea gardens sloping down to meet lush paddy fields

**The three chortens at Chuzom**

further. A kilometer or so after this town, at the T-junction, you have to turn left to Dalgaon. Around 43km further on, before Hashimara and 2km after the Torsa River bridge, turn left on to the slightly rough surfaced road that joins the road to Jaigaon/Phuentsholing (18km ahead).

Shorts are best avoided while visiting the immigration office.

The overall smooth road surface and light traffic allows you to make good time and you can be at Phuentsholing's Central Hotel by 8.30 for breakfast. This is a convenient place to connect with your guide and then proceed to complete the immigration and vehicle entry formalities

which can take a couple of hours.

While engaged in this exercise you cannot help but notice the change in people's appearance – gone are the dhotis, lungis and baniyans (undershirts), replaced by attire that seems almost like a uniform, albeit a rather dignified one. This is the Bhutanese national dress and it is compulsory for citizens to wear it while attending government offices, schools and official ceremonies as also when visiting a dzong or monastery. The men folk wear the gho; a long robe akin to the Tibetan chuba. It falls just below the knee and is held in place by the kyera — a woven cloth belt wound tightly around the waist. The gho comes in a variety of patterns and the plaids are very similar to the Scottish tartan. The socks are worn long with covered shoes and a scarf (kabney) is draped over the left shoulder. The women wear the kira which is an elegant full length wrap-around dress made from beautiful hand woven fabric. It is caught at the shoulder by a pair of exquisitely worked silver clasps (koma) and belted at the waist with the keyra. The inner blouse is called a wonju and the jacket, tego, completes this striking ensemble. The scarf (rachu) is worn over the left shoulder when entering a religious place or government institution. (The traditional attire for young girls is an ankle-length tunic — the gochu.) The jewellery is mostly of silver and precious stones such as coral, turquoise and the 'zee', a rare etched agate. Interestingly, in the Laya valley, both men and women wear turquoise earrings that they believe represent water that will help them negotiate their after-life journey!

This practice of wearing the national dress not only reinforces their identity but also ensures the

There are two gompas in Phuentsholing — the Zangto Pelri Monastery and the Kharbandi Gompa which overlooks the town.

**Paro valley**

continued importance of their traditional art of weaving by providing an assured market.

Phuentsholing is at a lowly 1700ft/518m but in the next 36km the road climbs to a cool 6600ft/2012m. At Gedu, 8km further, you will be impressed to note that the striking building complex you pass is no important government office but that of Tala Hydro-electric Project

## NATIONAL SYMBOLS

Bhutan's rectangular national flag is divided diagonally – with the golden yellow upper half representing the secular power of the king and the lower orange part symbolising the Buddhist faith. A white dragon in the center represents the purity of the country and the jewels held in its claws depict the wealth and perfection of the nation.

The national emblem is circular and in its center is a lotus with a double diamond thunderbolt placed above it. This is surmounted by a jewel and framed by two dragons. The lotus symbolises purity, the jewel expresses sovereign power and the double diamond thunderbolt signifies the harmony between secular and religious power while the dragons represent the country's name Druk-Yul.

The national flower is the high altitude blue poppy and cypress is the national tree, chosen since it grows straight and strong even in inhospitable terrain. The national animal is the extremely rare and unusual takin and the national bird is the raven. The raven represents Gonpo Jarodonchen (Mahakala with a raven's head), one of the country's most important guardian deities.

underway! All buildings in Bhutan follow the traditional style and this certainly lends a distinct character even to the latest urban development.

For the next 30-35km the valley you pass through is almost perpetually shrouded in a fine mist, lending it a mysterious quality. However, do look out for the magnificent Vince waterfall that comes up 20km beyond Gedu.

If you are looking for a break, the Border Road's (DANTAK) facility is around 16km before Chukha. At Wangkha you will catch a glimpse of the Chukha dam and 6km further you can tank up at Chukha if you failed to do so at Jaigaon. Or else, proceed to the Tourist Hotel at Bunakha (100km or 3-3.5 hours from your entry into Bhutan) and enjoy your first Bhutanese meal – served buffet style.

If you are running late, postpone all sightseeing and try to make it to your hotel before dark.

Resuming your journey you ascend 17km to 8350ft/2546m, the highest point on this route. There is a check point 8km before the top, followed by another when you drop down to the river confluence at Chuzom. The route runs along a river of the same name but before you reach Chuzom look upwards to your left and spot your first dzong – the Dobji Dzong which is currently under renovation but once served as a jail.

Chuzom marks the confluence of the Paro Chu and the Wang Chu. Opposite you, at the confluence, are three protecting chortens each built in a different style. From left to right these are the Nepalese, Tibetan and Bhutanese and this is one place where you can easily spot their architectural differences. The Nepalese chorten resembles the classical Indian stupa most closely and the four sides are painted with eyes which represent Buddha's all-seeing eye and what looks like a nose is actually the number

'one' in Sanskrit, depicting the absoluteness of Buddha. In the Tibetan chorten the rounded section angles outward instead of following the classical dome shape. The Bhutanese chorten, though based on the principles of the classical

You may not realise it but at 8000ft your body needs to acclimatise, so don't overdo it!

stupa, is unique in its style. It is square in shape and has a sloping roof. Painted under the eaves is a broad red band called the khemar which identifies the religious character of a building. There are tablets or slates embedded in the

**Tachogang Gompa, Paro valley**

## GOMPAS

The gompa, or 'solitary place', are buildings where monks can isolate themselves from the world to further their meditative process. Gompas were therefore built in remote locations. Their concept can be traced to the caves hollowed out of sheer rock, which monks used for retreat and meditation during the time of Gautam Buddha. The growing acceptance of Buddhism, and the patronage it received from the state, led to gompas evolving

into large, magnificent edifices that served both as places of worship for devotees and also as residence and teaching centers for monks. Each gompa held its own treasure of holy relics. According to a scriptural couplet, the gompa should be built with its back to the hill face and the front facing a water body. The approach to all gompas is lined with rows of fluttering prayer flags, gleaming white chortens and mani (medong) walls. People choose mani stones, preferably beautiful and unusual ones, and etch them in the graceful calligraphy with mantras — the most common being 'Om Mane Padme Hum'. The stones are piled on each other and form walls of prayer. Local belief holds that picking and carrying away one of these offerings of prayer brings bad luck.

Inside a gompa, one first enters the 'Dukhanq' or assembly hall, where monks are found engaged in various rituals or in chanting prayers. The most sacred place in a Bhutanese gompa is the 'Genkhag' (god's room), where the central deity with his attendant images is enshrined. Butter lamps provide beautiful, soft illumination and the walls are adorned with a variety of paintings and tangkhas. The interiors are vibrant with rich colours and the glowing images of Lord Buddha and the boddhisattavas. Being centers of learning, most gompas have extensive libraries, with xylographs of the 'Kanjur' (holy book of Buddha's teachings). Depending on the time of day, a gompa can be a beehive of activity but the overall aura is one of peace and tranquility.

**The country's only airport at Paro**

khemar with images of deities carved on them.

At Chuzom the road bifurcates – Paro lies to the left, only 24km away while Thimphu is 31km to the right.

After a couple of kilometers you enter the stunningly beautiful Paro valley which extends

Check out the flight timings and position yourself on the road leading to Olathang Hotel to watch the Druk Air flight landing.

all the way from mighty Jhomolhari on the Tibetan border in the North right down to the confluence at Chuzom. A side valley leads to the high pass Tremo La (16,400ft/5000m), which was once a major trade link with Tibet but also the route followed by marauding Tibetan armies. The

Paro valley is truly enchanting – a patchwork of lush green rice fields with a clear crystalline river meandering graciously through it, delicate pink and white blooms on fruit trees, azure skies and sunlit air.

The countryside is dotted with elegant farmhouses and traditional homes that are considered the most beautiful in the country. Their size as well as the elaborately carved and painted rows of windows at three levels is testimony to the prosperity of this valley. Much of its wealth went into a prolific building of monasteries and temples – there are as many as a hundred and fifty-five in Paro district.

Around 6km after Chuzom you pass the striking Tachogang Gompa located on the opposite bank of the river. This private temple was founded by the Tibetan saint, Thangtong Gyelpo (1385-1464), the 'Iron Bridge Lama'. It was built around 1420 after he saw a vision of Avalokiteswara in the form of a horse and the gompa's name means 'Temple of the Excellent Horse'. He is credited with building the first iron bridges in the country – in locations as far apart as Paro and distant Trashigang at the eastern end.

He also constructed the chorten-shaped Dungtse Lhakhang and is believed to have composed many of the folk songs still sung by people when engaged in chores such as threshing or compacting mud for house building.

Your journey now takes you past the village of Bondey, with Paro's magnificent airport complex coming into view shortly after. Hopefully, the 310km journey to your destination has not been too arduous and it is now time to locate your hotel and settle in for a relaxed evening ■

Just out of town there are stretches where you can sit by the river with your thermos of coffee.

## DAY 2
### ▶▶ Visit Paro Dzong, Dungtse Lhakhang, Ta Dzong (National Museum) and Kyichu Lhakhang

With the only airport in the country located here, one would naturally assume Paro to be a somewhat bustling township. Fortunately, nothing could be farther from the truth – the 'town' of Paro consists of under 3000 souls! In reality Paro is a village now transforming itself into a small town. It is undeniably going through a construction boom with numerous homes, shops and guest houses being rapidly added but since all buildings have to follow

**Young archers on the prowl!**

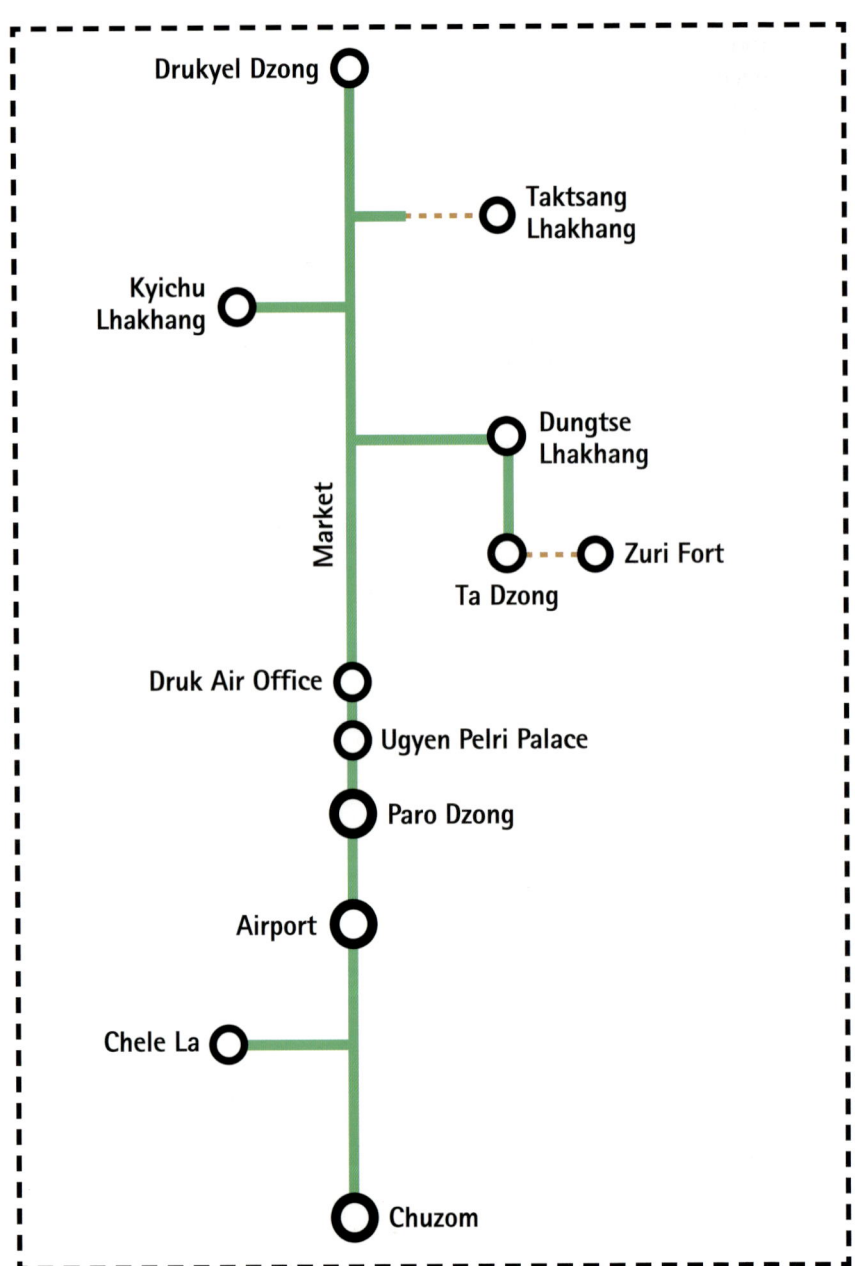

Drukyel Dzong

Taktsang Lhakhang

Kyichu Lhakhang

Dungtse Lhakhang

Zuri Fort

Ta Dzong

Market

Druk Air Office

Ugyen Pelri Palace

Paro Dzong

Airport

Chele La

Chuzom

the traditional Bhutanese architecture, there is a symmetry and harmony maintained. The market center was built as recently as 1985 and stretches for about 500m. The neatly arranged shops and houses are only a couple of blocks deep on either side of the main thoroughfare and the only petrol pump is located here. This is as 'downtown' as Paro gets and the rest of the region is charmingly rustic and tranquil. The willow-lined roads cut through cultivated fields tended by sturdy hard working farm folk with their colourful clothes and ready smiles. Roughly in the center of the valley lies the Paro Dzong – an awesome and impressive introduction to the world of dzongs that lies ahead of you. (As in the case of Europe where there is a danger of being 'castled or churched out', in Bhutan it is possible to get 'dzonged'!) Just ahead of the dzong the valley bifurcates; continuing North-West is the main valley which has a road running though it for 16km, ending at the Drukyel Dzong. The other valley runs northward along the Do Chu for the same distance.

There is not much to shop in Paro, but walking around the market place is an enjoyable experience.

The correct name for the Paro Dzong is Rinchen Pung Dzong (more commonly shortened to Rinpung Dzong), which means 'Fortress on a Heap of Jewels'. According to history, in the fifteenth century a man called Gyelchok, who was a descendant of Phajo Drukgom Shigpo (the founder of the Drukpa Kagyu school in Bhutan), went from the Paro valley to Tibet to study theology. Shunned as a pauper on his return, he constructed a little retreat by the river at Humrelkha, so named to honour Paro's guardian deity, Humrel Gompo. His descendants came to control a large part of this valley and were known as the 'Lords of Humrel'. In 1645 they accepted the authority of Zhabdung Ngawang

If you are in Paro at the time of the tsechu parking can be a bit of a problem.

Namgyal as their religious and political leader and handed over their small fort to him. The Zhabdung commenced construction of what is even today a most impressive building and on completion the dzong was consecrated in 1646. Being strategically located to thwart Tibetan incursions into the rest of the country as well as to protect the valley's inhabitants, this dzong

became one of Bhutan's strongest and most important fortresses. In 1907 it was severely damaged by fire but was almost immediately rebuilt by the Paro Penlop Dawa Penjor. The dzong is approached by crossing a quaint cantilevered wooden bridge with a shingle roof. Flanked by guardhouses and wreathed in bright fluttering prayer flags this cuts a rather striking

**Paro Dzong**

picture. This bridge was rebuilt in 1969 after the earlier one was washed away by a flood. The path curves around the building, ascending quite steeply to the entrance that lies along the North wall.

The courtyard (dochey), that you enter is actually at the third level of this massive structure and has two interesting figures on

**Taking it easy**

either side of the entrance — a Mongol holding a tiger on a leash and a man holding a black yak. The central tower (utse) is an imposing five-storey high structure that is adorned with fine woodwork and regarded as one of the best in the country. It houses four temples within. A flight of stone steps leads down to the monks' quarters where nearly two hundred monks

If you want to check out the very best accommodation in the country take a detour up to the Uma Paro Hotel.

reside. The Kunre is a large hall where they study and eat and its external walls are decorated with numerous instructive and finely executed paintings. In this area do look out for an unusual set of mandalas (cosmic diagrams), two of which depict the cosmos as it is visualised through the teachings of the Kalachakra. In the first mandala, on the left, the cosmos is shown as four circles – each representing the elements – and divided into further concentric circles with Mt. Sumeru shown in the middle as the central pillar of the world. The mandala on the right is painted according to the cosmology of a fifth century text by the Indian scholar Vasubandhu.

The famous Paro Tsechu is performed inside the dzong on the first day but subsequently moves to a larger open space, just beyond the outer wall. Archery competitions are also held during the festival and on the last day a giant thongdrel that covers an entire wall is unfurled and it bears a striking image of Guru Padmasambhava.

Coming down from the dzong, across the road, you will see a group of five large and very impressive Bhutanese chortens midst a copse of willow trees. These were built in memory of King Ugyen Wangchuck and you often spot devotees here, turning prayer wheels and silently mouthing their prayers. On the opposite side of the road from these you can catch a glimpse of the Ugyen Pelri Palace behind its high walls. It was built in the early 1900s by the Paro penlop as his version of Zangto Pelri (Guru Padmasambhava's heavenly abode), on earth. This palace is now one of the Queen Mother's royal residences and is off bounds for tourists. The town temple Druk Choeding, built in 1525, lies a little to the left and was established by the first Zhabdung's great-great grandfather.

One of the most popular places for lunch in Paro is the Chharo Restaraunt that is located at one end of the market, bordering the fields.

Chortens opposite
Paro Dzong

**Kyichu Lhakhang**

Your next stop is the Dungtse Lhakhang that lies just out of town, across the river and en route to the National Museum. Dungtse Lhakhang is possibly the only ancient temple built in the shape of a chorten and is literally chained down since local belief holds that it will otherwise fly off to heaven! It was constructed in 1421 by Thangtong Gyelpo who came to Bhutan in search of iron ore to be used for constructing bridges in his homeland Tibet. He was also

There is a track which takes you to a smaller dzong above Ta Dzong — the view is impressive but the climb is not easy.

known as Drubthob, 'The Realised One' or Chazampa (Builder of Iron Bridges). At that time a demoness had risen from deep within the earth and was terrorising the inhabitants of the valley. He built the temple in chorten form to overcome her, locating it on a small hill which was in reality her head. A massive restoration effort was undertaken in 1841 under the orders of the 25th Je Khempo and the paintings inside the temple were redone. These paintings are possibly the

There is a good view point overlooking the airport on the road leading to Chele La.

most extraordinary collection in all of Bhutan. The chorten temple was conceived as a mandala with the three different storeys corresponding to different levels of initiation. The ground floor is dedicated to historical figures, boddhisattavas and other protective deities. Various representations of Avalokiteswara and the five Buddhas of Meditation are located in the inner sanctum. On the first floor are scenes from the Bardo (the intermediary stage between life and death) and also many forms of Mahakala, the main protective deity of the country. Images on the second and third floors belong to the highest tantric cycles and depict the main teachers of the Drukpa Kagyu lineage. On the top floor do not miss the splendid lacquered wood image of the

**Paro market**

great twelfth century saint, Milarepa. You will need to carry a torch and allow yourself a good hour to absorb the magnificent interior of this somewhat plain looking building.

The road then continues up another 5km or so till you reach the Ta (watchtower) Dzong that lies above Paro Dzong and dates back to around 1650. It is a circular shaped building that lay in a state of disrepair till 1965 when the third monarch decided to establish the National Museum here. Open six days of the week (it is closed on Mondays), it consists of six floors of galleries all of which must be negotiated in a clockwise direction because of the enormous religious significance of the objects within.

The National Museum is a repository of not only precious works of art but also costumes, armour and other hand crafted objects of daily life that provide a good snapshot of the rich cultural traditions of the country. Carrying your torch is advisable. Of special interest is the gallery of tangkhas which exhibits exquisite pieces of different vintages – those depicting Zhabdung Ngawang Namgyal, the first Je Khempo and first Druk desi are of particular significance. For those interested in stamps, head to the philatelic exhibition on the top floor. The other galleries concentrate on statues, engraved slates, silverwork, armoury, stuffed animals, traditional receptacles and items made of bamboo. Exiting the museum you will come to the Tshogshing Lhakhang (temple of the Trees of Wisdom) which was built in the late 1960s and its centerpiece is a four-sided carving depicting the history of Buddhism.

Having spent some time indoors you would probably welcome a walk around Ta Dzong, stretching your legs a bit before heading back

Soak in the views.... with a beverage of your choice.

It doesn't get any better!

Check out Olathang
Hotel for a drink and
a meal.

to your vehicle. This is a good spot to catch
a clearer view of the Ugyen Pelri Palace and
appreciate the grandeur and entire shape of the
Paro Dzong.

If you are up to more of a 'stretch', a thirty
minute uphill climb from here would bring
you to the Zuri Fort which stands like a silent
sentinel, surrounded by cypress trees believed
to be 400 years old. This site is revered as

**Ta Dzong — the National Museum**

it is believed to have been blessed by Guru Padmasambhava. Built in 1352, this massive six-storey fighting fort was ideally located to protect the valley. It is approached by a narrow bridge and stone steps lead up to giant wooden doors. Its thick walls have narrow slits through which soldiers could shoot arrows and the top floor was used for storage as well as to target attackers with cannon balls! There are temples within but it is the stunning panoramic valley view that really recommends visiting this place.

Your last stop for the day is the historic Kyichu Lhakhang which is located approximately 5km up the valley from the bridge spanning the Paro Chu. This lhakhang has twin temples that stand together in a low-walled courtyard; the two are almost identical to look at but built thirteen centuries apart! The first and older

For those interested in local art, the Vajrayana Gallery, located in the main market, is definitely worth a visit.

temple, as well as the Jambay Lhakhang in Bumthang, are believed to have been built as early as the seventh century and are venerated as the first outposts of Buddhism in Bhutan. As the story goes a gigantic ogress lay supine, sprawled over entire Tibet and the Himalayan peaks surrounding it, preventing the spread of Buddhism. The Tibetan King Songsten Gampo was not a man who gave up easily and ordered

**Inside Paro Dzong — an unusual pet!**

**Ugyen Pelri Palace, Paro**

the simultaneous construction of hundred and eight temples which would be placed at key parts of her body to pin her down and subdue her for all time to come. This enormous task was undertaken around AD 650 with the temple of Jokhang in Lhasa situated over the very heart of the demoness. Kyichu Lhakhang was built over her left foot while Jambay Lhakhang pins the left knee. This first imprint of Buddhism was later used by Guru Padmasambhava as a place for meditation. It subsequently came under the sway of the Lhapa sect till the ascent of the Drukpas in the late thirteenth century. The structure fell into disrepair but was superbly restored in 1839 by the 25th Je Khempo. He also contributed the outstanding statue of Avalokiteswara, with eleven heads and a thousand arms, which is located in the sanctuary.

In 1968 another temple was constructed adjacent to the first, on the orders of the Queen Mother Her Majesty Ashi Kesang Choden Wangchuck. It was built in the same style and so skillfully executed that it is virtually impossible to discern any difference between the two — what better testimony that the art and cultural heritage of Bhutan has been well preserved! The walls of the small courtyard leading to the temples are adorned with paintings of the Kings of the Four Cardinal Directions and other protecting deities. As you enter, the ancient structure stands directly opposite with the modern temple to the right. The older temple is held in great reverence and carries depictions of the twelve acts of Buddha and his previous lives as also murals of the first sixteen disciples (arhats). Statues of Avalokiteswara dominate, but look out for the one of the Tibetan King Songsten Gampo, recognisable by his white hair worn in a knot. The new temple is dedicated to Guru Padmasambhava and the secret teachings, given only to his closest disciples, which make up the basic tenets of the Nyingma sect.

After a day abounding in culturally and visually rich experiences you will probably be ready to head back to the hotel. Try and turn in early as the next day promises to be exciting and possibly a little tiring ■

A good place to stop for a meal is the Red Rice restaurant which is located just short of Olathanq Hotel.

### DAY 3
### ▶▶ Visit Drukyel Dzong and climb up to Taktsang Monastery

We recommend a reasonably early start – the drive to Drukyel Dzong will take only half an hour but if the majestic Mt. Jhomolhari is visible you will want to linger and the best views are before 9 am  Seen at the North-West end of the Paro valley, Jhomolhari is a towering 24,000ft/ 7314m pyramid-shaped, snow clad massif that lies on the border with Tibet and is revered as the abode of Goddess Jhomo. First climbed in 1937, it is believed the mountaineers stopped short of the summit in deference to local sentiment and this mountain is now a 'protected peak'.

Driving out of Paro, through a narrowing valley, the road ends around 16km further and this is where the ruins of the Drukyel Dzong (Fortress of the Victorious Drukpas), are to be found. To mark his victory over the invading Tibetans in 1644, Zhabdung Ngawang Namgyal built this dzong in 1647 at a strategic point where the route from Tibet enters the Paro valley. Once the invasions ceased, this was the route used for trade between Tibet and Bhutan. Unfortunately, the dzong was destroyed by a fire in 1951 and only the shell remains (though a roof added in 1985 has prevented it from total ruin). Skirting the dzong and walking towards the end of the valley, a three-day walk would bring you to the base camp of Mt. Jhomolhari.

It is now time to embark on your somewhat arduous adventure for the day – ascending the 3000ft/915m cliff to reach the most spectacularly located gompa in all of Bhutan. To get to the starting point you will have to drive back around 8km and then turn left for 3km to reach a large

Visiting Taktsang requires a special permit to proceed beyond the view point. Check that your travel agent has arranged this.

parking lot decorated with prayer flags.

You need to keep in mind that the trek to Taktsang is quite an uphill task and it takes around three hours, at average speed, to climb up to this temple perched atop a cliff at 9700ft/2950m. The path is well laid out and you will be impressed with the efforts made to preserve the environment — there are receptacles for garbage placed all along the route and inspite of a large number of visitors and pilgrims, there is hardly any litter.

**Offerings en route to Taktsang**

If you are using the ponies it is advisable to reconfirm the arrangements with your guide/travel operator.

It is a continuous and fairly steep climb up to the meadow where a tea house is located — but beyond this point the trail ascends very steeply till you reach a fantastic vantage point above the monastery. And, if you think that's the end, you're in for a rude shock! You now have to go down four hundred steps, cross a narrow gorge and ascend another three hundred before you reach the base of this collation of six temples clinging to a vertiginous hill face. Needless to say, the return involves the same steps and a knee-jarring descent. Since you probably have not had time to acclimatise, you are likely to get breathless and will have to take it a little slowly.

The intention is certainly not to put you off visiting Taktsang — indeed if there is an 'absolutely must see' place in Bhutan, this is it! All the same, you do need to know what to expect and to be prepared for it. If you feel the need, an option you could consider worth taking is riding ponies up to the vantage point, negotiating the steps and maybe even the downward journey on your own steam. Regardless of the way you chose to go, you will not regret making this journey. Remember to carry some sunscreen, water and a hat as the sun beats down relentlessly once you are out of tree cover.

The first 100m or so is deceptively easy and you walk through pines, catching occasional glimpses of the fascinating monastery and struggling past a collection of dedicated 'mani' stones — but, after crossing a pretty meadow the real climb begins and sharp switch backs bring you up to a ridge. It takes around an hour if you are walking — and a little less on horseback — to reach a flat section with bright prayer flags flapping in the breeze. From here a path veers off, leading to a

**Taktsang from the view point**

restaurant nearby. This is where you can take a welcome break for drinks and snacks or even a buffet lunch that your guide will gladly organise for you. Across the chasm-like valley you see an imposing, glossy-brown sheer cliff with the monastery impossibly positioned at its very edge — a most memorable and awesome sight!!

**The Taktsang Temple complex**

Beyond this point, the oak and rhododendron forest gives way to a somewhat sinister one – the branches of the trees have wispy tendrils of Spanish moss trailing from them, waving delicately with even a breath of wind. On cloudy days, a swirling vaporous mist weaves through these eerie looking trees and your heart, already

Do not forget to carry a water bottle with you when you are making the climb to Taktsang.

pumping hard from your exertions, suddenly speeds up even more!

As you walk along you will pass a shallow meditation cave with many tsa tsa (small conical offerings) spread over its floor. After arriving at the vantage point you descend the four hundred steps that follow the natural curve of the rock face, down to a bridge spanning the gorge. After descending around a hundred steps there is a path leading up on the left that leads to the Machiphu Lhakhang – it is a fifteen minute walk. As you cross the bridge a steep flight of stairs lead up to Singyephu, a small gompa tucked impossibly into the gorge and used as a retreat. Before Guru Padmasambhava arrived, a deity called Singye Samdrup lived here and it is his consort's shrine that you see on the left as you enter Taktsang's courtyard. Nearby is a sacred spring that is believed to have gushed forth when Guru Padmasambhava's consort, Yeshe Tsogyal threw her rosary against a rock – the water is considered holy and your guide will help fill your bottle if you want to collect some.

The last three hundred steps are an absolute killer and you struggle up these to the entrance of one of the most venerated temples in the entire Himalayan region. Having caught your breath, you begin to absorb it all – the stupendous bird's-eye view, the ornate and dignified building, the evocative fragrance of burning juniper and the powerful spiritual vibrations. According to legend Guru Padmasambhava came to Taktsang in the eighth century, flying from the East of the country on the back of a tigress (a form that one of his consorts is believed to have taken). He meditated for three months in a cave here and then donning his terrifying form of Dorje

Carry an empty water bottle to fill with 'holy water' at the complex.

Droloe subjugated the evil spirits. He then went on to Tibet and one of his disciples, Langchen Pelkyi Singye came to Taktsang to meditate in AD 853. The cave was named Pelphug (Pelkyi's Cave) and later when he died in Nepal his body was miraculously transported here by the deity Dorje Legpa and sealed in a chorten located in a room on the left as you climb up the first flight of stairs. In the following years, many prominent saints came here to meditate; notably Milarepa,

**He could have been in the movies!**

the Tibetan yogin Machig, Labdoenma and Thangtong Gyelpo.

The first sanctuary was built by Nyingmapa lamas in the fourteenth century and in 1645 the site was offered to the Zhabdung. He intended to rebuild the temple but his untimely death resulted in his wish being fulfilled only in 1692 by the fourth Desi Tenzing Rabgye. The edifice was restored in the 1860s and again in 1982 but a mysterious devastating fire in 1998 led to the death of the caretaker monk and almost complete destruction of the complex and most of its relics. A long and extremely delicate rebuilding process was started under the supervision of the Dasho Zepon Wangchuck and completed only in 2005. Fortuitously a young reincarnation of Desi Tenzing Rabgye, the original builder of Taktsang, conducted the consecration ceremony and this monastic complex is rejuvenated once again.

Though small, the most important temple is the one that contains the cave where Guru Padmasambhava and his disciple meditated and it is opened only once a year. Dorje Droloe standing on the tigress, guards this sacred cave. The next two temples are dedicated to Guru Padmasambhava and hold fine statues and paintings. Besides the four mentioned so far, there is a temple with a striking statue of Amitava (Tshephame) and another above this complex called the White Palace or Zangto Pelri. Special permission from the Department of Culture will allow you to visit most of these temples but the catch is finding the monk in charge of each as the doors are generally closed!

The way down will take much less time so you should be back in your hotel for a well deserved afternoon siesta ■

After your hard day's work treat yourself to a relaxing traditional hot stone bath.

## DAY 4
### ▶▶ Drive up to Chele La

Since your first two days have been steeped in culture and history, its time now to take a break and indulge your visual senses with some natural beauty and give yourself some time to relax and soak in the atmosphere. Make a leisurely start and carry a picnic lunch as well as a beverage of your choice. It is just over 40km to the pass; you drive 5km to Bondey and take the ascending road that leads to Haa (61km) via Chele La. The pass is at a cool crisp 12,200ft/3720m and your route takes you through a spectacularly lovely forest of pine, oak and rhododendrons that are ablaze with blood

**The ubiquitous yak**

red and pink blooms in April and May. The heady scent of daphne permeates the air and the sun-dappled forest floor is carpeted with swathes of lilac primulas – as enchanting a drive as you could have hoped for! Around 10km from the

For your last night in Paro check out Dagmar Restaurant in town for dinner in a cosy atmosphere.

top you can spot the Kela Dechen Yangtse Anim Dratshang, a nunnery perched on the opposite hillside with prayer flags lining the walking path to it and surrounding the complex. Once you cross the tree line, you are likely to come upon

**Prayer flags at Chele La**

yaks grazing in the alpine meadows. The pass itself is marked by a multitude of prayer flags that seem to spear the intense blue skies! On a clear day you can get a breathtaking view of Jhomolhari and other Himalayan giants.

On the other side, the road descends to the remote Haa valley. If you decide to visit it, your return would be a two-hour drive.

This brings your delightful sojourn in the Paro valley to an end and unless you are flying out of the country, it is now time to head eastwards – the first stop being the largest city and capital of the country, Thimphu ■

**Primulas en route to Chele La**

## ⏵⏵ Journey to Thimphu and local sightseeing

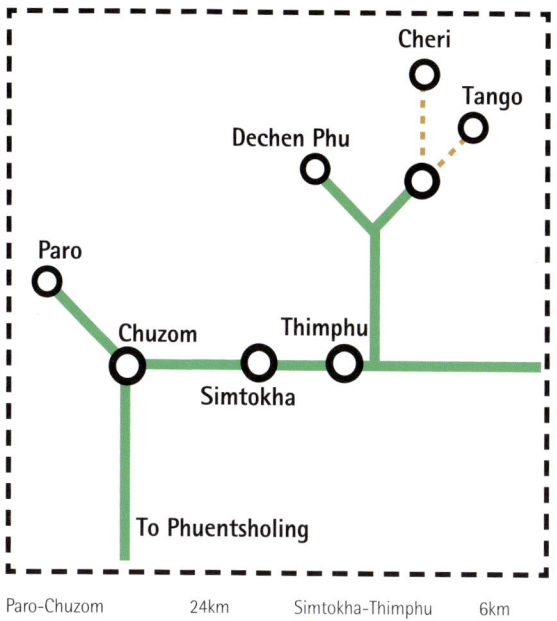

Paro-Chuzom    24km    Simtokha-Thimphu    6km
Chuzom-Simtokha    25km

The road between Paro and Thimphu is being broadened and till early 2008 there are specific times for movement of traffic.

The drive to Thimphu (7700ft/2350m) is only 55km long and is easily negotiated in 1.5 hours. You have to backtrack to Chuzom where your papers are checked before you can proceed to cover the balance 31km to your destination. Compared to Paro the valley along the Wang Chu is arid and has mainly scrub as vegetation. The countryside from Chuzom to Thimphu is less forested than what you have been seeing so far and the valleys are narrow except for two sections where it widens into gentle slopes, terraced rice fields and lovely strands of conifer trees. Around 12km before Thimphu you hit the first expressway in the country – a glorious new four-lane black top that allows you to enter the capital in style. If you continue on this road you bypass the mighty Simtokha Dzong strategically located at the crossroads of routes to Thimphu, Paro, Phuentsholing and Punakha/Wangdi. However, since the dzong is only 6km out of town, you can easily visit it later or even when you travel to Punakha or back to Paro.

The place where Simtokha Dzong is located was originally called Simmo Dokha (Demon on the Stone) till the Zhabdung cleansed and purified it and built the dzong whose complete name is San Ngay Sabdon Phodrang (the Palace of Profound Tantric Teaching). This was the first of the many dzongs constructed by the Zhabdung and was tested soon after its consecration in 1631 as it had to withstand an attack by the Five Groups of Lamas in 1634. In 1961 the third monarch, King Jigme Dorji Wangchuck decided to convert this dzong into a school for traditional studies. It was originally meant for lay people who would be trained as teachers of Dzongkha. At the time of writing it was under extensive renovation and is expected to reopen in 2008.

Having entered Thimphu (population: 80,000), you will soon notice that it is unlike most capital cities of the world. There are no high rise buildings and all structures — even the petrol pump — are built according to the traditional style. The traffic density is low and there are no traffic lights! Traffic is directed by policemen, standing on highly decorated boxes, who employ exaggerated but elegant gestures to guide you forward. Coming in on the expressway, you enter Thimphu over a new bridge spanning the Wang Chu (the old one, Lungten Zampa — Bridge of Prophecy — lies between the petrol pump and two schools). There are several streets that run

A good place for lunch is Plums, located near the clock tower and just off Norzim Lam.

A magnificent cypress in front of Pangri Zampa

on the North-South axis and have smaller streets crossing them and weaving up the wooded hillsides. However, there is one main street, Norzim Lam which leads to the town center and the clock-tower square with its adjoining hotels, shops and restaurants. New shopping complexes are coming up and the commercial hub is shifting. The government offices, golf

The dzong can only be visited after office hours and the best time is just after 5 pm so you still have sufficient light for photographs.

course and posh residential area of Motithang can be reached from the northern of the two intersections on Norzim Lam. Though the valley was inhabited even before the Zhabdung came to power, Thimphu remained a village till the decision was taken to make it the country's capital. Even so, it retained its rural character till the 1970s but the population grew dramatically

**Trashichhoe Dzong — the seat of power**

in the '90s and it is now quite the 'happening' (in the western sense) city with several bars and even a couple of discos livening up the nightlife!

If you get in early, you can make one quick stop before lunch and visit the impressive National Memorial Chorten. It was built in 1974 in memory of the third King Jigme Dorji Wangchuck by his mother. With its golden spires gleaming in the sun and its large white dome framed by the lazuline sky it is definitely worth

**Mani wall near Pangri Zampa**

a 'dekho'. A unique feature is that it is a chorten-chapel with the three shrines representing the main spiritual themes of the Nyingma school. The paintings depict tantric Buddhism in all its complexity and your experience will be enhanced if you are accompanied by someone schooled in its traditions. The complex is visited by people of all walks throughout the day and is one of the most public religious places in the country.

After lunch you can take the road (Gaden

Thimphu has a pretty active night life, particularly on weekends — if you want to disco check out Space 34, Buzz Club, Gravity and Destiny.

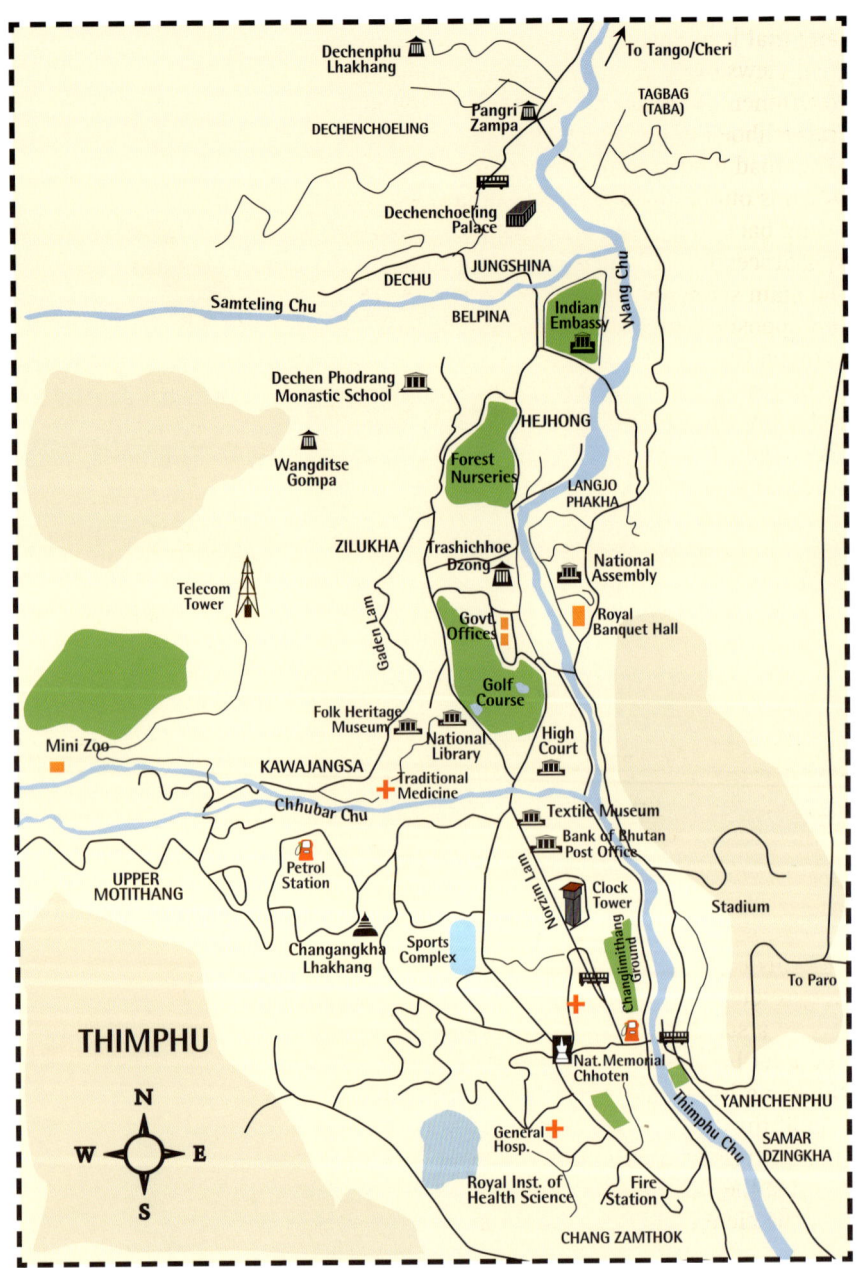

Lam) that leads you above the city, affording great views of the valley as also the seat of government – the magnificent, symmetrical Trashichhoe Dzong.

This road takes you to Changangkha Lhakhang which is one of the oldest temples in Thimphu, dating back to the fifteenth century. It was built by a descendant of Lama Phajo Dukgom Shigpo. The main statue here is that of Avalokiteswara and opposite the entrance is a large painting of Tsangpa Gyarey Yeshe Dorje. The place has an air of peace and tranquility, located as it is above and away from the city. With colourful flags festooned all over, carrying their prayers on the wings of wind, there is a meditative calm about this place and time seems to stand still!

Your last stop for the day, the Trashichhoe Dzong, can be visited only after 5 pm on weekdays, when the government offices close – or then during the day on Saturday/Sunday.

The Trashichhoe Dzong, in its present incarnation, was consecrated as late as 1969 and this building is a visual delight. With its superb sense of proportion and space, it carries an aura of regal dignity. Its history dates back to the thirteenth century but the original dzong was not on this flat stretch of land that offers no defensive merit. The old dzong was built in 1216 or so by the founder of the Lhapa school and was located on a spur to the North-East of the present one. This dzong was badly damaged during a subsequent struggle with the Drukpas and later became the property of Zhabdung Ngawang Namgyal in the 1630s. In 1641 he rebuilt the dzong, christening it Trashichhoe (the Fortress of Auspicious Religion). This became the summer residence of the Zhabdung and the clergy and Punakha the winter retreat.

There are some beautiful artefacts that you can buy here and Lungta Handicraft, opposite the GPO, has a great selection.

The wooded area above the mini zoo makes an excellent spot for a coffee (even though you have to carry your own!).

A fire in 1772 resulted in severe damage and the desi and Je Khempo of that time decided to rebuild it at the bottom of the valley where it now stands. This new structure too was damaged by fire in 1886 and yet again by the terrible earthquake of 1897 which damaged the five-storey tall utse (central tower). After the capital was moved to Thimphu, the king ordered a complete renovation and expansion in 1962, leaving the central chapels and the utse untouched. The entire dzong was rebuilt using traditional methods – planning without any blueprints (everything stems from the mind of the architect!) and building without using a single nail.

The dzong originally housed the National Assembly along with the secretariat and the king's throne room. The northern section serves

**The National Library, Thimphu**

## ARCHERY

Archery (datse) is the official national sport but is much more than just a sport — the Bhutanese have been intensely passionate about this activity since time immemorial. The sport is practiced at all levels — amateur as well as professional; in small hamlets, villages and towns and in all regions of the country. The basic requirements are quite simple: a level 150m stretch of ground, bows and arrows, the target and of course, competitors ever willing to take up a challenge and an audience whose full throated appreciation is guaranteed!

The traditional long bow and arrows are made of a special kind of bamboo, but today you are more likely to come across state-of-the-art carbonite bows with a pulley system that imparts great impetus to the arrow.

The target is a rectangular wooden piece, approximately 30cm by 120cm (1ft by 4ft) and lies at the end of the range, some 140m (550ft) from the archer. (Interestingly, the target for Olympic shooters is only 50m!) Indeed the target is so distant that spectators perform the function of spotters — standing close to the target, ducking and weaving away from the many wayward shots and guiding the archer closer to his mark. A good shot is rewarded with a resounding cheer while those not near the mark invite ribald comments questioning the archer's sexual prowess!!

A major competition is a serious event; eleven archers comprise a team and each is allowed to shoot two arrows. The system of scoring is somewhat complicated with near misses also being awarded points. Each team is accompanied by its 'secret weapon' — women bedecked in their finery who dance and sing, distracting the opposition with suggestive remarks while encouraging their team to excel — definitely a far cry from cheerleaders with their micro-skirts and pom poms!

According to tradition, an archer will not have sex the night before a competition and women are not allowed to handle the bow. Bhutan has not won an Olympic medal as yet, but don't be surprised if this happens soon.

Archery competitions are a colourful and extremely festive 'ceremony'. It is well worth checking out if there is one scheduled somewhere near where you are travelling and experience it first hand.

However, just a few words of caution. It is quite likely that you will find a table laden with spirits and competitors and their supporters imbibing the same! Naturally as the day goes on some shots become quite wayward, so be careful while approaching the competition field and follow instructions on where you should position yourself.

as the summer residence of the Je Khempo and
the central monk body (dratshang). The attention
to detail and finish given to this building adds
to its grand appearance – the outer walls are of
well dressed and fitted granite, the courtyard is
paved with rectangular stone slabs and on the
four corners are elegant three-storey high towers.
Unlike other dzongs this 'peace time' one has
three entrances; one for common folk, leading
to the administrative establishment; another to
the monastic section in whose courtyard the
tsechu is performed annually and the third only
for royalty. Unless you have official business,
you can only enter the monastic section to visit
the main lhakhang through the vast courtyard.

**Ready, Steady and
Let Go!**

This new Lhakhang Sarp (built in 1907) is in the center of the courtyard. You are allowed to enter this temple and should visit the top floor which has outstanding mandalas on its ceiling and a striking statue of Guru Padmasambhava. There are more mandalas and a magnificent 'Wheel of Life' painted on the exterior of the building that serves as the assembly hall for the monks (located to the right as you enter the courtyard). Before you leave, don't miss the well crafted wooden bridge that spans the river at the base of the dzong.

You can take the road past the elegant High Court complex and then cross the river to get a good view of the SAARC Convention Center which now houses the ministries of Foreign Affairs and Planning as well as the National Assembly. This impressive edifice was built to serve as the meeting hall for the heads of state of the seven countries that make up the South Asia Association for Regional Co-operation. If you can manage to get permission, visiting the elaborately decorated chamber of the National Assembly is a treat.

You now loop back to the town center and can either take a stroll through, soaking in its ambience or head for the shops for some hard-to-resist shopping! There are exquisite fabrics and unique handicrafts on sale.

On the next day your excursions involve a bit of driving, with some walking thrown in for good measure. For the first half you could drive past the dzong, cross the river and head up the valley. You will pass Dechencholeing Palace, which serves as the residence of the royal grandmother, on your way to the Pangri Zampa Temple Complex which is about 10km from town. This complex has two imposing

The Indian cuisine served at Druk Hotel and Jhomolhari Hotel is possibly the best you will experience in the country.

The National Memorial Chorten, Thimphu

white buildings approached by a path that runs past enormous cypress trees and along a mani wall. There are intricately etched and painted stones embedded along the sides of this wall. Pangri Zampa was the residence of Zhabdung Ngawang Namgyal when he arrived in Bhutan in 1616, directed here from Tibet by a divine vision. Entry into the building is prohibited so you will have to content yourself with enjoying the scenic setting. You can now proceed around

**The Clock Tower and market, Thimphu**

4km further, forking uphill to the right to reach Dechenphu Lhakhang which is at a cool 8900ft/ 2713m. You can catch an external view of this eye-catching tall red gompa which is dedicated to the powerful protective deity Gyenyen who looks after the country in times of need. Proceeding beyond the courtyard is not allowed but you can admire the 'sinking rock' after which Thimphu is named.

Coming down, turn onto the left prong of the

For those proceeding beyond Thimphu it is advisable to stock up on provisions from the supermarket located in the Clock Tower area or Lhatshog Shop No. 7 in Motithang.

The stray dogs in Thimphu are fast asleep during the day but their howls resonate through the night.

fork till the road ends 15km further, in front of a parking lot. Crossing the Wang Chu on another beautiful wooden bridge with a shingle roof, you can take the 1.5 hour walk up to Cheri Gompa. This was built by the Zhabdung in 1620 and is the place where he established the first body of monks. However, if you are short on time — or enthusiasm — we recommend taking an alternate, and shorter, path from the parking lot up to the Tango Gompa. This is a 300m hike and takes around one hour to ascend on the regular trail — or half the time if you elect to take the steep short cut. This monastery sits at the edge of a richly forested hill at Thimphu's northern end. Its great white walls appear stunning in contrast to the surrounding foliage and dominate the entire hillside. The gompa's austere frontage is broken by finely carved and painted windows. Although founded by Lama Gyalwa Lhanangpa, it was further developed by Lama Drukpa Kinley in the fifteenth century. Nearby is a cave where the Zhabdung meditated and believing that his spiritual powers had helped repel the Tibetan invasion, this gompa was presented to him in appreciation. Desi Tenzin Rabgye renovated and added to the structure in 1688, bringing it to its current magnificent form. Subsequent additions were made when a golden roof was added in the nineteenth century.

There are some fine images within of great saints and the hillside has several meditation huts where senior students choose to go into solitary retreat. Tango is now one of Bhutan's main Buddhist institutes and has over two hundred student monks.

In 1998, a tulku was identified in eastern Bhutan and after passing stringent criteria, was recognised as a reincarnation of Desi Tenzin

Rabgye. Although only twelve years of age, he now presides, with great dignity, over rituals at Tango and enforces a schedule of study and discipline at the institute.

It is now time to return to Thimphu for lunch after which you can take in some more attractions that this quaint capital city has to offer.

We would suggest starting at the top — you take the road to Motithang but turn right, heading towards the telecom tower which is at 8807ft/2685m and provides a vantage point for brilliant, clear views of the town and surrounding countryside. Heading back, stop for

**Monks at play**

**Who let the dog out!?**

a few minutes at the 'mini-zoo' which is now only a large outdoor enclosure that holds one of the strangest looking creatures you are likely to see — the takin. (Actually the best time to see them is when they come to the fence for food in the early morning so if you are really interested, you can reschedule your day accordingly.)

Proceeding downwards you will pass the Drubthob Gompa, a small building surrounded by prayer flags that now houses the Zilukha Nunnery. Located above the dzong, this gompa is believed to protect it from fires. Descending further, you arrive at Dechen Phodrang which was the original site of the dzong and is now occupied by the state monastic school. You often spot a procession of monks, in their ubiquitous maroon robes, moving between the dzong and this building. Your drive will now take you past the rolling greens of the golf course with the grand National Library coming up on the opposite side. This was opened in 1967 to preserve the ancient Dzongkha texts and act as a repository for thousands of old religious books and manuscripts as well as the wooden blocks used for printing. An altar located in the entrance lobby has statues of some of the most important historic figures – Zhabdung Ngawang Namgyal, Pema Lingpa and Guru Padmasambhava. Just above the library is the Painting School, known more formally as the National Institute of Zorig Chusum which offers a six year course on Bhutan's traditional crafts for those who are artistically inclined. Almost adjacent is the Folk Heritage Museum with its interior styled to resemble a typical farmhouse as it would have been a hundred years ago. The Museum offers not only a glimpse into the past but also depicts the present reality of many remote rural hamlets.

Visiting the Institute of Traditional Medicine is a rewarding experience – the herbs and other ingredients are neatly showcased and a guide book is on sale.

The National Institute of Traditional Medicine is not far away and has an impressive laboratory and production facility which turns out high quality traditional medicine in the prescribed manner. It also has a day care facility and an out patient clinic where diagnosis and treatment is handled by trained doctors. So, go ahead and give it a shot if you are feeling under the weather!

Your last stop could be the National Textile Museum which showcases the traditional methods of weaving, and also offers items for sale. Since Bhutan is known for its creative and exotic stamps, those interested would find a

If you want a change of cuisine the Thai Restaurant opposite Hotel Pedling is a good option.

visit to the Post Office an extremely rewarding experience.

If you are in Thimphu over the weekend, try and visit the local open market with its vast array of fresh produce, handicrafts and other items. These are brought in by villagers, from hamlets near and afar, who come to town to make purchases and sell their wares. It is over

the weekend that archery competitions are held **Willows by the river**
and it would be exciting to be able to watch this
much-loved sport.

Thimphu is also the base for several walks
– naturally most of them involve climbing and
on some you can visit a picturesque gompa
besides enjoying the stunning countryside (See
the Trekking section for details) ■

## SOWA RIGPA — BHUTANESE TRADITIONAL MEDICINE

In ancient times Bhutan was called Lho Jong Men Jong — Southern Land of Medicinal Herbs since many ingredients of Tibetan and Chinese medicine were found here. Akin to the Tibetan system, the Sowa Rigpa owes its origin to the Indian system of Ayurveda and was brought here by Guru Padmasambhava in the eighth century when he introduced Buddhism to Bhutan. The Buddha of Medicine is always shown with a terminalia plant in his hand.

Guru Padmasambhava had translated Indian medical treatises to Tibetan and influenced the development of Sowa Rigpa which later absorbed some Chinese traditions. Based on Ayurveda, this system follows the theory of the 'three humours' — bile, wind and phlegm — and believes it is the imbalance of these that leads to illnesses. From the Chinese system it adopted the expertise of reading the pulse — not just for the heart and circulatory system, but a far more detailed and sophisticated reading of twelve pulses for all body organs. This, combined with a visual examination of the eyes, tongue and urine makes Sowa Rigpa a unique diagnostic system. Making it even more holistic is that they factor in non-physical causes of imbalances; bad karma, evil spirits, all aspects of the person's life etc.

The patient is treated with medicines derived from over four hundred plants found in Bhutan as well as minerals and a few animal parts. Most of the ingredients required to make its range of medicines are found within the country, at altitudes above 13,120ft/ 4000m. Minerals used include gold and precious stones. Traditionally, animal parts like bear bile, rhino horn, musk, and elephant's gallstones were used but they no longer use parts from endangered species and have substituted these with plants that have similar properties (in fact, they use a rare high altitude herb that smells like musk pods).

The medicines take the form of pills, syrups, powders and lotions and are also accompanied by spiritual counselling to subjugate evil spirits and ameliorate bad karma. The system does not offer surgery and cannot help in acute conditions.

The Bhutanese set high value to hot mineral baths. There are numerous hot springs to be found here — like Gasa which is known to help with blood pressure and has separate pools for asthma, sinus and rheumatism. The Dunmang hot spring is believed to cure rheumatoid arthritis and skin ailments while the one at Dur supposedly cures as many as thirteen ailments. From this comes the custom of taking stone baths that offer a cure closer to home. These are usually a large wooden trough which has a separate section at one end where heated stones are placed. Medicinal spring water (high in mineral content), is piped over the stones, the heat releasing the healing minerals. You find these near many monasteries; like the Dechenphu in Thimphu, at the base of Cheri valley and even at Dobji Dzong close to Chuzom.

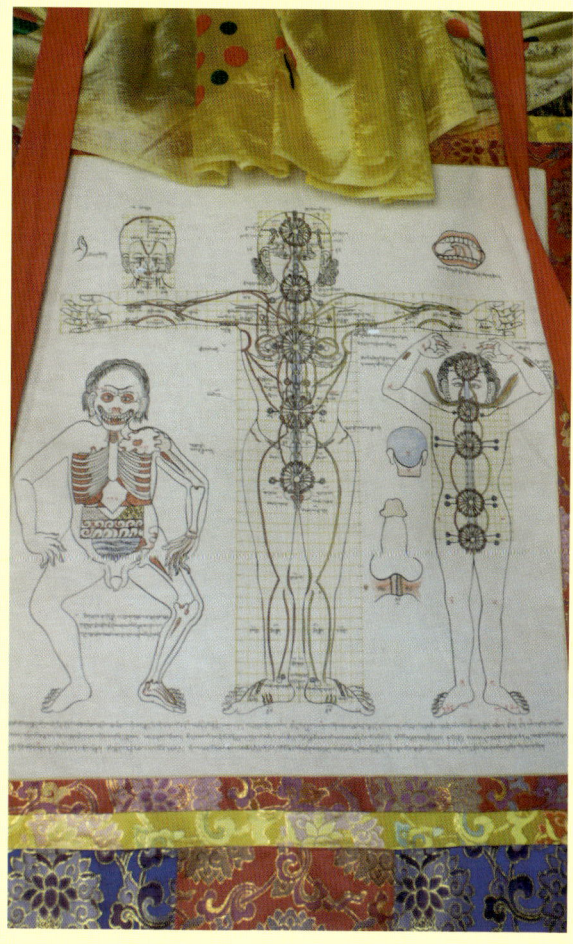

Sowa Rigpa is recognised today as the official medicine tradition and incorporated into the country-wide health system with over three hundred drugs that have been standardised at the National Institute of Traditional Medicine. The Institute runs hospitals, laboratories and dispensaries besides having its own hygienic manufacturing facility and offering a rigorous five-year training programme for doctors (dungtsho).

### DAY 7
### ▶▶ Journey to Punakha and Wangdiphodrang via Dochu La

The mountain views from Dochu La are spectacular but unpredictable — the early morning is your best bet but sometimes the view does improve after 8 am.

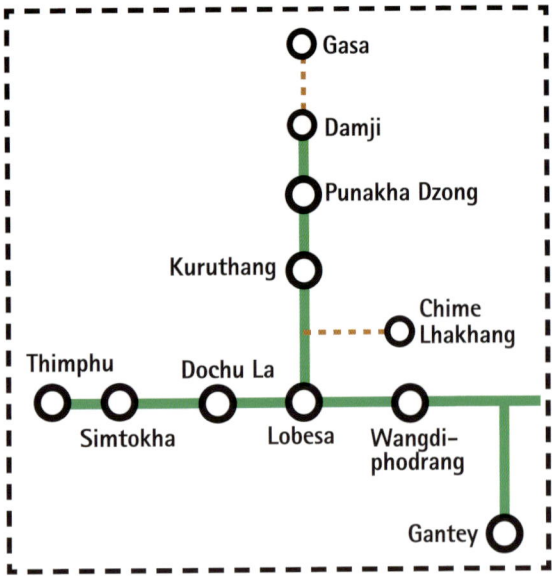

| | | | | |
|---|---|---|---|---|
| Thimphu-Dochu La | 22km | | Lobesa-Wangdi | 8km |
| Dochu La-Lobesa | 38km | | Punakha-Wangdi | 20km |
| Lobesa-Punakha | 12km | | Wangdi-Gantey | 65km |

We suggest making an early start since, on a clear day, the view of the eastern Himalayas from Dochu La is possibly one of the best in the country. It is only 22km to the top but allow 45 minutes for the journey as the road has many a twist and turn! The route takes you past Simtokha Dzong but you turn left at the crossroads and as you ascend there is a good overview of the dzong. The pass lies at 10150ft/ 3100m and is reached after negotiating the check point at Hongtsho village — the gompa of the same name clings to the hillside above.

Rhododendrons in full bloom in April

The top is unlike that of any other pass you will encounter here or for that matter anywhere in the world! The road bifurcates forming a large island which is populated not by people or animals but by striking chortens. There are a hundred and nine chortens in three tiers of forty-five, thirty-six and twenty-seven circumscribing a single larger chorten. These were constructed as recently as 2004. This group is known as the Druk Wangyel Chortens or 'Chortens of the Victory of the Druk Gyalpo'. The building of these chortens was initiated by Queen Ashi Dorji Wangmo Wangchuck when her husband, the fourth king, travelled to the

**Chortens at Dochu La**

South-East of the country in December 2003 leading his army against insurgents from India. These insurgents had set up numerous camps in the jungles of South East Bhutan and were using Bhutanese territory to launch hit and run attacks on targets in India as part of their separatist agenda. The thought of war was disturbing to the peace-loving people of Bhutan and the queen picked Dochu La as the site for the construction of a chorten – it was to be a visible symbol of prayers to the deities to protect their country. The area was consecrated by the Je Khempo himself and the intricate work of chorten building began. When the chorten is around a meter tall, an opening is made in the ground and offerings of grain and a bronze vessel filled with butter are put in. The most important stage is the installation of the sokshing or 'life tree', a symbolic linking of heaven and earth within the chorten. This is a square-sectioned long pole made from juniper wood. It is painted red and prayers in gold are inscribed on all four sides along its length. Sacred objects are then tied to the sokshing which is wrapped in silk and placed inside the partially complete chorten – in this case offerings were made by different generations of the royal family as well as by the Bhutanese people.

Stop for coffee and a snack at the cafeteria perched on a hilltop just below the pass.

The forces led by the king launched their attack on 15th December 2003 and succeeded in destroying thirty camps and routing the insurgents, many of whom were captured or fled leaving their arms and ammunition behind. The chortens were finally consecrated and sanctified in June 2004.

Besides these magnificent chortens in an amazing setting you will be able to spot some of the great Himalayan peaks starting on

# TRAVEL PLAN

## DRUKPA KINLEY

Born in 1455, Drukpa Kinley lived till the ripe old age of seventy-four and earned the reputation of being one of the county's most enigmatic characters. Revered as a saint today, he was never formally part of the clergy. He was a rebel with a cause — that of spreading the Buddhist doctrine without the formality and social conventions enforced by the clergy. Drukpa Kinley's origins were in Tibet and he was trained at the great Ralung Monastery. He travelled throughout Bhutan as a yogi using songs, humour and provocative behaviour to attract people to his teachings. His sexual prowess was legendary and the many flying phalluses that you see painted on homes and hanging from rooftops are not just symbols of fertility but signs of the people's continuing respect for him. His unconventional behaviour and sexual antics were a device to provoke and stimulate people to discard their preconceived notions. The creation of the national animal, the takin, is attributed to one of his many miraculous deeds. A verse attributed to him best encapsulates the essence of this eccentric but much-loved character:

*I, the madman from Kyishodruk,*
*Wander around from place to place;*
*I believe in lamas when it suits me,*
*I practice the Dharma in my own way.*
*I choose any qualities, they are all illusions,*
*Any gods, they are the emptiness of the mind*
*I use fair and foul words for mantras; it's all the same,*
*My meditation practice is girls and wine;*
*I do whatever I feel like, strolling around in the void.*

the left with Masangang (23,5012ft/7165m), which dominates the region of Laya. The next is Tsendagang (23,288ft/7100m) and the following peaks are Terigang (23,944ft/7300m), Jejegangphugang, Kangphugang, the 'Table Mountain' Zongaphugang (all at 23,288ft/7100m) and finally by the high peak of Gangkar Punsum at a towering 24,735ft/7541m.

From this lofty spot it is downhill for 38km till you reach the small village of Lobesa where you turn off for Punakha that lies at a somewhat lowly 4430ft/1351m. The descent is mainly through virgin forest with the magnolia tree blossoming in April and lending its beauty and

**Masangang and other peaks seen from Dochu La**

**Punakha Dzong**

fragrance to the air. As you near Lobesa the dense vegetation gives way to comparatively barren hills. The Punakha Dzong is only 12km from here and en route you can spot the Chime Lhakhang atop a small hillock. It is a pleasant

You can request the lama at Chime Lhakhang to bless you with Lama Drukpa Kinley's bow and arrow and wooden phallus.

30-40 minute walk from the road head, through cultivated fields and up a gentle slope. This lhakhang dates back to 1499 and was built by Lama Drukpa Kinley when he visited this valley. Permission is not required to visit Chime

Lhakhang and you pass a charming village set in lush terraced fields as you approach the temple sitting serenely at the crest of the hill with only the gently rustling leaves of a gracious tree and the fluttering of prayer flags breaking the silence wrapped around it. You will not fail to be impressed with the beautiful slate carvings and the row of prayer wheels at the entrance. Lama Drukpa Kinley is believed to have subdued the demoness residing at Dochu La with his 'magic thunderbolt of wisdom' and a wooden effigy of this is preserved within. There are also statues of him and his dog Shachi, along with those of the Zhabdung, Sakyamuni and Avalokiteswara. Devotees receive blessings from his wooden phallus and iron archery set that lie here and childless women are said to have their wish fulfilled after visiting this lhakhang.

Be prepared for almost gale force winds in the afternoon — particularly in the area lying below the Wangdi Dzong.

Around 4km before the Punakha Dzong you will pass through the new township of Kuruthang with the center of attraction being the newly constructed Zangto Pelri Monastery with its large Nepalese style chorten.

The Dzong straddles the confluence of two rivers and resembles a giant battleship. Its full name is 'Punthang Dechen Phodrang' or 'Palace of Great Happiness'. This extremely impressive fortress was built as far back as 1637. It was the second of the mighty dzongs built by the Zhabdung and was the seat of government till the end of the reign of the second king. The site is believed to have received Guru Padmasambhava's blessings — in the eighth century he prophesied the building of the dzong: "...on the front edge of the hill that looks like an elephant's trunk, a man named Namgyal will come and build a fortress..."

However, even before this dzong came up, this

Inside the Dzong

**Geometric poem in Punakha Dzong glorifying Zhabdung Ngwang Namgyal**

was a hallowed site as the Saint Ngagi Rinchen meditated here in the thirteenth century and built a small temple which stands opposite the main dzong and is known as 'Dzongchung' or 'little dzong'. The serene and beautiful Buddha image within is much revered by visiting pilgrims as is a site a few kilometers away where there is an enormous rock believed to have been split by Ngagi Rinchen to release his mother's entrapped spirit.

When the Zhabdung visited this region, he chose the confluence of the Mo and Pho rivers to set up camp. At night he had a dream in which Guru Padmasambhava's prophecy was revealed to him. He decided to build a dzong here and asked the architect to sleep at the foot of the Buddha statue in the Dzongchug. That night the Zhabdung led the architect to Zangto Pelri in his dreams. Inspired by the vision of Guru Padmasambhava's heavenly palace he conceived the dzong's design but never committed the same to paper! The Zhabdung also decided that this dzong would hold the most sacred of all relics, the Ranjung Karsapani, which was a self-created image of Avalokiteswara that he carried with him when he left Ralung Monastery in Tibet. This statue is believed to have miraculously emerged from a vertebra of Tsangpa Gyarey, the founder of the Drupka school, when he was being cremated. Punakha thus became a prime target for attacks by the Tibetans as this unique relic was extremely significant and precious to them as well. In 1639 during an epic battle the Zhabdung's small army, though vastly outnumbered by the Tibetans, managed to thwart the enemy through the art of deception. The Tibetans were led to believe they were confronting a large force as Bhutanese soldiers marched out of the dzong in an endless stream – they were actually circling back in through a secret door to march out again! When victory seemed imminent, the Tibetans observed an orderly procession head down to the river where the Zhabdung solemnly threw in the casket believed to hold the coveted relic. This was the last straw and considering the Ranjung Karsapani lost, the frustrated Tibetan army withdrew! This scene is enacted

Because of its low altitude and relative lack of forestation Punakha gets warm in April and May, so try to finish the sightseeing before lunch.

with great pageantry every year at the Punakha Domchoe by dancers attired in battle gear and accompanied by musicians. At the festival's conclusion, a grand procession of monks (serda) is led by the Je Khempo who ceremoniously throws in a handful of oranges representing the Ranjung Karsapani. On the last day of the domchoe a gigantic silk thongdrel, with an appliqué of the Zhabdung's image, is unfurled over the outer wall of the utse.

The Punakha Dzong cuts a striking picture with its imposing walls rising up from the tumbling clear waters of the river and framed against startling blue skies — the row of delicately flowering jacaranda trees around it provide a beautiful colour accent! Approached by a suspension bridge over the Mo Chu, you have to climb a flight of steep wooden stairs to the great entrance door that leads you to the first courtyard. The entire dzong is 180m long and 72m wide and the gold–domed central tower (utse) is six-storey high with temples on each floor — the embalmed body of Jambey Dorji, the Zhabdung's son, is kept in this utse.

The second courtyard beyond the utse is for the monks and is surrounded with prayer halls and temples while an additional third courtyard at the southern end holds the kunrey or assembly hall of the monks. This is quite spectacular with its fifty-four magnificent pillars and beautiful statues of Buddha, Guru Padmasambhava and Zhabdung. The Je Khempo's living quarter and temple is here. This hall was constructed twenty years after the completion of the dzong to meet the growing needs of the monk body that the Zhabdung had established. There are around six hundred monks here and Punakha continues to be the winter headquarters of the dratshang

There are no restaurants of note in this region, so meals are best enjoyed at your hotel or at another resort.

(central body of monks) with the Je Khempo
residing here for close to six months of the year.

Besides its historical significance, the Punakha
Dzong is held in reverence since it holds the
embalmed body of the Zhabdung who died
here in 1651. His remains are enshrined in
the Machen Lhakhang (Temple of the Sacred
Embalmed Body) in a sealed casket and only the
king, Je Khempo and two caretaker lamas are
allowed to enter. The Ranjung Karsapani is also
kept here and the remains of the great terton,
Pema Lingpa, are interred here. As per tradition,
the incumbent king and Je Khempo offer prayers

**At the Dzong entrance**

**Chortens by the river below Wangdi Dzong**

and are blessed here by the Zhabdung before they begin their reign. It was at Punakha that Ugyen Wangchuck received his ceremonial title of Knight Commander of the Indian Empire and was later crowned the first King of Bhutan on 17th December 1907.

The dzong was damaged by fire in the eighteenth century and with each reconstruction several new temples were added, and this vast complex now houses twenty-one lhakhangs. Unfortunately, visitors are not allowed to visit most of these but can go to the first courtyard, dominated by a large new chorten (circa 1981), as well as the main temple. The entrance is decorated with some spectacular carvings and a geometric poem glorifying the deeds of the Zhabdung.

Having spent time admiring the dzong you can drive up the valley past Puntsho Pelri Palace and other homes of the nobility. Around 7km ahead on the opposite side is the large Khamsum Yuelley Namgyal Chorten which was consecrated in 1999 after a mammoth eight year construction period. The road has now been completed up to Damji and is expected to extend to Gasa. There are many beautiful spots along this valley to enjoy a quiet picnic lunch.

You now retrace your tracks, climbing back to Lobesa (5000ft/1525m), and then proceed 8km to Wangdiphodrang (colloquially referred to as Wangdi), with its dzong strategically positioned atop a hill. The route takes you along the Puna Tsang Chu which later joins the Mangdi to form the Wang Chu that flows below the dzong. Crossing the river, as you climb up to the spur on which the dzong is perched, on the opposite bank you can see the quaint and ancient village of Rinchengang renowned for producing the best

If you don't feel up to it you can give Wangdi Dzong a miss – it's actually more impressive viewed from below.

stone masons in the country. The slopes below the dzong are covered in cacti and although it enjoys a remarkably commanding 360° view of the valley, this hill is constantly buffeted by winds that raise clouds of dust!

The dzong was founded by the Zhabdung in 1638 at a spot that controlled the routes to Trongsa, Punakha, Dagana and Thimphu and the dzongpen here was regarded as a very powerful political personality. Currently this is the headquarters of Wangdiphodrang Dzongkhag.

However, popular legend ascribes other reasons for the selection of this spot. It appears that when the Zhabdung arrived in the area he spotted a boy building a grand sand castle on the banks of the river. This was taken as an omen and when the dzong was built it was named after the boy — Wangdiphodrang or Wangdi's Palace. Another legend, a part of religious lore, holds that the great protective deity Mahakala gave instructions to the Zhabdung in a dream — 'At the top of a rocky spur where two rivers meet, at the place where a flock of ravens fly off in the four directions, there you will build a dzong'. While searching for the site four ravens were spotted flying off in different directions and their take-off point was selected to be an auspicious spot.

Complex and different in shape, the dzong comprises three separate but linked structures. However, the interior of the dzong does not offer much of interest to the visitor and after a quick look you can proceed to your hotel for a relaxed evening. Since this area is not only warm in summer but also subjected to strong dusty winds, our recommendation would be to push on for another 65km (2.5 hours) to the cooler climes of Gantey ■

Petrol is available at Lobesa and Wangdi after which it's a 'dry run' till Trongsa.

## DAY 8
### ▶▶ Drive to Gantey

| Punakha-Wangdi | 20km | Nobding-Lawala | 10km |
| Wangdi-Nobding | 42km | Lawala-Phobjika | 13km |

An excellent place for a break is the scenic Kuenphen Café at Nobding which is around 11km before Lawala.

The drive, albeit a short one (65km), is dramatic due to the range of scenic beauty that unfolds along its route. Undoubtedly you will want to stop as photo-ops abound so factor in three hours for this journey that transports you from 4400ft/1342m to a pass just under 11,000ft/ 3354m. After a few days steeped in history and architectural splendour, it is time now to savour the enchanting pristine natural beauty of this land. The only place of historical importance here is the Gantey Gompa which at the time of writing was under renovation and is expected to open only in 2008. For the first 8km the road runs high above the Dang Chu through grassy

**Mountain views en
route to Gantey**

slopes till Chuzomsa (the confluence of Dang
Chu and Pe Chu), where it is almost at level with
the river. The Kyichu Resort is picturesquely
located close to the confluence. From here it is
a steady steep ascent to Lawala, 3km short of
the Pele La which is the cross-over point into
central Bhutan. The road clings tenaciously to

The view of the snow peaks gets more expansive and even better as you ascend, so there is no need to stop at every bend!

the very edge of the valley and it is a spectacular – though sometimes unnerving – drive up to the pass. Though clear days are rare, if you luck upon one you will be rewarded with views of Jichu Drakye, Kang Bum and other peaks en route. In summer the hill slopes are alive with vibrant blooms of pink, white and red

rhododendrons and you may even encounter some yak and the odd barking deer or red panda!

Just after Lawala you turn right, off the main road, and crest a ridge at 10,800ft/3293m to make a gradual descent into the glacial Phobjika valley famed for the migratory black-necked cranes that make it their winter home. This endangered species arrives from Tibet towards the end of October, marking the end of the harvesting season and the time for cattle and their herders to move down to warmer climes. The Bhutanese call the bird 'thrung thrung karmo' and as many as three hundred of these visitors arrive here every winter. The people have great affection for these beautiful winged creatures and they are featured in many folk songs. Local lore has it that these birds circle the gompa three times on their arrival and also when they fly out. Their departure towards the end of February is marked by songs of lamentation! The cranes have an elaborate mating ritual and they mate for life; according to locals when one bird lost its mate, it stayed on in the valley desolate and heart broken, for a whole year! Details of their habitat and habits, backed by some great photographs are available at the Crane Observation and Education Center. This facility is operated under the aegis of the Royal Society for the Protection of Nature. If the birds are in residence when you visit Gantey you may be able to get a close view from the hides specially constructed for this purpose.

The Gantey Gompa is on a small promontory overlooking the lush green valley. While visiting the area the great terton, Pema Lingpa prophesied that a gompa would be built on a gang-teng (hilltop) and that his teachings would

There are no eating options in Gantey — it is best to order lunch in advance at Hotel Dewachen or carry a well loaded hamper.

be carried forth from here. In 1613 a monastery was established by Pema Lingpa's grandson who became the first Gantey Tulku. The gompa was enlarged subsequently by the second reincarnation Tenzing Legpa Dhendup. Gantey is affiliated with several other important gompas in this region, including Tamzhing in Bumthang. Currently the ninth reincarnation, Kunzang Pema Namgyal is the abbot here. Besides the gompa there are several schools, a Tibetan style chorten and meditation centers where monks

**Picture perfect mustard fields at 8000ft!**

**The Phobjika valley**

retreat for periods ranging from three days, three months to three years. There is also a Buddhist college nearby that offers a nine-year course in Buddhist studies (For details on Pema Lingpa refer to Page 236).

The Phobjika valley is lush green and extensively cultivates potatoes which are the region's primary cash crop and an important

While walking around remember you are about 10,000ft high so take it easy on the first day.

export to India. The expansive peaceful pastoral environment here makes it an ideal place to chill out for a few days – there are no intruding cell phones and no electricity either.

From here your route takes you across the Black Mountains via Pele La, on to Trongsa and the Bumthang region that certainly qualifies as the cultural capital of the country ■

## ARTS AND CRAFTS

The country has a very strong artistic tradition which flourished in the fifteenth century under the great terton, Pema Lingpa who lent his expertise to structure and formalise this burgeoning activity. He was an accomplished sculptor, painter and architect and took the arts to a higher plane. The Bhutanese name 'Zorig Chusum' is an apt description — 'zo' is the ability to make, 'rig' is the science or craft, and 'chusum' is thirteen.

The thirteen disciplines are painting, sculpture, carving, blacksmithing, casting, carpentry, gold and silver smelting, weaving, embroidery, masonry, leather work, bamboo work and paper making. Each receives continuous on-going support from various segments of Bhutanese society.

When you visit Bhutan you begin to understand how traditional crafts that have flourished for centuries are not just alive but are thriving even in this era of globalisation. The country remained relatively isolated till the twentieth century and currently follows a cautious policy of integrating with the world economy on its own terms and pace to protect its culture and heritage. As a result of this deliberate choice the economy remains dependant on local skills and produce for the bulk of its day-to-day needs thereby not only providing employment but protecting the crafts.

The exquisite jewellery here is not like the mass-produced products you see in large showrooms elsewhere — it is finely handcrafted by local artisans. All the hectic building activity visible in Paro follows traditional architecture, with stone quarried locally and using masons trained in the craft for generations.

There are no stainless steel-and-mirror buildings nor pre-fab doors and windows here but rather carved wooden ones stunningly painted with symbols and floral patterns, thus ensuring the carpenter remains very much in demand.

All Bhutanese are required to wear their traditional attire to offices, monasteries and on all formal occasions and this gives a fillip to their wonderful art of weaving as also to the time-consuming but beautiful hand embroidery.

Utensils for cooking are made locally — in many places bamboo receptacles are used for serving. Tools for construction and agricultural implements such as ploughs, axes, shovels etc. are made by the blacksmith and there is even a thriving local paper industry. With a conscious policy to maintain the social fabric by not destroying traditional occupations, the country

is a live laboratory of a hitherto successful experiment of coping with 'modern times'.

Like all Buddhist art, in Bhutan too art is usually religious and anonymous. Unlike western art where the painter is expressing himself or herself, the emphasis here is on the subject and the aim is to bring out the deep inner symbolism of the person or scene being depicted.

You will come across many paintings that are 'beautiful' or 'outstanding' but this is not of consequence to the artist — his satisfaction lies in successfully portraying the 'message'.

Paintings and sculptures are commissioned by royalty, the clergy as well as lay persons, with the former two being the main patrons. When a Buddhist commissions a painting or statue he, as the 'jinda' or patron, gains merit as this is considered a pious act. His name may appear on the work but the artist's name is almost never mentioned! The artist also strictly adheres to the iconographical conventions laid down and his own personality can only be expressed in

minor scenes or unimportant details. (Most of these guidelines were established by Pema Lingpa in the fifteenth century)

Paintings can be grouped into three categories; tangkhas or thongdrels, mural paintings and painting of statues. The art of painting is called 'lhazo' and proficiency in this is basic to all other arts. The portrayal of human figures in paintings are subject to strict rules of iconography, with the proportions and features being precise and no artistic liberty being allowed. Tangkhas are created by painting on canvas sheets stretched taut and attached firmly to a wooden frame. Once the painting is complete it is detached from the wooden frame and a double border of colourful brocade fabric is stitched to its edges in a manner that resembles an exotic 'frame'. Wooden slats are attached to the top and bottom so that it can be hung up and displayed. Some tangkhas are displayed while others are rolled up and stored — these are brought out on special occasions.

Although many monks are well versed in this complex art, most paintings are executed by artists who are laymen. Traditionally, vegetable dyes and minerals were used to make colours but now there is an increasing dependence on chemical based oil pigments which are cheaper.

When painting statues, the artist usually paints only the face on a metal statue where as clay statues are completely painted over. The body is painted a golden hue which often makes the statue appear to be a bronze but in reality these are clay statues painted from head to toe!

The murals on temple walls are painted on pieces of thin, finely woven cloth which is then affixed to the wall by adhesive with so much care that it is impossible to detect. In addition, a paste of pepper and flour is applied to prevent termites from eating the 'invisible' fabric!

Bhutanese religious painting was greatly influenced by the Tibetan style which in turn drew inspiration from the Indian Pala-Sena dynasties of Bengal. The style sponsored by these dynasties was the dominant art form between the eighth and twelfth centuries. From the beginning of the eighteenth century, the influence of Chinese art is clearly discernible. The reds and yellows were then replaced by aquamarine from ground turquoise and other stones and there was an increased use of gold paint. Whereas in the earlier form the background of the painting was usually of other deities, they were now filled with mountains, landscapes, clouds and flora reflecting the style followed in Chinese paintings.

### DAY 9
#### ▸▸ Drive across Pele La to Trongsa onto Jakar (Bumthang)

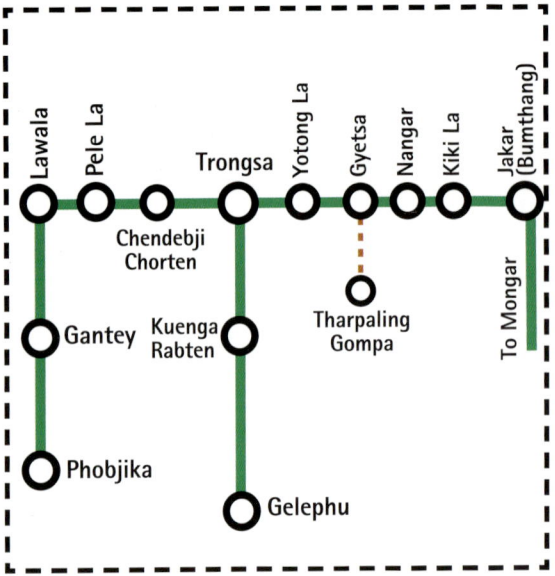

Including stops, you are likely to be on the road for 6-7 hours so carry enough snacks and beverages.

| | | | | |
|---|---|---|---|---|
| Gantey-Pele La | 16km | | Trongsa-Yotang La | 29km |
| Pele La-Chendebji | 27km | | Yotang La-Kiki La | 32km |
| Chendebji-Trongsa | 41km | | Kiki La-Jakar | 9km |

Your journey involves travel of around 150km (5hrs), so we suggest making a start by 9 am You have to trace your way back to the junction and then ascend 3km to the high pass Pele La (11,070ft/3375m), which is marked by chortens and prayer flags. Approaching the pass you find the hill slopes covered in bamboo, locally called 'ham', which is the favourite meal of the resident yak population. The road now descends gradually to the Langthel valley, passing through groves of fir trees to the evergreens and finally the broadleaved varieties. On the opposite

side of the road is the village of Rukubji with its clustered homes and a gompa. The land is well cultivated with crops of mustard, wheat, barley and potatoes. You then drive past Sephu village known for the bamboo baskets and mats produced here and temptingly displayed along the roadside. The next village is Chendebji, and two kilometers further on your right lies the spectacular Chendebji Chorten on the banks of the Nikkar Chu. This startling white stone chorten is built in the Nepalese style with eyes painted on all four sides. A large mani wall leading to the chorten tells the story behind its founding. It was built in the eighteenth century by Lama Shida of Tibet to suppress a demon

**Weaving beauty!**

# TRAVEL PLAN

Trongsa Dzong

who had been troubling the inhabitants of the valley. It is an extremely serene spot and this chorten is one of the most picturesquely located in the country. A smaller Bhutanese style chorten was constructed nearby by the royal grandmother in 1982. Chendebji, till recently, marked the western end of a series of chortens with Chorten Kora, located at Trashiyangtse, being the eastern end but in 2005 a new chorten was built at Kuruthang, Punakha, making it the western-most.

The drive to Trongsa from here is only 41km and the last section is along the Mangde Chu with a precipitous drop of almost 3280ft/1000m on the right hand side for much of the way! The awe-inspiring Trongsa Dzong can be seen before you reach it – there is a view point around 14km short of town from where you get a good overview of the dzong on the opposite hill face with the river rushing below. In this region grows a cherry that flowers in autumn and at that time the whole valley is prettily covered in pink blooms. The road then curves away to cross the Mangde Chu at a check point and then climbs to the small township at 6800ft/2073m.

The Trongsa Dzong is possibly the most impressive in the country – it is intricately layered into the hillside, in complete harmony with its surroundings. The structure is aesthetically designed and its clean lines boast a superb sense of proportion and space while finely carved woodwork and elegant paintings suitably embellish it. Of its collection of buildings, the first, Chorten Lhakhang, was built at this strategic location as recently as the mid-sixteenth century and lies at the southern end of the dzong. The Zhabdung's great grandfather, Drukpa Lama

The best view of Trongsa Dzong is from a point on the road around 14km short of the town!

Ngagi Wangchuk resided in Yueli village which is located above the current dzong. One evening while meditating he observed a strange light on the spur below. Perceiving this as an auspicious omen he clambered down to investigate and found footprints of the guardian deity Palden Lama's horse. He built a small meditation center here and subsequently others came up around it. Viewed from Yueli this cluster of buildings resembled a small village and was referred to as Trong-sa meaning 'new village'. While he was in the process of unifying the country, the Zhabdung ordered the construction of a dzong at the location found by his ancestor. Following these instructions, the dzong was built in 1644 by Chhogyel Minjur Tenpa who later became the third desi. He named it Druk Minjur Rabten Tse Dzong. The structure was enhanced by Desi Tenzin Rabgye in 1771 and now contains twenty-three temples. It is a veritable maze of corridors, courtyards and passageways leading to the multiple levels contained within the great outer impregnable shell.

Ensure that your guide takes you to the main lhakhang whose interiors are quite spectacular.

Today Trongsa is just one of the twenty districts but till the very recent past played a pivotal role in the history of the country. In the nineteenth century it was the de facto center of authority as the penlop controlled all of central and eastern Bhutan, including the rich fertile southern duars. The royal family has its antecedents here — the father of the first king, Jigme Namgyal, as the penlop of Trongsa exerted his authority across the country. Before becoming the monarch, Ugyen Wangchuck became penlop of Trongsa thereby establishing a tradition that continues — the present fifth king was appointed Trongsa penlop in 2004.

Besides wandering around the incredibly well

maintained stone-flagged courtyard, you will find a visit to the main lhakhang (kuenrey) particularly interesting. The complex has temples to the great tantric deities Yamantaka and Kalchakra as well as one dedicated to Maitreya with a large statue within. There are some superbly executed paintings and the dzong even has its own printing press where the traditional xylographic method is used to print texts.

You can also clamber up to the Ta Dzong which is now being converted to a museum. It has an unusual tower section with wings extending in front of the main building. Entering this you can visit the chapel dedicated to Jigme Namgyal and enjoy a bird's-eye view of the dzong stretched out below you.

**Outside the lhakhang**

# TRAVEL PLAN

Trongsa is also the point from where the southern road begins its 237km journey to the border town of Gelephu. For those interested in a one hour (each way) diversion, a 28km drive allows you to check out Kuenga Rabten, the winter palace of the second monarch King Jigme Wangchuck. This building is now under the aegis of the National Library and one does not need permission to visit this splendid structure with its intricate woodwork and decorations. There is

**Another scenic drive**

also a large nunnery nearby and a little further down is Yurung Choling, the first king's winter palace. If you plan on taking this diversion carry a picnic lunch as you won't be able to make it to Bumthang for a proper meal.

Having taken in the sights of Trongsa the road now leads you on to the Bumthang region which comprises four major valleys; those of Tang, Ura, Chumey and Choekhor. Agricultural activities predominate in the Chumey and Choekhor

The best place to stay at in Trongsa is the Yangkhil Hotel and this is also the best option for a meal en route.

valleys while in Tang and Ura sheep and yak breeding is more popular.

The town of Jakar is the administrative center and is located in the Choekhor valley. It is in this valley that the Jakar Dzong and most of the important lhakhangs are located — hence, in popular parlance, this represents Bumthang. The origin of the name is ascribed to the shape of the valley — that of a 'bumpa', the oblong vase which contains the holy water placed at the altar of the lhakhang, while 'thang' means field or flat place. Sacred in character, the Bumthang region has the highest concentration of temples and monasteries. Bumthang embraced Buddhism in the eighth century when Guru Padmasambhava visited the region and its religious significance was enhanced when venerated Nyingmapa saints — Longchen Rabjamba, Dorje Lingpa and the Bumthang-born Pema Lingpa made this their home. In the seventeenth century the Drukpas gained power here. This gentle green valley with its wide terraces enjoys a sense of space that is fairly uncommon to Bhutan and is thus an ideal place for hikes and light treks.

While climbing out of Trongsa do stop for an overview of the labyrinth-like structure of the dzong.

The road climbs steeply above Trongsa for around 7km and then more gradually for another 22km till you reach the high point of the drive — the pass Yotong La at 11,000ft/3354m. As you descend, the road passes through dense forest of fir, followed by blue pine and then bamboo. The wide cultivated Chumey valley marked by the village of Gyetsa (8850ft/2698m), comes up around 13km after the pass. Besides wheat, barley and potatoes, the most important crop grown here is buckwheat which is used to prepare the staple diet of the region — noodles and pancakes. Just after Gyetsa you pass the fourteenth century Buli Lhakhang perched on

a small knoll. Visible in the far distance above are the Tharpaling Monastery and even higher, the Choedrak Gompa. A rough 9km track allows you to drive up to Tharpaling (11,810ft/3600m), if you are so inclined. The monastery was constructed in 1352 by Longchen Rabjampa who was an eminent philosopher of the Dzongchen sect. There are two temples with the one on the upper floor having been restored by King Ugyen Wangchuck. This contains some exquisite paintings of the Zhabdung, Longchen Rabjampa,

**Often a multi-use vehicle!**

Water-driven prayer wheel

Amitava's heaven and Guru Padmasambhava in his rarely depicted form of Guru Dewa. There is a monastic school above the main monastery.

From here you can climb up to Choedrak Gompa, built on the spot where Guru Pabmasambhava had meditated. The temple was built by Lama Lorepa of Tibet in 1234. When the lama returned to Tibet a demon is said to have taken over the premises. It lay abandoned till this bad element was eventually vanquished in the eighteenth century by Ngawang Trinley, a renowned monk from the Punakha region. He then rebuilt the monastery and the great terton Pema Lingpa discovered several terma (hidden treasures) from around these gompas.

Back on the road you reach the village of Domkhar after a few kilometers. Perched on a small hillock to your right is the Domkhar Tashicholing which served as the summer residence of the second king. Just beyond this you encounter something rather unusual for Bhutan — an almost 1km straight stretch of road with three speed breakers, the only ones we came across in the whole country! You then cross the river and enter the settlement of Zugney which is well worth a stop so you can watch the many weavers working arduously at their looms. The women here generally have scarves tied on their heads in 'the Bumthang style'! This is a sheep rearing area and yields high-quality wool that is used to make the 'yathas' that this village is famed for. The yatha is a twill-weave woollen cloth in bright coloured stripes and geometric patterns and is used to make cushions and bed spreads and even garments. Yathas are a Bumthang speciality and the Chumey valley is famous for the quality of its produce. While driving through Zugney, take

In Bumthang you will be back at a cool 8500ft — keep the woolies handy.

in the small temple on the right hand side of the road which is attributed to the seventh century King Songsten Gampo from Tibet.

Around 2km further, you will skirt the scenic village of Pra or Prakhar which traces its antecedents to the sixteenth century. According to legend it was founded by Pema Lingpa's grandson Tenpe Nyima who was directed by a vision to construct a temple here. After putting in a hard day's work, when he returned to the site next morning, the temple seemed to have literally grown overnight! An investigation by the villagers revealed that white monkeys continued his job of construction through the night – the place was thus called Prakhar (white monkey). Tenpe Nyima's father, Lama Dawa Gyeltsen is embalmed in a chorten that is in the main temple and this lineage has provided the country with many great reincarnations and personages of eminence. The gompa is a ten minute walk from the road.

Stop to watch the women at work on their looms once you enter the Chumey valley.

The road now climbs past Nangar, the last village in the Chumey valley, through apple trees and blue pines on to Kiki La at 9300ft/2835m. Your destination, Jakar, at a cool 8450ft/2576m, is only 9km from here and you should be in time for a relaxed albeit slightly late lunch. You are now in the broad Choekhor valley, which not only abounds in mesmerising natural beauty but is peerless in the rich religious and cultural heritage it allows you to view. A number of ancient lhakhangs that are accessible to visitors are scattered over a 10km radius. Relax and unwind after your drive and then if you are up to it, you can begin your exploration of this cultural hot spot with a visit to two lhakhangs.

To visit Tamzhing Lhakhang you have to leave town over the bridge spanning Bumthang Chu,

White rhododendrons

**Tamshing Lhakhang**

turn left and drive around 5km. This lhakhang was founded in 1501 by Pema Lingpa who was personally involved in its construction. It took four years to build and even today remains, along with Gantey Gompa, the premier center for teaching Pema Lingpa's tradition of Buddhist studies. It is believed that he was assisted in his task by khandums who are female celestial beings. The outer courtyard holds the monk's quarters while the inner courtyard leads to the lhakhang. The Dunkar Lhakhang is to the East of this courtyard which also accesses the assembly hall. In this hall is a separate structure – the main chapel. A low balcony wraps around the upper floor which also has a chapel, located just above the lower one, which holds a statue of the Buddha of Long Life.

There are thirty-six paintings on the inner walls at the ground level – these are attributed to Pema Lingpa himself and are the oldest extant paintings in the country. Each has a central deity surrounded by attendants, the figures conforming to the iconographic canons established by him. These early sixteenth century paintings are of special value and interest in the fields of both art and history as they are in their original form and not 'restored' as most others.

The inner sanctuary is dedicated to Guru Padmasambhava and his eight manifestations. His statue is believed to have been sculpted by the khandums and has the eyes sloping upwards watching the angels in their flight! Another unusual aspect is the fact that Guru Padmasambhava is not wearing shoes. Pema Lingpa's original coat of mail (that he possibly made by himself), is kept on this floor and it is supposed to bring good luck if you can carry it three times around the gompa. (Warning: It weighs twenty-five kilograms!) To the front of the assembly hall are three thrones for the body, mind and speech reincarnations of Pema Lingpa who attend all important ceremonies.

Moving to the upper floor, be prepared to stoop as you walk around the balcony – apparently Pema Lingpa was quite short and the ceiling was designed keeping his height in mind! The walls are elaborately illustrated with 1004 paintings of Buddha (The Thousand Buddhas) and those of the twenty-one Taras and striking yellow-on-red depictions of the Three Bodies of Buddha – Amitava, Avalokiteswara and Padmasambhava.

If you don't feel like stopping, the sights en route can easily be accessed from Jakar where you will be staying.

Carry a torch while visiting Tamzhing Lhakhang so that you can fully appreciate the magnificent art.

On the inner walls are paintings of the religious cycle with the eight forms of Guru Rinpoche, the eighty-four Mahasiddhas and a continuation of the Thousand Buddhas. The collection is one of the most remarkable pertaining to this period, in the country and indeed anywhere in the Himalayas. The temple on the upper floor is dedicated to Amitayus, but do look out for the

small statue of Pema Lingpa in a glass case by the entrance.

Tamzhing affords great views of the Kurjey Lhakhang complex across the river and it can be accessed on foot from here. Just short of the bridge there is a path leading up to the small Padmasambhava Lhakhang which was erected to mark one of his meditation spots. The original

**Our entry — a welcome distraction!**

'Chorten wall' at
Kurjey Lhakhang

shrine was built in 1490 by Pema Lingpa around a cave and was known as Dekyiling – it was subsequently expanded and has recently been restored.

On your return, around a kilometer from Tamzhing look out for the unassuming and almost unmarked Kenchosum Lhakhang which is believed to date back to the eighth century and subsequently restored by Pema Lingpa in the fifteenth century. In the lhakhang is an ancient bell believed to have been cast for the Tibetan royalty and there is an interesting tale about it – the bell was spirited away to Bhutan but its chimes could still be heard in distant Lhasa! An army was sent from Tibet to retrieve the bell but it weighed so much that they dropped and cracked it and returned empty handed. It is made of a unique alloy of gold, silver, bronze and tin. Various terma, dating back to the tenth century, were also revealed from this place. Pema Lingpa also discovered religious treasures from a subterranean water body below the lhakhang. He is supposed to have sealed the entrance with a large stone bearing his lotus insignia – this stone can still be seen in the center of the courtyard. The antiquity of this temple is attested by the main statue which is of Vairocana Buddha surrounded by Avalokiteswara and Guru Pabmasambhava. There are also images of Pema Lingpa and Longchen Rabjampa, the great philosopher who sought refuge in Bumthang.

Before returning to your hotel stop and check out the Swiss Farm products available at their outlet located 500m from the bridge where the road curves up to the Swiss Guest House. Besides gouda and emmenthal cheese, you can sample the Red Panda beer brewed here as also the brandy and apple wines ■

Even if the caretaker at Kenchosum Lhakhang is missing when you visit, it's worth returning to see its interior.

## DAY 10
### ▸▸ In and around Bumthang
### (Visit Jakar Dzong, Kurjey and Jambay Lhakhang, Membartso and beyond)

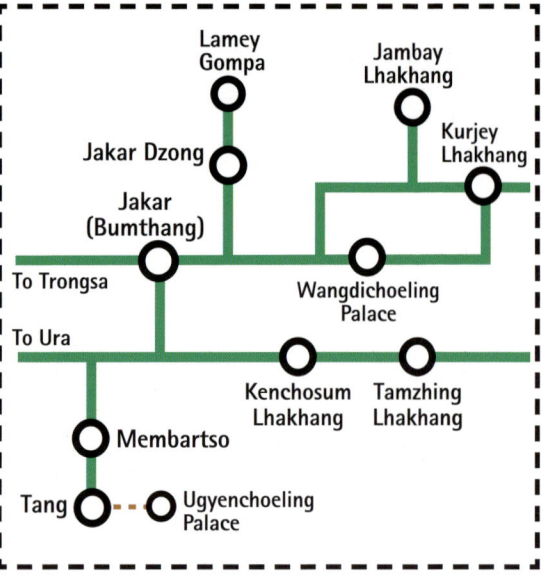

| | | |
|---|---|---|
| Jakar-Membartso | 11km | Tang-Jakar  28km |
| Membartso-Tang | 17km | |

The dzong at Jakar is one of the few that you may give a miss — the other sights more than compensate.

Make a leisurely start and begin your day by visiting Jakar Dzong which was initially built as a monastery and later converted to a dzong in 1646. Scenically located on the crest of a hill spur, it overlooks the Choekhor valley. This 'Dzong of the White Bird' was so named by the Zhabdung's great grandfather Ngagi Wangchuk because one day, while building the monastery, a great white bird flew directly over the site and landed on this spur. Interpreting this as an auspicious omen the site of the monastery was immediately shifted and it was later converted into a dzong. This building was damaged by fire and then again by the earthquake of 1897 after which it was rebuilt by King Ugyen Wangchuck in 1905. The dzong is the administrative seat of the district. The lhakhang at Jakar is one of the oldest temples in Bhutan and contains some fine paintings. However, all said and done, you will not need to spend much time here and can take a short 4km drive further to the end of the road to see the Lamey Gompa. This charming gompa was actually built as a palace in the nineteenth century by the Trongsa penlop. At present this building houses the Forest Institute but traces of its original grandeur are visible and there is a great view to be had from here.

**The Kurjey Lhakhang complex**

**Memorial chorten in Kurjey Lhakhang**

You now head down to the main road below the dzong and proceed up the valley for around 7km till you reach the exquisite Kurjey Lhakhang complex at the end of the road. This is the country's most historical holy place – the complex is surrounded by 108 chortens, transforming it into a three dimensional mandala patterned on the lines of the Samye Monastery in Tibet. 'Kur' means body and 'jey' its print – it is here that Guru Pabmasambhava meditated when he first visited the country, leaving an imprint of his body on the rock enshrined here. The story behind this event is as remarkable as any you will come across in the country and marks the first stage in the establishment of the Buddhist faith in Bhutan.

In the eighth century the ruler of the Bumthang region was the Indian King Sendhaka, popularly known as Sindhu Gyab. His capital was in the Choekhor valley where he ruled from a nine-storey iron castle known as Chakhar. This was rebuilt in the fourteenth century by Dorje Lingpa and the present building came up in the beginning of the twentieth century and is called Chakhar Lhakhang.

Sindhu Gyab was feuding with his southern neighbour Na'oche (Big nose!) and was unfortunate to lose his son while engaged in battle. Distraught with grief, he omitted to worship his personal deity Shelging Karpo for some length of time. Greatly angered by this very human failing, the deity decided to punish the hapless king and withdrew his life force. The king soon took gravely ill and was on his deathbed when his ministers decided to invite Guru Padmasambhava – whose exploits were legendary – to intervene. Fortunately for Sindhu Gyab, Guru Padmasambhava acceded to the request and arriving in Bumthang proceeded to a huge thunderbolt-shaped rock near Chakhar that was the abode of Shelging Karpo. The Guru meditated here awhile, leaving his body's imprint on the rock. He then transformed himself into his eight manifestations and performed a celestial dance on the meadow before the rock. This magical performance was watched in awe by all the local deities except for Shelging Karpo who continued to sulk in his abode above the present temple. Undeterred by this 'no show', Guru Padmasambhava then transformed the king's daughter who was carrying water in a golden

Jakar is a small bustling township – if you are out shopping, check out Sonam Handicrafts.

If you have been doing weights try lifting and carrying Pema Lingpa's coat of mail at Tamzhing Lhakhang.

ewer into five princesses, each with a golden ewer. The rays of the sun reflected off the five ewers engaged the attention of Shelging who emerged in the form of a white lion to check out what was happening in his domain. This was the moment that Guru Padmasambhava was waiting for — he now took the form of the holy garuda (griffon) and swooped down, catching Shelging Karpo in his talons. Subsequent moral persuasion made the deity not only restore the king's life force but to also pledge not to cause further harm and to become a protective deity of Buddhism in the region. Beholden to Guru Padmasambhava and guided by him, both Sindhu Gyab and Na'oche embraced Buddhism and agreed to end their discord in the interest of peace. Guru Rinpoche planted his personal staff in the ground here and this is believed to have

**Jakar Dzong**

Heading home after a pious round of Kurjey Lhakhang

grown into a giant cypress and a descendant of this tree is believed to stand sentinel even today, in front of Kurjey Lhakhang!

The complex comprises three temples, two of which are old while the third was constructed by the royal grandmother in the 1980s. The first temple on the right is the oldest and is built around the rock where the meditating Guru Padmasambhava left his body print. This dates back to 1652 and was built by the Trongsa Penlop Minjur Tenpa. As you enter, looking up, do not miss the carved depiction of the garuda subduing the white lion. There is also a small opening in the rock at the entrance – you can try and squeeze through to the other end and if you succeed, by Guru Rinpoche's grace, your sins will be absolved! (Warning!! If you get stuck only intense prolonged meditation will set you free!) An easier feat to tackle is crawling through the small rock below the steps in the courtyard – an easier option for sure but one not guaranteed to help you with your misdeeds!

There are two sanctuaries within the lhakhang; one contains images of the past, present and future Buddhas enclosed by walls painted over with the twenty-one Taras and other deities representing wealth and prosperity. The second is the holiest spot within the complex as it contains the rock cave where Guru Padmasambhava meditated. To the left of the entrance is an image of Shelging Karpo and an altar dedicated to him. On the right side there are a thousand statues of Guru Padmasambhava along with three larger ones. The opposite wall has paintings of him in all his eight manifestations and of his twenty-five key disciples. The wall paintings are often draped with a protective cloth covering. The main statue at the altar is also of the Guru,

If you want a break from Bhutanese cuisine, Swiss Guest House offers excellent western fare.

surrounded by his eight manifestations, and it is behind this that the rock bearing his imprint lies concealed.

The second temple dates back to 1900 having been constructed by Ugyen Wangchuck when he was still penlop of Trongsa. This was built to house a large 33ft/10m tall statue of Guru Padmasambhava, modelled under the supervision of a senior lama who prophesied

**Jambay Lhakhang**

that the vibrations emanating from the statue would contribute greatly to the stability and prosperity of the country. The statue is surrounded by the eight manifestations with an image of the historical Buddha on the left side and that of Zangto Pelri on the right side. The entrance porch is decorated with paintings of the Kings (or Guardians) of the Four Cardinal Directions, Shelging Karpo and the other deities

In the white 'chorten wall' around Kurjey Lhakhang are four chortens, on each side, that are of different colours — these mark the four cardinal directions.

**'Bamboo Factory' on the road!**

who were converted to Buddhism by Guru Padmasambhava.

The third temple is a private one belonging to the royal family and visitors are not allowed inside. This was built in 1984 by the royal grandmother who also had the courtyard paved in stone and commissioned the '108-chorten-wall' that encloses the complex. In front of the temples are three large memorial chortens – including one that is a heap of stones – and these are dedicated to the first three kings of Bhutan. An interesting feature in the beautiful symmetrical white chorten wall is the presence of one coloured chorten on all four sides, representing and marking the great cardinal directions.

There is no permanent monk body resident in Bumthang but the Trongsa monks spend the summer here at Kurjey and perform ceremonies and rituals, including the festival.

The Kurjey Tsechu is held in June and includes a spectacular masked dance symbolising Guru Padmasambhava overcoming Shelging Karpo. A large thongdrel depicting Guru Pabmasambhava and his eight manifestations is also unfurled during this event.

You will now have to backtrack for around 3km to a junction that leads you to Jambay Lhakhang. You may want to make a quick stop, around 500m before the junction, to visit Dechen Phodrang Lhakhang. Although this building looks like an ordinary house it is reputed to be the site of the Iron Palace (Chakhar) of Sindhu Gyab. The original is believed to have been an awe inspiring iron-clad, nine-storey high structure that held 'all the treasures of the world'! The current building dates to the early twentieth century and the main statue is of Guru Padmasambhava. What is particularly interesting is the display of numerous and varied masks that are still used during the annual festival held here in October.

You may get some rain in Bumthang so keep an umbrella handy

Jambay Lhakhang was supposedly constructed on the same day as Kyichu Lhakhang in Paro, by the Tibetan ruler Songsten Gampo as part of his successful effort to subdue the ogress preventing the spread of Buddhism. It was one of the 108 strategically located temples and was placed on the left knee of the ogress, 'to subjugate the frontiers'. The temple is dedicated to Maitreya or Jampa and the central shrine holds a large statue of this Buddha of the Future, surrounded by four boddhisattavas. The statue is guarded by iron chain mail handcrafted by Pema Lingpa himself

The local brew is called 'ara' but you may find the flavour too strong.

and the walls of the circumambulation path are painted with the Thousand Buddhas — actually 1004 Buddhas. From here Guru Padmasambhava is believed to have preached to Sindhu Gyab and his courtiers the teachings of the Kagye cycle of Buddhist philosophy and in an alcove inside there is a statue of him, marking the place where he meditated and left a footprint. Inside the main temple are three stone steps depicting the ages — the first symbolises the past, the age of the Historical Buddha, and has sunk into the ground and is covered by a plank. Visible are the 'present step', at level now with the floor and the 'future step' — the belief being that when the present step sinks, the gods will descend and the world will no longer be as we know it! According to popular belief there is a subterranean lake below this lhakhang where Guru Padmasambhava secreted away many terma.

Over the years this lhakhang was restored many times by various Trongsa penlops and in the mid-ninteenth century four more temples were added. Of these, one is the sanctuary of Dukhor (Kalchakra) — with the Chorten Lhakhang in its extension wing — and the other is the Guru Lhakhang. The Dukhor was built by King Ugyen Wangchuck and dedicated to Kalchakra (the Wheel of Time) which is regarded as the most complex of tantric teachings. These were preached by the Buddha and then kept secret for centuries till they were divulged in the late tenth century in India and reached Tibet in the early eleventh century. The temple holds the Kalchakra deity embracing his consort. The Guru Lhakhang was built in the mid-nineteenth century and its temple holds a statue of Guru Rinpoche flanked by Avalokiteswara and Amitayus. The annual Jambay Lhakhang Drup is

held here every October and is one of the most spectacular festivals in the country. A highlight is the fire dance performed to bless infertile women so that they may bear children.

Membartso lake

Before heading back for lunch you can make two quick stops – the first for a bit of shopping (which may not so be quick after all!!), at the 'Handicrafts Emporium' run by an NGO. Located in a charming traditional building by the river, this emporium promotes the crafts of the region and you will find a good selection and range of products to choose from. For the next stop you need to head close to the river to visit the historic but now closed Wangdichoeling Palace. Built in 1857 by the Trongsa Penlop Jigme Namgyal, it was the first palace not designed to be a fortress as well. When his son Ugyen

**Hanging out to dry
— clothes and dinner!**

Wangchuck became the first king of Bhutan, this was chosen to be the principal residence. The second king continued to live here with the court moving to Kuenga Rabten Dzong (near Trongsa), for the winter. It was only in 1952 when the third king moved the court to Punakha that the palace fell into disuse. It is now being restored as a family residence and the imposing entrance, beautiful murals and the three-storey utse with its chapels will be brought back to their former elegance.

After lunch, it is only a short 11km drive to the Tang valley where you can visit the site of some of Terton Pema Lingpa's greatest finds — Membartso or 'Flaming Lake' which is one of the great pilgrim sites of Bhutan. For those of you who are planning on travelling further East, or plan to spend more time exploring the Ura region (which starts from the pass Shelthang La, 37km from Jakar), this can be combined with either.

The route takes you across the bridge that lies beyond the market, after which you turn right onto the road leading to Ura and Mongar. About 9km or so further on you will come to the Dechenpelrithang Sheep Farm. Just under a kilometer ahead there is a rough track on the left and another kilometer ahead you come to a junction where you can park your vehicle. From here it is a ten minute walk down to the river rushing below you. The path is lined with prayer flags and ends up above a gorge where the river forms a pool before it rushes on. Images of Pema Lingpa and his two sons are carved on a rock here. This is where the great terton found many treasures hidden by Guru Padmasambhava – you're tempted to peer in to see if you can get lucky enough to make a discovery yourself but please don't fall in! (See box on Pema Lingpa for details of his discovery at Membartso)

For those in the mood for a little rough driving, followed by a good walk, you can continue on the same unpaved track for 17km to the village of Tang. The road climbs up past Chhelwa Rithrang where Pema Lingpa's birthplace is marked by a small chorten. Perched high on a cliff (10,990ft/3350m) is a gompa built by Pema Lingpa in 1490. It contains many sacred relics but is a stiff two hour climb. This gompa consists of Pema Lingpa's living quarters and three temples of which Khandroma Lhakhang stands out for its seemingly impossible perch, clinging to a vertiginous cliff side – legend has it that its construction was only possible with the help of khandums, the female celestial beings!

The road to Tang is rough and you won't miss much if you turn back from Membartso.

If you are not going further East, you might consider driving an hour or so towards Ura, to experience the 'highs' of the Shelthang La.

After climbing for around 5km from the base of the Kunzangdra cliff, the road descends into the Tang valley with the motorable section ending at a large village of the same name. From here you proceed on foot for 3km to the Tang Rimochen Lhakhang which has body imprints of Guru Padmasambhava and two khandums on a rock in front of it.

A further 45-minute uphill walk from here takes you to the sixteenth century

**School at Tang village**

Ugyenchoeling Palace which was restored in the nineteenth century. It is privately owned and has been turned into a museum depicting the life of Bhutanese nobility and also serves as a retreat for those engaged in religious studies. If you seek to spend a night or two away from civilisation, there are six rooms available here. Having ventured – or rather, adventured – this far, we suggest you pace yourself so you get back to the road before dark! ■

## PEMA LINGPA

Pema Lingpa is possibly one of the country's greatest spiritual masters and his lineage can be traced back to the ninth century.

Lacham Pemasel, the daughter of the Tibetan King Trisong Detsen, died unexpectedly in her eighth year but Guru Padmasambhava, moved by the king's extreme sorrow, drew her consciousness back into her body. When she regained awareness the Guru transmitted to her the secret doctrine of Khandro Nyingtig (the 'Three Heart Practices') and blessed her with the prophecy that in the future she would be reborn as a terton king Pema Lingpa and reveal to him these precious hidden teachings. These teachings were expounded widely in her next incarnation as Pema Lendreltsel who in turn was reborn as Longchen Rabjampa — the 'all-knowing Lord of the Doctrine' — who could read and write at the age of five and mastered the Buddhist precepts before he was twenty! During his lifetime he was made aware that his destiny was to be reincarnated as a great terton king — Pema Lingpa — so that he could serve an even greater number of beings.

Though Guru Padmasambhava was more than successful in confronting and converting forces opposed to Buddhism in his lifetime he was also able to foresee that in the future these teachings would get confused and separated from their core essence. He therefore blessed the region with thousands of termas — teachings in the form of hidden treasures which would be revealed by the tertons (treasure revealers). The most profound and subtle of these were the teachings on Atiyoga or dzogchen. These esoteric teachings were secreted over the vast and varied landscape of the Himalayas — in lakes, rivers, caves, trees and mountains, as well as in the psyche of disciples who, as reincarnated spiritual gurus, would be led to discover the 'terma' through dreams, visions, and spontaneous realisation.

Pema Lingpa (1450–1521), was born in a small hamlet called Drangchel, located in Bumthang's Tang valley. He was an extremely gifted student but did not go through extensive formal religious training. As a young lad his grandfather taught him the crafts of blacksmithing and carpentry — he is believed to have personally crafted the iron chain mail fencing Maitreya's statue in Jambay Lhakhang as well as his own chain mail coat that is now preserved in Tamzhing Lhakhang. In his early adult years his dreams and visions became the medium through which he received instructions to extract one hundred and eight treasures — texts and relics spread through the Himalayas, over Bhutan and parts of India and Tibet. However, due to the karmic disposition of sentient beings living during that era, he only revealed thirty-two of these prophesied treasures. Even so, these thirty-two encapsulated the essence of all one hundred and eight and pertained to the cycles of the Three Heart Practices initially transmitted to Princess Pema by Guru Padmasambhava.

His first discovery was made at the age of twenty-five after he dreamt of a monk coming up to him and giving him a scroll that instructed him to go to the Tang Chu, accompanied by five companions, to reveal sacred treasures hidden there in a rock called Naring. At night, guided by a full moon, he and his companions went to the river and reached a point where they could see a huge

rock overlooking a large natural pool in the otherwise fast flowing river. Peering down into the waters, he was able to discern a temple with multiple entrances of which only one door was open. He plunged into the pool, passed through the door, and found himself in a cave that held a life-size statue of Buddha on a throne and surrounding him were many large boxes. A one-eyed old lady handed one of these to him and in the next instant he found himself back on the rock with the treasure! He returned with this to his home at Kunzangling which is perched high on a cliff in the Tang valley. The scroll in the chest took considerable time deciphering as it was in 'fairy script', where one word is equivalent to a thousand and each has a deeper meaning. This became the basis of his teachings, but his second discovery was the more famous one.

The first terma provided instructions to retrieve treasures from the same spot, and this time Pema Lingpa was accompanied by a swathe of onlookers, many of whom questioned his divine powers. Amongst them was the penlop who accused him of being a common trickster. Cut to the quick Pema Lingpa took a lighted butter lamp in one hand and proclaimed to the largish gathering, "If I am a genuine revealer of your treasures, then may I return with it now, with my lamp still burning; if I am some devil then may I perish in the water."

He jumped into the lake and when a considerable time passed without him appearing, the skeptics began to gloat thinking they had been right. They were astounded when Pema Lingpa suddenly appeared on the rock with the butter lamp still alight and a statue and chest in the other arm. This pool became known as Membartso, or 'Burning Lake'.

In his dreams, he was often transported to Guru Padmasambhava's celestial abode, Zangto Pelri, where he was privy to the dances of the khandums and yidam (tutelary deities). He incorporated some of these movements into three dances which are an integral part of tsechus even today. He built two important gompas — that of Kuzangdra in his village, and later in 1518 the Tamzhing Gompa in Bumthang.

Pema Lingpa had a large family of six sons and a daughter and after his death was reincarnated in three forms — that of the body (kur), speech (sung) and mind (thug). His lineage is an important part of Bhutan even today... his son Kuenga Wangpo settled in the Lhuentse region and his great grandson founded the Dungkhar Dzong. Descendents of this clan became powerful personages and today's royal family the Wangchucks, are from his lineage. A reincarnation of Pema Lingpa founded the Gantey Gompa and this lineage continues with the ninth reincarnation Kuenzang Pema Namgyal having been born in 1955.

## DAY 11
### ▸▸ From Jakar to Mongar via Ura and the Thrumsing La

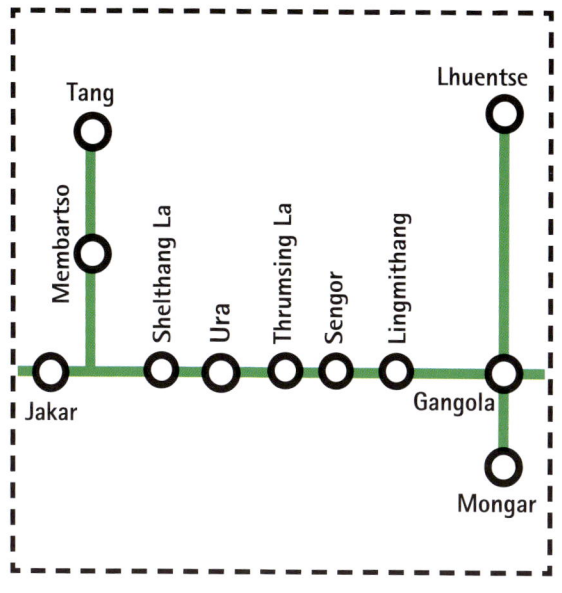

You will need warm clothes for the first part of the journey.

| | | | | |
|---|---|---|---|---|
| Jakar-Shelthang La | 37km | | Thrumsing La-Sengor | 20km |
| Shelthang La-Ura | 10km | | Sengor-Lingmithang | 56km |
| Ura-Thrumsing La | 35km | | Lingmithang-Mongar | 29km |

This journey is a bit long but the route is quite scenic and, including a short stop at Ura village, takes around 7-8 hours. You can make a leisurely start as your day's destination does not offer any sight-seeing opportunities and actually serves as a transit point en route to Trashigang, your last port of call. Located towards the eastern end of the country, Mongar also serves as your base for a day excursion to the enchanting Lhuentse region. For those who want to give Mongar a miss and press on, an early start will enable you to negotiate the additional

**Ura village**

125km to Trashigang in about 10 hours.

The route takes you past the turn off to Tang valley, climbing up to the lofty Shelthang La (11,500ft/3506m) that is 37km out of Jakar. If you are lucky, just before you get to the pass you will be rewarded with a view of the famed 'Table Mountain' and Mt. Gangkar Punsum (24,735ft/7541m), which lies in a north-westerly

You may miss spotting the Namling waterfall because of mist but the sound will tell you when to stop!

direction. Cresting the pass you loop down gradually into wide open countryside. Ura village (10,168ft/3100m) is on the right and you can easily spot the Geyden Lhakhang at one end. A 500m-long cobbled road leads to the temple which appears rather isolated and if you wish to enter you will probably have to locate the caretaker! The village homes are built close to each other and the cobbled pathways leading to each dwelling are unique to this place. The Ura valley is touted as a success story of what progressive development can achieve — in thirty years they have graduated from bare subsistence farming to an enviably prosperous region. They now grow potatoes as a cash crop and, combined with cross-bred dairy farming, this has resulted in greatly enhancing income levels.

From Ura you drive 35km through conifers and rhododendrons to the 'high point' of the day — Thrumsing La (12,000ft/3659m), which is usually wreathed in swirling vaporous mists. Though the ascent is not difficult, the next couple of hours promise high drama as you plummet breathtakingly from heights above the tree line down to balmy semi-tropical jungle at 2100ft/640m! Beyond Thrumsing La you pass through thick forest for 20km till you emerge on to a plateau at Sengor (9700ft/2957m) which is an excellent place to stop for an early picnic lunch. Descending sharply from here you again enter a forested stretch and the road clings precariously to a sheer mountain side that drops away precipitiously from its very edge, disappearing into a thick bottomless fog so you can't see what lies below (most often, nothing at all!!). Several cascading waterfalls fling themselves off the sides and tumble across the road that is lined with dripping ferns and delicate orchids and you are overtaken by the sense of human endeavour barely holding its own in the face of Nature's uncompromising majesty. You pass several chortens by the road and these are dedicated to the three hundred or so Indian and Nepalese workers who lost their lives hewing out this section of the road from the vertical cliff face. There is no human habitation here and the road

After passing the waterfall you can begin to shed your layers of warm clothing.

maintenance camp at Namling (22km further on), certainly has its task cut out.

A quick stop around 8km before Namling is a 'must do'; this is the best place to view the impressive Namling Dra waterfall as it explodes off the mountain side and crashes down into a gorge. Approaching the place where it actually drops down from under the road you can barely see it though the sound here is thunderous and a fine mist sprays tantalisingly over you as you peer down. You are still above

**The lhakhang at Ura**

8000ft/2440m and the real descent begins from Yangkho La from where you plunge to the low points of Lingmithang (2525ft/770m) and Kuri Zampa (2241ft/683m). Fortunately, the road is broader in this section, making the journey far more relaxed! The valley opens out now, the vegetation is semi-tropical and there are more houses visible. There are clumps of bamboo and when you reach the valley floor the road meanders through large cultivated fields of the staple crop corn as well as of rice. After your descent from great heights the rise in temperature is immediately discernible. Short of Lingmithang you can see the ruins of the twelfth century Zhongar Dzong, once the most powerful of eastern Bhutan's dzongs.

**A symbol of fertility**

At your lowest altitude you cross the Kuri Chu on a bailey bridge with a large Nepalese style chorten at its eastern end. There is a mini-hydro plant nearby as also a factory where paper is manufactured. This valley is famed for its production of lemon grass oil which is distilled in several thousand homes under a government sponsored project. The oil is exported to Germany and this activity provides much needed incremental income to the denizens who hitherto were solely reliant on agriculture and herding to survive.

Your destination is only 20km away and you climb through pine forest up to a very pleasant 5400ft/1646m. En route, 12km before town, you pass a junction at Gangola and the road to the left leads to Lheuntse which is 65km from this point. Look out for the rare exotic looking golden langurs after you start the climb from Kuri Zampa. The bamboo forest is their prime habitat and they can often be seen swinging from branch to branch like dare-devil trapeze artists!

Mongar does not have much to offer in terms of restaurants, so stick to your own hotel and your rations.

Mongar is the district headquarters and true to the trend in eastern Bhutan this town is situated on the mountainside instead of the valley. Parts of this district used to belong to the ancient region of Khyeng where people engaged in agriculture and many observed shamanistic Bon practices. The language spoken beyond Mongar is Sharchopa and this area is more densely populated than the western and central sections. There is not much to see or do in Mongar – it is a town in transition, with a spanking new hospital having come up and several new hotels under construction. The dzong here is a new one that was built in 1953. It has a most 'un-dzong-like' exterior but is still a pleasant two-storey building located half way up the hillside ■

### DAY 12
#### ▸▸ Explore the Lhuentse valley

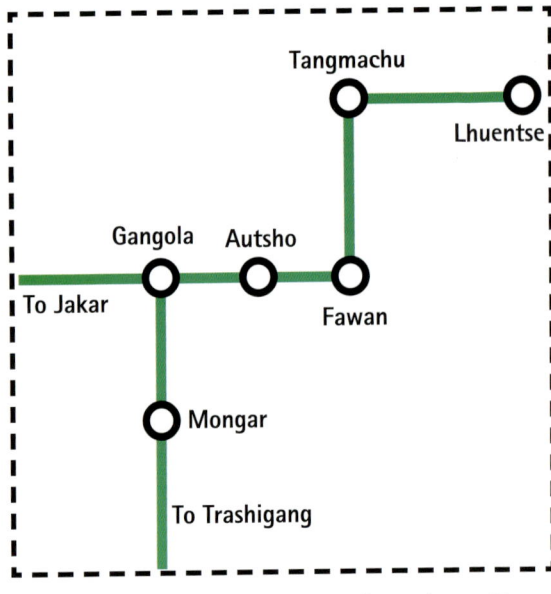

| | | | |
|---|---|---|---|
| Mongar-Gongola | 12km | Autsho-Tangmachu | 25km |
| Gongola-Autsho | 24km | Tangmachu-Lhuentse | 13km |

Look out for golden langurs around the junction at Gangola — they are very shy, so approach slowly.

You can sleep in and start your day's outing after a leisurely breakfast. The drive is 74km each way and is a comfortable 6-7 hour excursion at a relaxed pace. Carry a picnic lunch as there are no restaurants and the river below the dzong offers some great spots for a quiet sojourn with Nature, sitting by the swirling waters and letting their sound and wind-tossed spray sooth you.

You backtrack 12km to the junction at Gangola (3608ft/1100m) and turn on to the road to Lhuentse. You travel another 12km, initially through open landscape, then sweeping down a tighter valley till you are at level with the fast flowing Kuri Chu. Before you reach the small hamlet of Rewan the road deteriorates into a dirt track for a stretch of at least a couple of kilometers. Yet another 12km drive brings you to the slightly larger village of Autsho with its cornfields. En route you pass a startling white chorten surrounded by a hundred and eight smaller ones laid out in concentric circles. Marked by a series of narrow valleys and sinuous ravines, the villages here are perched on ridges and although the region supports a

**Wall painting in the Lhuentse Dzong**

**A precarious crossing**

fairly dense population this is not evident from the road. With its headwaters in Tibet, the Kuri Chu later joins the Drangme Chu to form the Manas that flows into India. The route through the Lhuentse valley was a natural and important trade link between India and Tibet in the past.

The road follows a roller-coaster route along

Lhuentse is not much more than a small village, so don't count on getting anything to snack on here!

the river till you reach Fawan, offering many opportunities to stop and soak in the grand vista. You now ascend to 3700ft/1128m and can see some dramatic soaring vertical cliff faces on the opposite side while the river hurtles through the gorge with its waters turning and flipping into white-flecked turmoil when it hits the 'rapids'.

You then cross the river on another bailey bridge, just before the large settlement of Tangmachu that is 25km from Autsho. Your destination, the dzong at Lheuntse, is now only 13km away. The first six kilometers of this section are once again along the mesmerising river that beckons you to stop awhile and sit on the bleached brown boulders with your feet dangling in its tumbling waters! There are also a couple of 'beaches' — one is 6km from Tangmachu and makes an ideal spot for lunch on your way back. You now climb rather sharply up to the small town of Lhuentse that is dominated by the dzong perched at 5000ft/1524m, commanding a majestic view of the Kuri Chu valley.

The headquarter of this district is in Lhuentse which is also the ancestral home of the royal family — Jigme Namgyal, father of the first king, was born in Dungkar village which is a full day's hike from here. Two family manors are still maintained in this small village that sits on a conch-shaped ridge and it is difficult to believe the monarchy had its origins in such humble surroundings. The terraced hill sides grow mainly maize though some millet is grown too and used to brew the local alcohol 'ara'. The conifers yield turpentine and lemon grass is also grown for its oil. The area is reknowned for its weavers who follow a brocading technique, using bright coloured silk to make some of the best 'kushutara' dresses in the country.

Pema Lingpa's son established a small gompa here in the early sixteenth century but the picturesque structure you see today was built by the Trongsa Penlop Minjur Tenpa in 1654. The Lhuentse Dzong is strategically positioned on a rocky outcrop with sheer vertical drops on all four sides plunging down to the rushing Kuri

The river is extremely inviting but don't wade in too far — looks are deceptive and the current is strong.

Separating the chaff

**Mongar — a town in transition**

Chu. Reached by a stone paved path, this dzong encloses an administrative section, five temples — besides the gonkhang that is dedicated to Mahakala — and houses a body of monks. The woodwork here is exceptional and you can see statues of Guru Rinpoche, Avalokiteswara, and the Buddhas of the Past, Present and Future.

After a quick look around you can locate a beautiful spot to relax over a well deserved lunch before tracing your way back to Mongar ■

## DAY 13
### ⏩ From Mongar to Trashiyangtse via Drametse and then to Trashigang

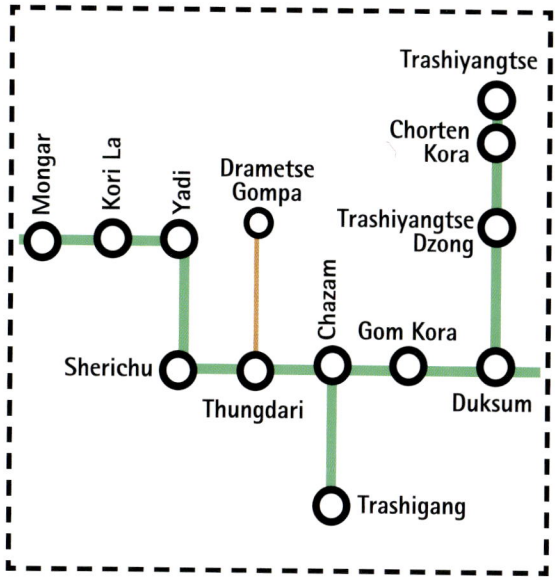

Drametse is 'off' the tourist map and the monks are more than happy to spend time showing you around.

| | | | | |
|---|---|---|---|---|
| Mongar-Kori La | 20km | Thungdari-Chazam | 12km |
| Kori La-Yadi | 22km | Chazam-Trashigang | 10km |
| Yadi-Thungdari | 29km | Chazam-Gom Kora | 13km |
| Thungdari-Drametse | 17km | Gom Kora-Trashiyangtse | 29km |

If you plan to take the diversion to Drametse Monastery we suggest making a slightly early start — the total drive is around 200km and will take most of the day to negotiate. If you are not visiting Drametse, the time saved is a good two hours and allows you to make a more leisurely start.

It is a 70km drive from Mongar to the point where you turn off for Drametse and initially passing through cornfields, you enter a deep vibrant fern-lined forest of rhododendrons, blue pines and exotic orchids. The road hugs the tight contours of steep tree-covered mountain slopes and ascends sharply to the pass, Kori La, at 7800ft/2378m (20km from Mongar). The pass is marked by gaily fluttering prayer flags and a mani wall. You now pass through broadleaved forest, past the elegant Guru Lhakhang and a private temple at Nagtshang which is 11km below the pass but still at a lofty 6100ft/1860m. Beyond this are fields of corn and groves of bamboo as you negotiate the next 11km to the large village of Yadi (4900ft/1494m). Past this village are the well known 'Yadi Loops' — a series of ten hairpin bends which bring you down 1200ft in only 10km! Around 2km ahead of the village of Zalaphangma look out for the striking Sherichu waterfall with a village of the same name coming up 4km further. You are now down to a warm 2200ft/671m and pass a Nepalese chorten by the side of the road, overlooking the confluence of the Gamri Chu and the Sheri Chu. The merged river is known as the Drangme Chu and later referred to as the Manas Chu. The Gamri Chu starts its journey from Bhutan's eastern border with India and is one of the largest rivers of the country. From Sherichu it is an 11km run on almost level road to Thungdari where a side road leads up to Drametse.

The track up to the monastery is 17km each way but is largely unmetalled with treacherous loamy soil on the sides. If it is raining or the surface is wet, proceed with extreme caution (we went up in rain and got stuck!) The road is also extremely narrow and ascends quite rapidly to 6900ft/2104m from only 2600ft/793m at the turn off point!

Drametse is the largest and most important

If it is a clear day the views of the surrounding valleys and snow peaks from Drametse are dramatic.

monastery in East Bhutan and houses a body of around sixty 'gomchens'. The gompa dates back to the sixteenth century when it was founded by the great granddaughter of Pema Lingpa, Ani Choeten Zangmo and her husband. It is here that her brother, Kunga Nyingpa, had his vision of the famous dance, 'Drums from Drametse'. It is a striking three-storey structure with a large flagstone courtyard. Visitors are allowed inside the lhakhang dedicated to the 'Five Sisters of Long Life'. There is a three day festival held here in Sep-Oct as also a tsechu in November when a thongdrel with Pema Lingpa's image is unfurled. Drametse means 'the peak where there is no enemy' and this extremely serene, idyllic rural

**Drametse Gompa**

The elusive
golden langur

spot commands great views of eastern Bhutan. The region is famous for its potato crop and most of the produce makes its way to India in the autumn.

You now vend your way back down to the main road which soon opens into a wide valley with the rushing and comparatively broad Gamri Chu below you. It is only 12km to Chazam where the great 'Iron Bridge Builder' from Tibet, Thangtong Gyelpo built a cha (iron) zam (bridge) in the fifteenth century. Although the town and dzong of Trashigang is only 10km ahead, we recommend pressing on along the river to take in other sights the region has to offer.

Just after Chazam is the confluence of the Bamri Chu and the Gamri Chu. You now turn left and follow the former along its right bank for 13km to Gom Kora, passing a luxuriant waterfall midway to it.

Gom Kora or Gomphu Kora is a small gompa set in an undulating meadow along the river bank and was established in the seventeenth century. Kora means circumambulation while Gomphu is a sacred meditation site of Guru Padmasambhava. There is a small cave below the large black rock that lies adjacent to the temple amidst vibrant lush rice fields. This is where Guru Padmasambhava is said to have spent time in meditation and it bears an imprint of his body. According to legend, he subdued a demon – a snake – that dwelt within by taking the form of Garuda, the revered griffon depicted everywhere as a protector. The rock has a small narrow path that 'sinners' can wriggle through to shed the load of their misdeeds! Within the gompa the central figure is that of Guru Padmasambhava flanked by his protective angel and a thousand-armed Avalokiteswara.

The road after Notang La is narrow in sections and you may have to reverse if you meet oncoming traffic.

To the extreme right is a 'jangshu', a small chorten specifically found inside monasteries and dzongs. Below the main statue is a shelf that holds sacred objects believed to have been placed here by the Guru himself. There is a perfectly shaped large dragon's egg, which is stone-like in appearance and weight, as well as a hoof of Guru Padmasambhava's horse and the footprint of a khandum. A tsechu is held here in spring but unlike tsechus elsewhere the main activity at this one is circumambulating the rock throughout the night – besides being good for the soul, it appears that many romantic liasons are fructified here!

The road now goes all the way to Bomdeling and if you have the time, this is a very scenic drive.

Returning to the road, you come to the village of Duksum 2km ahead, with its large population of women weavers who turn out brightly patterned cloth on their waist looms.

You cross the raging Kulang Chu, a tributary of the Bamri Chu, following its path and ascending 23km up to an altitude of 6000ft/1829m. The entire drive is pretty barren but the forest reappears after Notang La and as the valleys narrow, signs of cultivation and habitation become rarer. The gorge is lush green and there is an impressive waterfall 16km after Duksum. As you approach the high point of this drive you catch a good view of the old Trashiyangtse Dzong built by Pema Lingpa on a spur across the river. You can reach it by taking a road down to the river and across but there is not much to see here and the action has shifted to the new town which lies 3km further on the main road. The magnificent and immense Chorten Kora lies like a gleaming white jewel set in a large flat field just before the township. This is what you are here for and the chorten marks the end of the road, in more ways than one – it is almost

Gom Kora

the culmination of your exciting and visually stunning Bhutanese adventure!

Chorten Kora is probably the largest chorten in the country and was constructed in the 1700s by Lama Ngawang Loday. It is modelled after the great Bodhnath Stupa in Nepal, the replica of which was carved out of a radish and brought to this sacred spot. Unfortunately, the radish shrivelled a bit on its journey, resulting in the Chorten Kora being built a little smaller than originally intended! Other blemishes, which are certainly not visible to the eye, are also attributed to the imperfection of the model. Legend has it that after Guru Padmasambhava had subdued several demons in the Bomdeling

valley he predicted that a great chorten and temple would be built at this spot which is at the southern tip of the valley. The chorten is completely white-washed and makes an impressive sight in its picture-perfect setting in a field below the road, next to the river. The

Trashiyangtse is a new 'planned township' with buildings spaced out neatly but still lacks a decent hotel.

building of this chorten fulfilled the needs of the deeply religious inhabitants of the valley who yearned to make the pilgrimage to Bodhnath but were unable to undertake the long and arduous journey. A great annual 'kora' is held here on two separate days with a fifteen day interval.

**Chorten Kora**

**Trashigang Dzong**

On the first day, people from the adjoining Indian state of Arunachal Pradesh come to walk around the chorten thereby gaining merit, while the second day is for the locals who come from every nook and cranny of eastern Bhutan. Adjoining the chorten is a small gompa with an unusual rendering of the 'Wheel of Life' in its porch.

From here you can proceed up the road, skirting the town, and cross the river for a picnic lunch on the opposite bank. The village and valley of Bomdeling is a three hour walk and a smaller flock of black-necked cranes visit the area every winter. There is not much to see in

Trashiyangtse but you can visit the Institute for Zorig Chusum which teaches the thirteen arts and crafts as part of a six-year course. At the institute you will see students at work and can even purchase handicrafts made by them at the small shop on campus.

You now retrace your steps along the scenic and easy drive back to Chazam and then climb 9km up to Trashigang (3725ft/1136m). This district is the most densely populated in the country and enjoys a mild climate. It is a pleasant unspoilt little town with friendly ever-smiling people milling around the small square that marks its center. There are several international development projects located here, including a major irrigation one. The highlight of course is the Trashigang Dzong that is built on a promontory overlooking the river confluence. This dzong was built in the seventeenth century, ordered by the third desi, Minjur Tenpa. Unlike other dzongs, this one has only one courtyard that both the administrative and monastic sections open on to. Protected by deep ravines and rivers, backed into a mountainside, this dzong enjoys an indomitable location and an outstanding view of the countryside. There are several temples within with statues of Guru Rinpoche, Mahakala and the Eight Great Indian Masters of Buddhism and of Yama – the wrathful form of Avalokiteswara who is a protector of the faith, god of death and king of law; many dances are performed here in worship and to appease him.

The accommodation and food in this far flung region of Bhutan is very basic but after a long day – and an early start slated for the next – you are unlikely to miss the comforts you have enjoyed till now ■

Accommodation in Trashigang is not great, but you can stretch your legs by taking the road leading up from the market.

# TRAVEL PLAN

## DAY 14 & 15
### ▸▸ Heading back....

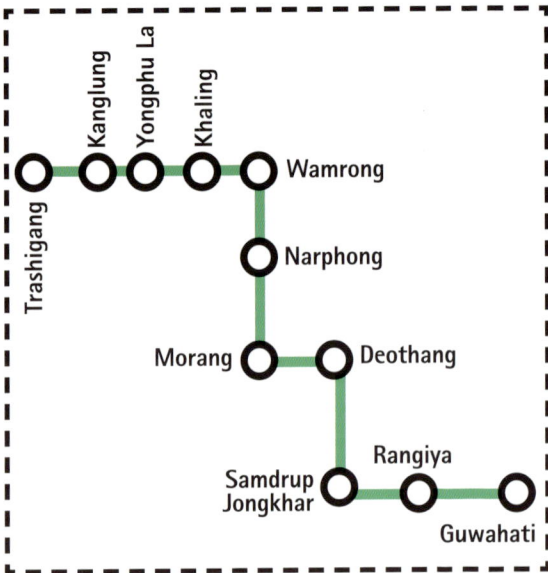

If you are exiting from Samdrup Jongkhar aim to be up and about by 5 am, so that you can make it to Guwahati well before dark.

| | | | |
|---|---|---|---|
| Trashigang-Yonphu La | 35km | Deothang-Samdrup | 13km |
| Yonphu La-Wamrong | 45km | Samdrup-Rangiya | 48km |
| Wamrong-Deothang | 82km | Rangiya-Guwahati | 52km |

Having reached the eastern end of Bhutan, if you are scheduled to fly out of the country it is certainly a long 550km haul back to Thimphu. For die-hards even this is possible – if you leave at 4 am, you should be in Thimphu at 9 or 10 pm! A slightly more palatable option would be to drive up to Wangdi which, with the same early start, will allow you to put your feet up at a more civilised 7-8 pm. However, in this case your drive to the airport the next day will be three and a half hours as opposed to one and a half from Thimphu. The more relaxed – but still pretty rushed – option is to drive the 275km to

Warding off the evil eye

**The protective Garuda (griffon)**

Bumthang (9 hours) and then roughly the same distance the next day to Thimphu or even push on to Paro for the night. Our recommendation is to add an extra day to your itinerary; drive into Bumthang, spend the fifteenth day relaxing and push on to Paro the next day so you can fly out on the seventeenth day of your exotic holiday.

For those of you who have chosen to exit Bhutan by driving into India, it is much simpler. The hill drive to the border town of Samdrup Jongkhar is only a 175km which takes around 6 hours. From there it is approximately 100km, on a flat and reasonably broad road, to

An old but sturdy bridge

Guwahati and it should not take more than two hours to negotiate this stretch. With an early start you can comfortably make the evening flight to Delhi or Kolkata and even make an international connection, after a good dinner, from either city!

From Trashigang it is a 22km drive to Kanglung which lies on a ridge at a cool 6000ft/ 1829m. This is a university town and Bhutan's only college is located here. Sherubtse (Peak of Knowledge) College started as a junior school, grew over the years into a senior school and eventually, with the assistance of Late Father

William Mackey, a Jesuit priest, evolved into a college. More than three hundred students are engaged here in pursuing studies in the Arts, Sciences and Commerce. You pass the Zangto Pelri Gompa opposite the college gate and after leaving town climb to Yonphu La (8200ft/ 2500m) that lies 13km further. Interestingly, there is a small airstrip on the ridge above and one day you may actually be able to fly in and out of here! From this height, you descend 19km to Khaling (6000ft/1829m) which is tucked into the verdant mountain and has a National Handloom Development project located 3km beyond the township. Driving through rich forest you remain at the same average height, cresting two ridges that lie above 7500ft/2287m, before reaching Wamrong (26km). There is a charming little private gompa here surrounded by trees and you now gradually descend to Deothang (82km) driving past the small villages of Narphang (42km) and Morang (4650ft/1418m) en route. The thick vegetation is more tropical now with a surfeit of teak, tall bamboos and swaying ferns but Deothang is at a lowly 2700ft/ 823m and you will soon start shedding layers as it grows increasingly hot and steamy. The cool misty heights of just a few hours ago now seem a figment of your imagination as you drop rapidly down 2000ft/610m in the next 13km to Samdrup Jongkhar!

After completing exit formalities here you bid adieu to your helpful Bhutanese tourist guide and proceed 49km to Rangiya — non-Indian nationals will first have to register their entry into India at the Darrang check point on the other side of the border. Once past Rangiya you get on to the National Highway and pass through the small crowded town of Baihata

Saying goodbye to Bhutan is hard — when crossing the border, pray for an early return to the 'Land of the Thunder Dragon'.

Chariali before crossing the mighty Brahmaputra, 40km ahead and short of Guwahati.

If you're not flying back immediately you can go 'big game spotting', looking for elephants and the one-horned rhinocerous in either Kaziranga or Manas — or settle for a nice cool shower, switch on the air conditioning, order a chilled beverage and try and adjust to life in the plains before heading home!! ■

**Even Madonna would agree!**

# SUGGESTED ITINERARIES AND COSTS

LIKE walking, driving holidays too are best enjoyed at your own pace. While the suggested itineraries cover all – or as much as possible – of the interesting sites along your route, you may like to exercise your choice of pace and time to be spent in each place, based on your own preferences and interests.

## ITINERARIES

| DAYS | SHORT 'N' SWEET | A LITTLE LONGER | ALMOST ALL THE WAY | THE FULL MONTY |
|------|-----------------|-----------------|--------------------|-----------------|
| 1 | Arrive Paro | Arrive Paro | Arrive Paro | Arrive Paro |
| 2 | Chele La/Paro | Chele La/ Paro | Chele La/Paro | Chele La/Paro |
| 3 | Taktsang/Paro | Taktsang/Paro | Taktsang/Paro | Taktsang/Paro |
| 4 | Thimphu | Thimphu | Thimphu | Thimphu |
| 5 | Thimphu | Thimphu | Thimphu | Thimphu |
| 6 | Day trip Punakha | Punakha/Gantey | Punakha/Gantey | Punakha/Gantey |
| 7 | Thimphu/Paro | Gantey | Gantey | Gantey |
| 8 | Fly back | Thimphu | Trongsa/ Bumthang | Trongsa/ Bumthang |
| 9 | | Thimphu/Paro | Bumthang | Bumthang |
| 10 | | Fly back | Bumthang/Gantey | Mongar |
| 11 | | | Thimphu/Paro | Lhuentse |
| 12 | | | Fly back | Drametse/ Trashigang |
| 13 | | | | Exit from Samdrup or drive to Bumthang |
| 14 | | | | Drive to Thimphu |
| 15 | | | | Relax |
| 16 | | | | Fly back |

## ITINERARIES

### INDICATIVE COSTS (FOR A COUPLE)

| DAYS | SHORT 'N' SWEET | A LITTLE LONGER | ALMOST ALL THE WAY | THE FULL MONTY |
|---|---|---|---|---|
| Luxury* | Rs 50,000 | Rs 65,000 | Rs 80,000 | Rs 101,000 |
| Budget** | Rs 30,000 | Rs 50,000 | Rs 62,000 | Rs. 76,000 |

* Assumes a hotel cost of 3500/- per night in Paro/Thimphu and 2000/- per night in other towns. Food costs around 1500/- per day and a car with driver-cum-guide at 1600/- per day. Savings are possible if you are a larger group as you can end up saving around 5000/- per couple on transportation costs.

** Assumes a hotel cost of 1000/- per night and food at 1000/- per day. Transportation costs are the same as above but for a large group can make considerable savings by using a 16-20 seater bus.

Neither of the above includes air fare which at the time of writing was Rs. 18,000/- (return) from Delhi and Rs. 8000/- (return) from Kolkata.

# TREKKING, RAFTING & MOUNTAIN BIKING

BHUTAN'S stunning natural beauty and the relatively isolated nature of its trekking trails make the country a veritable paradise for trekkers. It is one of the few places left in the world where you could trek for days on end without coming across any human habitation or better still, other trekkers. The number of trekkers has been growing slowly but steadily and in 2006 close to 2500 visitors indulged in the activity.

Although there are twenty-eight routes open to trekkers, since this book focuses primarily on visitors driving through the country, this section gives you a brief sketch of five popular treks.

For those interested in including a trek in their itinerary, undoubtedly the tour operator will provide all relevant information but a few general points to keep in mind are:

▸▸ In Bhutan you will be shouldering a rather light backpack as you only have to carry essentials like water, a jacket and a camera – the rest of your equipment, which should not exceed 15kg, is carried by pack horses or yaks.

▸▸ You will be accommodated in two-person tents equipped with foam pads that serve as mattresses and your luggage will be stowed in with you.

▸▸ The pack animals, guides and cooks will camp close by and hot meals are served in a dining tent.

▸▸ Due to the topography trekking in Bhutan involves more than the usual number of ascents and descents in a day and hence you could be on the move for 8-9 hours.

**Negotiating a high ridge**

- ▸▸ Your tour operator will provide tents and other basic equipment but you will have to bring your own sleeping bag and other specific gear.
- ▸▸ The trekking season is reasonably short: Mar 15 to May 15 and Sep 15 to Oct 30 are regarded the best periods as the weather is clear.

## THE DRUK PATH

This is possibly the most spectacular and popular trekking route in Bhutan. It takes you from Paro to Thimphu — or vice versa — traversing mountain passes, through lush green valleys and passing several small high altitude lakes. You are likely to spot the rare blue poppy besides other exotic flora. The duration of the trek ranges between 4 and 6 days and it is a moderately difficult one with the maximum altitude reached being 13,776ft/4200m.

The trek starts above Ta Dzong and on the first day you climb 3280ft/1000m to your camp site just below Jili Dzong (11,480ft/3500m). This dzong dates back to the fifteenth century and the large lhakhang has an impressive 4m tall statue of Sakyamuni. On a clear day there are stunning views of Jhomolhari and other peaks from here. Your next day's walk takes you to Jangchu Lakha where you camp at 12,300ft/3750m. The following day's walk also promises good views of Jhomolhari and Jichu Drakye, ending up on the shores of a scintillating lake – Jimilang Tso (Sand Ox Lake) at 12,694ft/3870m. You then walk past Janye Tso and camp above Simkotra Tso at the end of the day. This is your highest camping point at an altitude of 13,448ft/4100m. The last two days of your trek are spent descending into the Thimphu valley and visiting the Phajoding and Thujidrag gompas.

## JHOMOLHARI TREKS

There are two versions of the Jhomolhari trek both starting from Paro and both of a longer duration – 8 to 10 days. The highest camp is at an altitude of 13,448ft/4100m. On this route the views of Jhomolhari's twin peaks, neighbouring Jichu Drakye and Tshering Ga are peerless (except maybe from the Druk Air flight!). The longer version takes one to Lingzhi, up to 16,236ft/4950m and ends up close to Thimphu while the shorter one returns to Paro albeit by a different route. Both treks are moderate to hard with the maximum altitude on the shorter version being 15,580ft/4750m.

The trek starts from the Drukyel Dzong at the head of the Paro valley and on the first day takes you on a gentle ascent through terraces of millet and rice, climbing midst blue pine and fir, to Sharna Zampa at 9348ft/2850m. The next day is a tough walk with an ascent of around 2460ft/750m punctuated by many sharp, short descents. In places you walk close to the river while other sections have you negotiating rocks as the trail climbs through oaks and rhododendrons and then through rich forest of birch and firs till you reach Thangthangka (11,808ft/3600m). This is a rolling alpine meadow with the majestic Jhomolhari peak looming at the valley head. It is 19km to the splendid view point and camp at Jangothang (13,448ft/4100m)

– crossing the river, rock-hopping along a muddy track past a couple of settlements to get here. The next day or two are usually spent at this camp, acclimatising and drinking in the magnificent views of Jhomolhari and Jichu Drakye. There are several half-day hikes from here that take you to other vantage points with breathtaking views. If you have a license you could even choose to go fishing at the high altitude lake, Tshophu. Trekkers taking the shorter route now return via a different scenic route, camping close to 13,120ft/4000m for two nights, before joining the trail at Sharna Zampa. Those with a quest for more excitement will proceed from Jangothang to Lingzhi, enjoying brilliant views of Jhomolhari, Jichu Drakye and Tserim Kang en route.

The region is isolated but incredibly beautiful and you traverse a large glacial valley with several moraines and climb over a windy pass to your camp at Chha Shi Thang (13,153ft/4010m). The trail leading to the Jichu Drakye base camp is from here.

The next day is an arduous and tiring one as you cross the Yeli La (16,236ft/4950m) and descend to Shodu. Subsequently, you have to ascend to Barshong before descending over the last two days

via Dolam Kencho to the road head at Dodina which is opposite the bridge leading to Cheri Gompa.

## THE LAYA–GASA TREK

The Laya-Gasa trek is quite a popular 14-day trek that is rated a medium-hard one. It takes you through diverse terrain and mountain villages down to Gasa. The hot springs here are famed for their medicinal properties. For the first five days this trek follows the route of the Jhomolhari trek till Lingzhi. For the next five days you walk 6-7 hours each day, making numerous ascents and descents as you traverse meadows laden with flowers, juniper and medicinal plants. The valleys and hill sides are cloaked in deep forests of oak, rhododendron, fir and birch and you trudge over moraines, past glacial lakes, catching awesome views of Kang Bum, Gangchhenta (Great Tiger Mountain) and cresting passes as high as 16,416ft/5005m. Routing through Chebisa, Shomulthang, Limithang to Laya you now descend to Gasa and finally to Damji.

The best time to undertake this trek is Apr -Jun and Sep- Nov.

Since the hot springs are such a popular destination, a short three day trek can be organised to them from Phobjika through Zasa and Chorten Karpo to Tikke Zampa.

# TREKKING, RAFTING & MOUNTAIN BIKING

## SNOWMAN TREK

This is a 25-day trek that is best undertaken in Sep-Oct and is regarded as one of the most difficult treks in the world because of the altitude – in fact trekkers often find they are unable to complete the route due to heavy snowfall on the high passes. The trek starts from Drukyel Dzong and follows the route of the Laya – Gasa trek till Laya, after which you climb to Tarina crossing two high passes and catching views of Tsendagang, Jhomolhari, Gangla Karchung (20,976ft/6395m),

When the going gets tough, the tough get going!

Kang Bum (21,405ft/6526m), Terigang (23,944ft/7300m) and Jejegangphugang (23,288ft/7100m). The best views of the entire trek are past Gangla Karchung La from where you also see a glacier sweeping down from Terigang and ending in Lugi Tso, the brilliant

glacial lake that burst in the '60s and again in the '90s, causing a flood that destroyed part of Punakha Dzong. For the next three days you negotiate steep ascents past lakes and moraines, battling sharp cold winds in Lhedi till you reach Thanwa for a well deserved day of rest. You then make a long hard climb, cresting Jaze La (16,892ft/5150m) to reach Tsochena lake (16,302ft/4970m). The route then takes you over a ridge at 16,728ft/5100m that offers the most dramatic 360° panoramic mountain view, up to Loju La (16,859ft/5140m) and down into a wide glacial valley. The following day you crest the highest pass on this route – Rinchen Zoe La (17,450ft/5320m) and then descend past a number of lakes down to the tree line and finally over one last pass down to Sephu and Bumthang where your trek ends.

### THE DAGALA THOUSAND LAKES TREK

This trek starts above Thimphu and takes you to several mesmerising high altitude lakes – but unfortunately no where close to the fabled thousand! The duration of the trek is six days and this is not a much frequented route. Although your highest camp at is 14,104ft/ 4300m the route takes you up to a lofty 15,416ft/4700m from where you get spectacular mountain views. This is an excursion of medium difficulty.

To embark on this trek you need to drive almost up to Chuzom and then take a rough 8km track up to Geynikha Primary School which marks the beginning of your adventure. During the first two days you cover only 7km, crossing streams and walking through yak pastures and oak forests before ending up at Gur (10,824ft/3300m). There are ample opportunities for short hikes off this section of your trekking trail. The next day is tough as you now climb 3280ft/1000m in 12km, walking through fir, spruce, birch and rhododendrons, crossing the Pangalbasa La that affords great views of the Dagala range, to reach your camp by the Utsho Tso (14,104ft/4300m) – a lake well known for its golden trout. If you decide to spend a day here you can explore numerous small lakes in the vicinity. The next couple of days lead you to Talakha via Panka with the fifth day involving a descent of 3608ft/1100m. Vehicles can pick you up from Talakha from where it is only a short haul to Thimphu via Simtokha.

Besides these, there is a ten-day trek to Rodang La which is rated as a medium to hard trek reaching a maximum elevation of 13,645ft/4160m. This trek is best undertaken in Oct-Nov and starts in Toktu Zampa in the Bumthang area in the East and ends at Trashiyangtse.

A couple of shorter (and also easier!) options are the three-day Gangtey Trek which reaches a maximum elevation of 11,480ft/3500m and takes you to Gogona Lhakhang through rich varied forest of aspen, rhododendron, juniper and blue pine. This trek also affords great bird watching opportunities and is graded 'easy'.

The other short trek is the one that starts and finishes near Jakar in the Bumthang region. Again lasting three days and reaching a maximum elevation of 11,152ft/3400m only, it is rated 'medium to easy'. Besides the natural beauty, the trail takes you past several remote lhakhangs that very few people visit.

## WALKS OUT OF THIMPHU
### TO PHAJODING AND THUJIDROG GOMPAS
▸▸ From Motithang it is a 5km uphill trek to the Phajoding Gompa (11,939ft/3640m) with its commanding valley views. Although this gompa was founded in the thirteenth century it was in the eighteenth century that the ninth Je Khempo added the large complex you see within. This comprises ten lhakhangs and fifteen monastic residences. The Thujidrog Gompa clings to a cliff face some

984ft/300m above Phajoding and involves a stiff climb.

### TO WANGDITSE GOMPA

▶ It is a short one hour climb to this gompa starting from the telecom tower. Founded in 1750 this lhakhang was renovated in 2001 and houses statues of the protective deities – Mahakal, Mahakali and Tsheringma (the goddess of longevity)

### TO DROLAY GOMPA

▶ This gompa is approached from the same starting point as the one leading to Tango and is a 2-3 hour walk from the road.

### TO LUNGCHUZEKHA AND TRASHIGANG GOMPAS

▶ If you drive up to Dochu La you can make the 4 hour return trip to the Lungchuzekha Gompa or descend to the eighteenth century Trashigang Gompa and arrange for a car to meet you at Hongtsho.

The Thadrang Gompa lies on the hill face opposite Motithang and involves a stiff 2 hour climb through a blue pine forest.

## RAFTING

Rafting is still in its infancy in Bhutan with the wider, stronger and infinitely more challenging rivers of the eastern region remaining largely unexplored and uncharted. Rafting is mainly done in the Punakha region on the Mo Chu and the Pho Chu. The former involves a gentle 6km float starting upstream from the dzong and ending just before the confluence of the two rivers. The latter takes you through a couple of Class 3 rapids with a grand finale at the 'Wrathful Buddha' rapid next to the dzong.

## MOUNTAIN BIKING

This is another relatively new activity that is attracting visitors to the country. The flat, almost traffic free, roads in the Paro and Thimphu valleys make for excellent outings with some camping thrown in. The climb up to Pele La and Dochu La will test even seasoned bikers but the views will certainly mitigate the exertion! It is now possible to hire bikes in the country so you can leave your wheels at home. A keen enthusiast is Paro-based Wangda Tobgyal and you can contact him at www.bhutanprayerwheel.com for all the 'gyan' (information) that is available ■

# THE ENVIRONMENT AND YOU

*"Take nothing but pictures,
kill nothing but time,
leave nothing but footprints".*

THE importance of respecting, preserving and not polluting the environment wherever we travel cannot be over-emphasised. Whenever we travel overseas we marvel at the cleanliness, the lack of litter, the absence of plastic/foil wrappers and so on. Yet within our own environs many travellers treat the roads, pathways, forests, meadows, streams and lakes as a dumping ground!

The tourist is not entirely to blame for the litter that you come across in some places, but the onus falls on us to set the standard and certainly not make things worse.

Over the years some of the basics that one has followed are outlined below. Unlike the rest of the book, which offers suggestions, I would like to urge you to strictly adhere to some rules, (and ensure that your co-travellers do the same), so you leave the environment you came to see as beautiful and well-preserved, as it should be.

Carry a waste bag in each vehicle. Eating and drinking is an essential part of any road journey, but all empty packets, bottles, cans etc. need to be kept in the vehicle. Get rid of the bag when you reach your destination, (provided disposal facilities are available there), or in a garbage dump en route.

While walking through the forest, munching a chocolate or a biscuit, put the wrapper in your pocket and get rid of it later.

Apply the same rule while enjoying a drink and that great packed lunch by a rushing stream or a lovely meadow dotted with daisies.

If you are a smoker be extremely careful with cigarette butts as this is the cause of many an unintended forest fire.

Strongly discourage scribbling on trees, walls and buildings – we don't need to see cupid signs on every bench! Let the Himalayas make their impression on you and not the reverse!

Try to avoid blasting music while driving or picnicking.

For those who are going to be camping overnight, care has to be taken to ensure the use of kerosene or gas for cooking; toilet facilities should be away from a water source; combustible waste such as paper, plastic pouches etc. should be burned; bio-degradable items such as food, unlined cartons etc. should be buried; while non bio-degradables need to be carried back.

While using a stream or lake for bathing and cleaning utensils,

minimise use of soap and washing of clothes with strong detergents.

While visiting temples or gompas, shorts, skirts and tight-fitting clothes should be avoided. Shoes need to be removed and avoid touching religious books or relics.

In many places it is advisable to ask permission before taking a photograph of the locals; in some

**Segregated pits for biodegradable and non degradable waste en route to Taktsang monastery**

areas the older people are not familiar with cameras and taking photographs are a strict no-no.

Burn it, bury it or carry it out – be the invisible traveller! This is the best tribute you can pay the magnificent Himalayas ■

# STAYING AND EATING RECOMMENDATIONS

THE hospitality business is a sunrise industry in Bhutan. With the number of tourists growing by twenty percent per annum it is no wonder that there has been a veritable explosion of new hotels and restaurants mushrooming across the country. The bulk of this growth is naturally concentrated in Paro and Thimphu but, with the exception of Trashigang deep in the East, now even hitherto rustic eastern Bhutan has comfortable staying options in less frequented towns such as Trongsa and Mongar.

Multi cuisine restaurants have not really spread beyond Thimphu, though the *Swiss Guest House* in Bumthang is a notable exception.

A remarkable feature of Bhutan's hotel industry is the presence of high priced boutique hotels with the Aman group being at the forefront not only in terms of being the first but also the most expensive! They have a chain of four small exclusive properties, totalling around seventy rooms, located in Paro, Thimphu, Punakha and Gantey with plans to add two more in Trongsa and Bumthang. The rooms are priced around $1100 per night (inclusive of taxes, food, transportation and sightseeing) and their guests travel across the country with them on what is dubbed as the 'Aman Kora' (Literally speaking a misnomer as you don't circumambulate but pretty much travel in style in a straight line!) The Singapore based Como group also have a significant presence with their flagship Uma Paro which is a tastefully appointed and luxuriously comfortable resort. Zhiwa Ling is Bhutan's first indigenous super luxury hotel and is elaborately embellished in the traditional style. The Taj group of hotels from India is setting up a large deluxe facility in Thimphu. The presence of so many up market hotels is particularly significant when compared with neighbouring India where, despite a large number of visitors, there is no hotel in the $1100 tariff range and, for example, there is only one Aman resort (with another nearing completion)!

While categorising our preferred properties we have used a system based only on tariff. We have also included our personal observations and you may at times find a C category hotel preferred over one in the A or B list. The categories are:

A+ Rs.5000 + for a double room
A  Rs.3000 + for a double room
B  Rs.1500 + for a double room
C  Rs.1000 + for a double room
D  Below Rs.1000 for a double room

The Department of Tourism has provided a complete list of hotels given at the back of the book as Appendix B.

## BUMTHANG

This is one of the few places outside of Paro and Thimphu where you have multiple staying options.

## CATEGORY B

▸▸ *Swiss Guest House* lies around 3.5km out of town and is a charming place set in an apple orchard overlooking the valley and river – ideal for those looking for sylvan charm and a peaceful atmosphere. The rooms are wood panelled and comfortable albeit slightly small though the size makes the wood stove (bukhari) more effective. The excellent western cuisine here is a bonus, especially so as it's a welcome change from eating only the local cuisine available in eastern Bhutan.
P: 00975-3-631144/45
E: swissguesthouse@druknet.bt

▸▸ *Mt. Tourist Lodge* is a 22 room property also located out of town and overlooking the Wangdichoeling Palace.
P: 00975-3-631255
E: mtnlodge@druknet.bt

▸▸ *BTCL Wangdicholing Lodge* has been completely renovated and offers comfortable accommodation.
P: 00975-3-631452
E: wangdicholingresort@druknet.bt

▸▸ *Rinchenling Lodge* is just off the road leading to Jambay Lhakhang and is a more recent addition to the booming hotel industry in Bumthang.
P: 00975-3-631147
E: jampel@druknet.bt

## CATEGORY C

▸▸ *Mepham Guest House* is located a couple of kilometers out of town and has 18 comfortable rooms.
P: 00975-3-631738

## GANTEY
## CATEGORY A+

▸▸ *The Aman group outpost* here is situated in a pretty valley and, as is the case with their other properties, is in a stand-alone location. With 12 rooms this is the smallest, but boasts their hallmark attention to quality and service. P: 00975-2-490049
E: amankora@amanresort.com

## CATEGORY B

▸▸ *Dewachen Hotel.* This relatively new property is really the best staying option in Gantey. Located on a hillside with commanding views of the valley and a dense forest behind, this is the perfect place to relax for a few days. Although solar-generated electricity is limited to the evenings the rooms are comfortable and are equipped with bukharis (wood stoves).
P: 00975-2-490007/442550
W: www.hoteldewachen.com

## CATEGORY C

▸▸ *Hotel Gakiling* is a budget option with 8 basic rooms and is located above the Crane Center.
P: 00975-2-442540/442516

## MONGAR
## CATEGORY C

▸▸ *Hotel Druk Zhongar* is a recent addition and is your best option here. It is located on the road leading out of town towards Trashigang. Some rooms have decent valley views and the food is quite palatable. P: 00975-3-641587
E: drukzhongkar@druknet.bt

# Staying and eating recommendations

## PUNAKHA
### CATEGORY A+

▸▸ *The Aman group* has a hotel here and in terms of architecture this is the most interesting of their Bhutan properties. Originally a farm owned by the royal family the old farmhouse has been retained and converted into a dining area with a quaint library and sit out on the first floor. The rest is 'Aman' all the way but even they can't help the temperature in April and May!
**P**: 00975-2-58422
**E**: amankora@amanresort.com

### CATEGORY B

The two best staying options are both located on a hill face between Lobesa and the new township of Kuruthang that lies short of the dzong.

▸▸ *Hotel Zangto Pelri* is the older of the two properties. It has 45 rooms and is possibly the only non-super deluxe hotel with a swimming pool.
**P**: 00975-2-584125/584321
**E**: hotzang@druknet.bt

▸▸ *Hotel Meri Puensem* is a newer and smaller entrant with comfortable rooms many of which have good valley views. It is owned by Dodo Tshering, a former governor of Punakha, whose warm hospitality is enhanced by the wealth of information and interesting tales he imparts.
**P**: 00975-2-584195/584237
**E**: mpuensum@druknet.bt

### CATEGORY D

There are budget options such as *Welcome Hotel* (**P**: 00975-584106) and *Hotel Kuenga* (**P**: 00975-584123) which are located in Kuruthang.

## WANGDIPHODRANG (WANGDI)
### CATEGORY B

The two best options are both located a little out of town in picturesque locales. One lies above the river before the road climbs up to the dzong, while the other is 8km out of town on the banks of the Mangdi River.

▸▸ *Hotel Dragon Nest* has comfortable rooms overlooking the river and with a view of the dzong in the distance above. Sitting outdoors in the evening is a pleasurable experience and the service here is good.
**P**: 00975-2-480521
**E**: nest@druknet.bt

▸▸ *Kichu Resort* is located just below the road, 8km out of town amidst a grove of trees with the bubbling Mangdi River flowing alongside. This is a good option if you are going on to Gantey the next day as it cuts down travel time. **P**: 00975-2-481359

## TRASHIGANG

The standard of living here is of the extremely small hotel/guest house variety, with both options being located in the small market place.

### CATEGORY C/D

▸▸ *Hotel Drukdoetjung* (**P**: 00975-521214) and *Dzongkhag Guest House* (**P**: 00975-521145) are your only options and both have small clean rooms and attached bathrooms.

## TRONGSA
### CATEGORY B/C

▸▸ *Yangkhil Resort* is the best accommodation here. It is located 4km short of town and offers good views of the dzong. The rooms are a bit on the smaller side but the overall ambience is extremely pleasant.
**P**: 00975-3-521417-9
**E**: yangkhilresort@druknet.bt

▸▸ *Phuenzhi Guest House* is also out of town, located off the road to Mongar overlooking the dzong. Its 21 comfortable rooms perched on the hill side certainly make it the 'high' option in Trongsa! **P**: 00975-3-521197
**E**: puenzhi@druknet.bt

## PARO

There are numerous hotels here but unlike Thimphu almost all are spread around and out of town. The properties are quite large, in idyllic locations that offer good views of the dzong and valley and in a few cases both!
### CATEGORY A+

▸▸ *The Aman Paro Resort* is in a peaceful location almost at the end of the valley, short of Drukyel Dzong. Nestled in a grove of trees, this is the only property which gives you views of Jhomolhari from your bedroom! The rooms and other facilities are in keeping with the 'Aman standard' – interestingly on some evenings they hold lectures by renowned Buddhist scholars and you have an opportunity of direct interaction too.

**P**: 00975-8-272623
**E**: amankora@amanresorts.com

▸▸ *The Uma Paro* is the flagship of the Como group and enjoys a rather private stand-alone location on a hill face. The main structure is built in traditional Bhutanese style, modelled on the Paro Dzong. With its beautiful décor, attention to detail, warm hospitality and great service we rated this the best property in Bhutan. The cottages here are absolutely divine – however 'divinity' comes at Rs. 40,000/- or $1000 per night while the somewhat small but luxurious standard rooms are a more affordable Rs. 13,000/- or $325 per night. The resort also has an excellent spa with a large heated pool and traditional hot stone bath. If you want to indulge yourself for a few nights this is the place to do so.
**P**: 00975-8-271597
**E**: info.paro@uma.como.bz
**W**: www.uma.como.bz

▸▸ *Hotel Zhiwa Ling* is the new luxury kid on the block. Located close to Kyichu Lhakhang the main building is an impressive representation of traditional Bhutanese architecture with ornate interiors. It has its own lhakhang built using 450-year-old discarded wood from the Gantey Lhakhang. With 45 rooms in three blocks this is the country's only indigenous effort in the super luxury segment and also has a spa and multi cuisine restaurant.
**P**: 00975-8-271277 **W**: www.zhiwaling.com

# Staying and eating recommendations

## CATEGORY A/B

▸ *Olathang Hotel.* This BTCL owned property is the oldest and largest (over 60 rooms) in Paro. With great views of the valley and dzong this is the best non-super-luxury option in town. The accommodation is a mixture of cottages nestled among trees and rooms in the main block — the former are infinitely preferable and cottage numbers 438-442 are the best located. The bar is cosy and the food good — the one facility we missed in our comfortable stay was the traditional hot stone bath/massage facility, though we were told that this is planned.

P: 00975-8-271305
E: ohotel@druknet.bt

## CATEGORY B

▸ *Hotel Gantey Palace* is perched atop a small hillock with great dzong views, a nice garden and cute bar. The rooms are on the small side, but you can indulge in a hot stone bath/massage and visit their private lhakhang with its unique Shambala fresco. The building is 100 years old, originally owned by the Paro penlop who converted it into a royal residence in 1928. The property became a hotel only in 1995.

**P**: 00975-8-271301
**E**: chukie@gangteypalace.com
**W**: www.gangteypalace.com

▸▸ *Kichu Resort* is located a few kilometers out of town, almost opposite the lhakhang, spread along the bank of the river. The rooms and cottages are set amongst sprawling gardens and a few rooms actually sit on the river! This is the only property with 500m of river frontage. **P**: 00975-8-271647
**E**: kichuresort@druknet.bt

▸▸ *Pelri Cottages* are located just above Olathang Hotel. This is a relatively new property with comfortable rooms and good service. **P**: 00975-8-271683/272473

**CATEGORY C**

▸▸ *Hotel Samdencholing* is located mid-way up the road to Olathang Hotel and has 20 comfortable rooms. It offers sauna/hot stone baths and has a largish restaurant which overlooks the valley and dzong. **P**: 00975-8-271449/271509
**E**: samden_choling@druknet.bt

▸▸ *Hotel Jigmeling* is a newly opened hotel located in town. For those who want to be where the action is, this 10 room property is a great option.
**P**: 00975-271444/271669
**E**: jhotel@druknet.bt

## EATING IN PARO

Paro has a multiple choice of restaurants that you could visit for a good meal. In town the best are *Chharo* and *Dagmar* which offer traditional

Bhutanese cuisine tailored to cater to your preferences. For multi cuisine check out the restaurants at *Uma Paro* and *Zhiwa Ling Hotels*, while *Red Rice* restaurant located below Olathang has an interesting menu of fusion food. The grand old *Olathang Hotel* provides a good standard buffet lunch or dinner.

## PHUENTSHOLING
### CATEGORY B

▸▸ *Druk Hotel* is possibly the best option here with large comfortable rooms and good cuisine.
**P**: 00975-5-252426-8
**E**: h-druk@druknet.bt

### CATEGORY C

▸▸ *Central Hotel* has basic clean rooms and a multi cuisine restaurant.
**P**: 00976-5-252172/3
**E**: centralhotel@druknet.bt

## THIMPHU

Most of the hotels in the capital are located within 500m of each other around the clock tower area.

### CATEGORY A+

Unlike Paro where there are options in this segment, the Aman resort here rules the roost. This property is possibly the best located of their four resorts in the country. Very private and nestled in a forest above the Motithang area it offers commanding views of the valley and capital city. Expect all the comforts associated with the 'Aman experience'.
**P**: 00975-2-334224
**E**: amankora@amanresorts.com

# STAYING AND EATING RECOMMENDATIONS

## CATEGORY A

▸▸ *Druk Hotel* has a combination of 53 luxury rooms and well appointed suites. With a charming bar, super Indian tandoori cuisine, great service and a spa with a good massage facility, this is a good place to live in during your stay in Thimphu.
P: 00975-2-322966/322977
E: drukhotel@druknet.bt

▸▸ *Jumolhari Hotel* is a boutique hotel with 20 comfortable rooms and 6 suites. It is centrally located, next to the clock tower. Warm hospitality, exemplary service and a good multi cuisine restaurant makes this a popular place.
P: 00975-2-322747/325506
E: hoteljumolhari@druknet.bt

▸▸ *Pedling Hotel* is located next to the landmark Swiss Bakery and is barely a two minute walk from the clock tower. The rooms here are of a slightly older vintage but the restaurant offers excellent Indian cuisine. P: 00975-2-325714/324451 E: pedling@druknet.bt

## CATEGORY B

▸▸ *Hotel Dragon Roots*, a good option in this category is centrally located and has 30 rooms, some of which overlook the clock tower area.
P: 00975-2-332820/22
E: droots@druknet.bt

▸▸ *Wangchuk Hotel* has completed 10 years of its existence and has 20 comfortable rooms, some with river views. It also offers a spa facility, so that you can relax at the end of the day!
P: 00975-2-323532/325484

E: htlwchuk@druknet.bt
W: www.wangchuk.com

## CATEGORY C

▸▸ *Druk Sherig Hotel* also enjoys a central location and offers 20 basic but good rooms at budget prices.
P: 00975-2-322598
E: travelbt@druknet.bt

▸▸ *Yeedzin Guesthouse* overlooks central Thimphu and has 16 rooms which offer great value for money.
P: 00975-2-325702 E: yeedzin@druknet.bts

## EATING IN THIMPHU

There is no shortage of good eating places here; if you feel like a snack the old favourite, *Swiss Bakery*, offers both sweet and savoury snacks throughout the day. Adjacent to it is *Hotel Pedling* whose restaurant serves a great Indian spread while opposite it is the newly opened restaurant called *Thai Cuisine*. This is the only Thai restaurant here and is pretty close to the real thing. A stone's throw away is the ever popular *Plums Café* with its buffet being a lunch time favourite. Diagonally opposite it is another recent addition — *Sonam's Fine Dining* which offers multi cuisine options.

In the clock tower area *Druk Hotel* and *Jumolhari Hotel* offer great Indian tandoori and multi cuisine respectively.

There is a wide choice of bars with the one at *Druk Hotel* and *Benez* being popular options while disco action takes place at *Space 34, Gravity, Destiny* and *Buzz Club* ■

# WHAT TO CARRY

## FOOD

Paro and Thimphu offer a reasonable variety of cuisine; the most popular is of course Bhutanese, with Indian and Chinese vying for the second preference. Western cuisine is mostly confined to the larger hotels and Thai is beginning to make a presence. From Thimphu onwards, barring Bumthang, you will be offered local food only.

Phuentsholing and particularly Thimphu offer a reasonably large variety of canned food, pasta, sauces etc. and you can easily stock up here for any supplementary food items that you might want to carry for your journey eastwards. A good place to source these is the supermarket adjacent to Druk Hotel, in the clock tower area in the town square in Thimphu.

## DRINKS

Liquor is freely available throughout the country and served in all restaurants and hotels. The local rum as well as Coronation Silver Jubilee Whisky are very palatable and reasonably priced. Thai, American and Indian beers and a rather limited selection of imported wines are offered at restaurants. The local 'ara' and 'chang' are stronger than the equivalent brewed in parts of India

but Bumthang has a good cider. You are entitled to bring in one litre of alcohol into the country and Paro airport has a selection of Scotch whisky, gin, vodka and cognac.

Bottled water is available throughout and the brand 'Mountain Spring' is particularly good.

## CIGARETTES

For smokers who want to make an attempt to kick the habit, Bhutan is an excellent place to make a start! Smoking in public places and sale of cigarettes is banned throughout the country. However, you are allowed to bring in 200 cigarettes but will have to pay a duty of 200% on this import. You can smoke in the privacy of your room, vehicle but not in a bar or restaurant while having a drink.

## CLOTHING

Warm clothes to cope with very cold conditions albeit for short periods are a must, as also warm socks and sensible walking shoes. Ideally you should dress in layers so you can add or shed as per the conditions. From mid-March to mid-October a cotton shirt will suffice for most of the day but you do need to keep a light sweater or jacket handy. If you are visiting in the period May to September carry

# WHAT TO CARRY

some rain gear or do the local economy some good by picking up umbrellas from the market as the need arises!

## MEDICINES

There are chemists in all major towns but you should carry a small stock of essentials including paracetemol, combiflam, your choice of medicine for stomach upsets, motion sickness, antiseptic cream and band aids for minor cuts. Also add a good sun block lotion.

While walking through the forest, carrying a pouch of salt is a useful precaution to take — at certain times of the year, particularly the rainy season, leeches are common. If, unluckily, you end up as their victim the best way to rid yourself of these 'yucky' blood suckers is to sprinkle salt at the point where it has attached itself — it will fall off shortly. Pulling it off is a no-no as a part will remain under your skin and cause discomfort.

## GENERAL

Binoculars and cameras are essential — film is available in the major towns. A small torch and a Swiss Army knife may also come in handy.

## IMPORTANT TIPS

Carry your cell phone but get a local connection by paying Rs. 400 and use the Bhutan Telecom network which will cut your phone bills by something close to 70%! (Roaming charges are exorbitant in Bhutan)

You will need to carry cash or traveller's cheques as there are no ATMs and credit cards have limited acceptance — even where they are accepted there is a 2-5% surcharge. Carry the bulk of your cash (and it is a bulk!) in hundred rupee bills as in some places the Rs. 500 and Rs. 1000 denominations are not accepted.

If you are driving yourself, remember that local drivers are extremely polite and disciplined — there is no need to lean on the horn!

While visiting dzongs, bear in mind that these are religious institutions and hence noisy or boisterous behaviour is not tolerated ■

# SHOPPING

SINCE the Bhutanese have been particular about retaining their traditional lifestyle, one does not see the same decline of handicrafts and artisans that is evidenced elsewhere. In fact their markets and emporia are a veritable treasure trove for those seeking fine hand made products as much as for those just looking for something to remember a fabulous holiday by!

Bhutanese jewellery is stunning and though the designs are limited the work is intricate; you find pendants, ear rings, brooches, belts and bracelets in finely worked silver – and sometimes in gold. These are often set with semi-precious stones like coral, turquoise, pearls, amber and lapis lazuli. There is also an attractive range of affordable jewellery in both traditional and more modern designs but a lot of these come from India and Nepal.

Fine wood carving can be found on wall panels and furniture but is also done on easy-to-carry items such as picture frames, coasters and trivets – we found some really nice ones at the Crane Observation Center at Phobjika. Rich-hued lacquered bowls made from gnarled wood come in all sizes and some are edged and mounted with silver. Brightly painted traditional masks in wood as well as papier mache are to be had in both the regular as well as miniature size and you can also buy striking wall hangings made from wooden printing blocks carved with the text and figures used on prayer flags.

The *pièce de résistance* of Bhutanese handicrafts are their exquisite handloom fabrics. These are similar to those found in the tribal areas of North East India, Thailand and Laos and the finer pieces are much sought after by textile connoisseurs and collectors. Intricate designs are tightly woven with brilliant yarns of cotton, silk or wool and can take a long time to weave. Although running lengths of fabric are unusual, you can buy items like cushions, jackets, scarves and belts while the 'kira', 'gho' and Bumthang's speciality, the woollen 'yatha' can be used to sew into something of your choice or used as a throw.

Handicrafts like brass and copper ritual items, statues, dorjes, cymbals, bells, singing bowls etc. can be found with varying levels of workmanship. Bamboo and rattan products are popular gifts and you can buy mats, quivers, hats, a bamboo cylinder typically used for carrying alcohol or the famous 'banchung' basket made in coloured geometric patterns.

Tangkhas with their detailed depiction of traditional iconography can be bought either unmounted

or mounted on rich brocade.
Unlike the old ones that used
natural colours, these are made
with chemical based paints but are
beautifully done. A good place to
pick one up from is the Insititute of
Zorig Chusum in Thimphu and the
government-operated Handicrafts
Emporium. Also look out for good
contemporary art that seems to
be coming into its own recently
– we picked up a striking collage
of textured hand made paper,
weathered 'lungda' (prayer flags)
and calligraphy done by artist
Chhime Dorji from Vajrayana Art
Gallery in Paro.

Woollen carpets in bright colours
and dramatic Tibetan designs can
also be found in the market. There
is a carpet factory in Phuentsholing
and Tibet Art Collection in Paro has
a wonderful selection.

Exquisite, unusual and older
artifacts can be found in some
handicraft shops and in hotel
arcades but you can – and must
– only buy those pieces that carry
a government seal allowing their
export from Bhutan.

Besides these, you could choose to
carry back a selection of Bhutan's
innovative stamps or some
beautiful handmade paper products
or even some Bhutanese music
– there are some CDs featuring
musicians from the Royal Academy
of Performing Arts ■

## SOME GOOD OUTLETS
### THIMPHU
▶▶ Lungta Handicraft
(Opposite the GPO)
Tel: 00975-2-333855
▶▶ Handicrafts Emporium on
Norzim Lam
Etho Metho
▶▶ Ghasel Handicrafts on Norzim
Lam.
Tel: 00975-2-325688
▶▶ Druk Handicrafts
▶▶ Tashi Delek Handicrafts
▶▶ The Open Air Market

### PARO
▶▶ Tibet Art Collection, near Satsam
Chorten.
Tel: 00975-17111573
▶▶ Made-in-Bhutan Handicrafts
Tel: 00975-8-272886
▶▶ Bhutan Textile Collections
Tel: 00975-17614827
▶▶ Lucky Art Gallery
Tel: 00975-17627883
▶▶ Vajrayana Art Gallery

### BUMTHANG
▶▶ Sonam Handicrafts
Tel: 00975-3631370
▶▶ Handicrafts Emporium en route
to Kurjey Lhakhang.
▶▶ Swiss Dairy Farm outlet

# Driving tips

## SOME PRECAUTIONS THAT MAY PROVE VERY USEFUL

▸▸ If you are driving your own car, switching to tubeless tyres is strongly recommended. Both road conditions and new cars today make it possible to reach high speeds, even while cornering. A front tyre blowing out, in such situations, could mean very serious trouble. Tubeless tyres have the twin advantage of deflating slowly and being capable of inflation that would allow you to drive up to 60km or more till you reach a repair shop.

▸▸ One should also carry a do-it-yourself repair kit. This is a very handy, if not necessary, accessory to carry as small towns are not yet familiar with tubeless technology. A small air pump that plugs into the cigarette lighter socket is also available and, depending on the type, costs between Rs. 2000 and Rs. 6000.

▸▸ Carrying an additional spare tyre may seem a little extreme, but if you are not using tubeless tyres, can be very useful when travelling in remote terrain where one may not come across an air pump or repair shop for several hours at a stretch.

▸▸ Also carry a couple of spare tubes as the specific one for your vehicle may not be available everywhere.

▸▸ If you have a luggage carrier, add a 20ltr jerry can of additional fuel as a contingency measure – sometimes all does not go according to plan and the scheduled refuelling stop could be dry.

▸▸ Carry spare engine belts, if your car still uses them, as also clutch and accelerator cables.

▸▸ An invertor that plugs into the cigarette lighter socket is extremely useful for charging cameras and cell phones while on the move.

Above all, remember that in the tourist season there are many more vehicles on the road, so be cautious and take the curves carefully ■

# ACUTE MOUNTAIN SICKNESS (AMS)

ACUTE mountain sickness is a condition brought about by decreased oxygen content in the blood due to lower atmospheric pressure at high altitudes.

Oxygen normally flows from the alveoli (air sacs) of the lungs, into the blood as the pressure in the alveoli is greater than that in the blood. At higher altitudes, the lower pressure of oxygen in the atmosphere reduces pressure of oxygen in the blood – at 18,000ft/ 5500m, the blood oxygen pressure is 40–45mm, which is half the normal value.

The development of symptoms of AMS depend upon the rate of ascent, elevation attained, and most importantly–individual susceptibility. AMS can be of the mild (benign) or severe (malignant) type. Symptoms usually start twelve to twenty-four hours after arrival and begin to decrease in severity on about the third day.

The symptoms of mild AMS include headaches, dizziness, loss of appetite, lethargy, and difficulty in sleeping. The treatment calls for rest as much as for staying at the same altitude till the symptoms disappear – which they normally should by the third day. Paracetamol together with a Combiflam drowned with a litre of water can be taken for the headaches, while Stemitil (5mg)

helps nausea.

Malignant AMS can develop from mild AMS and can be fatal. The symptoms include breathlessness, double vision, severe headaches which do not respond to Paracetemol, confusion and irrational behaviour, and a dry cough that may progress to production of a pink frothy substance. The treatment for this

is immediate descent to a lower altitude – even 500m can produce substantial relief. In addition medication is also recommended – Decadron 8mg to start with, followed by 4mg doses six hourly as also Depin 20mg six hourly.

Whereas starting a course of a medicine called Diamox before going on your trip is a precaution recommended by some, others believe the medicine masks the symptoms if AMS does occur and can lead to delayed treatment. If you are an anxious traveller wanting to take additional precautions, we suggest you consult a doctor on this medication since there is some controversy over its use.

In order to avoid AMS besides ascending slowly and resting at progressively higher altitudes the following guidelines are very important:

» Fluid intake of 4-5 litres spread out during the day is essential and this can be started 48 hours before one's ascent to altitudes above 10,000ft.

» The diet should be carbohydrate rich and not high on proteins. Heavy meals should be avoided.

» As a general rule, one's night halt should be at an altitude lower than the peak achieved during the day.

» Avoid alcohol as it dehydrates one; remember what happens when one has imbibed on a flight — the cabin is pressurised at the equivalent of 5000ft but one still gets dehydrated pretty quickly!

» Similarly, you should abstain from smoking as it impairs one's breathing in the rarefied air.

» Your regular exercise routine is to be avoided till acclimatisation is complete and you feel absolutely normal.

Despite all precautions, it is still possible to have symptoms of AMS – the important thing is to recognise them and treat them accordingly. Generally AMS occurs at altitudes above 11,000ft/3500m but cases at 10,000ft have been known.

The writer undertook the journey to Leh by road with a large group of thirteen adults and six children (aged five to fifteen). We followed all the rules outlined above but one afternoon, which stretched into a long night, mild symptoms of AMS hit almost eighty percent of the group when we spent the night at 14,000ft. Treatment with Paracetamol, fluid intake and early to bed restored everyone to near normal by the next morning. The other strange thing about AMS is that it can hit even the most experienced mountaineer, who has had no previous history, at random – so please do not assume that if you have been there and done it that you are immune!!

## AMS AND HOMEOPATHY

Homeopaths recommend the use of coca for headaches caused by altitude.

Ferrum Phos 30C is a great remedy to 'give oxygen' – dose as needed. If seriously short of oxygen, use every five minutes to 'catch up'. Five to ten doses like that is usually effective.

Be sure to eat a diet supporting quick blood building – Lixotinic is a good supplement that not only has the iron to make haemoglobin but copper to help it absorb. Good aerobic fitness is also necessary to increase red blood cells ■

# DRUK AIR

A royal decree in 1981 introduced a new airline to the international skies and by 1983 Royal Bhutan Airlines, more popularly known as Druk Air, commenced commercial operations. Starting on a very modest scale with only two propeller-driven eighteen-seater Dornier aircraft, the airline underwent significant modernisation and expansion in 1988 with the acquisition of two BAe 146 planes. By 2004 two Airbus 319s were added to the fleet and these comfortable modern aircraft, coupled with the airline's impeccable and courteous service, catapulted Druk Air into the premier league.

The flight into the country's only airport at Paro allows you to enjoy the most incredibly beautiful and dramatic mountain views – Himalayan peaks stretch out in a magnificent chain, intriguingly close and yet imposing and distant in their sheer grandeur. Although a scenically spectacular flight Paro's location and weather often makes landing conditions difficult – in fact, keeping this in mind the aircraft manufacturer had to provide A321 engines with a A319 fuselage!

Initially the airline recruited experienced foreigners as pilots and flight engineers but systematic recruitment and intensive training has resulted in 'indigenisation' and around ninety-five percent of Druk Air's crew now comprises Bhutanese citizens. The laudable expertise of the pilots, the excellent care and polite demeanor of the attendant crew members that reflects traditional Bhutanese hospitality make your short flight a most pleasurable and comfortable experience.

Druk Air is the only airline operating in the country and a common misconception is to perceive it as a monopoly carrier. In reality all countries that it flies in and out of – India, Nepal, Bangladesh and Thailand – are entitled to fly into Bhutan. Possibly the need for dedicated aircraft and crew to cope with conditions at Paro, as well as the lack of around the year traffic, has been the deterrent.

The airline currently carries around 110,000 passengers per annum and the passage volume is growing by leaps and bounds. Druk Air has plans to add other international destinations like Hong Kong, Singapore and Dubai to its route ■

# DRUK AIR

## RESERVATION OFFICES

### BHUTAN
#### PARO
▸▸ **DRUK AIR CORPORATION LTD.**
(Head Office)
Royal Bhutan Airlines
Nemeyzampa, Paro, Bhutan
Tel    : +975 8 271856/57/58/271860
Fax    : +975 8 271861
Email  : reservationparo@drukair.com.bt
Airport : +975 8 271423
Fax    : +975 8 271855
Email  : parostation@drukair.com.bt

#### THIMPHU
▸▸ **DRUK AIR CORPORATION LTD.**
(Branch Office)
Chang Lam Plaza Building,
Chang Lam,Thimphu, Bhutan
Tel    : +975 2322215/323420/322825
Fax    : +975 2 322775
Email  : spccontrol@drukair.com.bt
        drukairthimphu@druknet.bt

### INDIA
#### NEW DELHI
▸▸ **DRUK AIR CORPORATION LTD.**
(City Office)
Ansal Bhawan Building, G Floor-3,
16 KG Marg, Connaught Place,
New Delhi – 110001
Tel    : +91 11 23357703-04/23358968
Fax    : +91 11 23357768
Email  : sales.delhi@drukair.com.bt

▸▸ **DRUK AIR CORPORATION LTD.**
(Airport Office)
Room No.43, New Visitor's Lounge
IGI Airport, Terminal II
New Delhi
Tel    : +91 11 25653207
Fax    : +91 11 25653147
Email  : delkkkb@drukair.com.bt

**PSA**
▸▸ **STONE TRAVELS**
IC-3, Taj Apartments
Rao Tula Ram Marg, New Delhi-110022
Tel    : +91 11 26711163-64/
        26176594/6597
Fax    : +91 11 26164928
Email  : drukinfo@stonetravels.com
▸▸ **ECO EXPEDITIONS & TOURS PVT.**
**LTD.**
505, Jaina Tower II
District Centre, Janakpuri
New Delhi 110058

Tel    : +91 11 41579134/35
Fax    : +91 11 55405772
Email  : akhilesh@visitbhutan.com

## KOLKATA

▸▸ **DRUK AIR CORPORATION LTD.**
**(City Office)**
Royal Bhutan Airlines,
51, Tivoli Court,
1A, Ballygunge Circular Road,
Kolkata-700019
Tel    : +91 33 22902429/22805376
Fax    : +91 33 22900050

Email  : reservation@drukairccu.com
         cityoffice@drukairccu.com

▸▸ **DRUK AIR CORPORATION LTD.**
**(Airport Office)**
Room No.16
(International Building) NTB,
N.S.C.B.I. Airport
Kolkata-700017
Tel    : +91 33 25119976/25111973
Fax    : +91 33 25117094
Email  : aic@drukairccu.com
         airport@drukairccu.com

# DRUK AIR

## PSA

### ▶▶ UNIQUE AIR TRAVELS (P) LTD.
G2, Circular Centre,
222, AJC Bose Road, Kolkata-700017
Tel : +91 33 22807419/22907917
Fax : +91 33 22807418
Email : uniqueair@hotmail.com

### ▶▶ STONE TRAVELS (P) LTD.
55BB, Mirza Galib Street
Kolkata-700016
Tel : +91 33 40059780-83
Fax : +91 33 40059784
Email : stplcal@stonetravels.com

### ▶▶ GAINWELL ENTERPRISES PVT.LTD.
Gainwell Manor, 11B,
Dr. Rajendra Road, Bhowanipur
Kolkata-700020
Tel : +91 33 24545000-10
Fax : +91 33 24545011
Email : gainwelltravel@rediffmail.com

### ▶▶ CAREWELL EXPRESS TOURS PVT. LTD.
Tobacco House, 1&2
Old Court House Corner, 3rd Floor
Kolkata-700001
Tel : +91 33 22107278/79
Fax : +91 33 22107280
Email : carewell21@vsnl.net

### ▶▶ A & A TRAVEL ZONE PVT. LTD.
13, Chowranghee Lane
Kolkata-700016
Tel : +91 33 22172792/22521076
Email : travel_zone@yahoo.co.in

## GAYA

### ▶▶ DRUK AIR CORPORATION
Happy Guest House,
Near Mahabodhi Society of India,
Bodh Gaya, Bihar 824231
Tel/Fax : +91 631 2200264
Email : peman@drukair.com.bt
        pemagaya@drukair.com.bt

## MYANMAR

### ▶▶ DRUK AIR CORPORATION LTD.
No.52, Phyapon Street
Sanchaung, Yangon, Myanmar.
Tel : +95 1 527724
Fax : +95 1 537873
Email : drukair@mptmail.net.mm

## NEPAL

### ▶▶ DANFETRAVEL CENTRE (P) LTD.
P.O. Box 4429, Dubarmarg
Kathmandu, Nepal.
Tel : +977 1 4239988/4239922/4239651
Fax : +977 1 4239658
Email : sales@drukair.danfetravels.com
Airport +977 1 4471712
Email : ktmkkkb@drukair.com.bt

### ▶▶ MALLA TREKS (P) LTD.
P.O.Box 5227, Leknath Marg
Kathmandu, Nepal.
Tel : +977 1 4410089
Fax : +977 1 4423143
Email : info@mallatreks.com

## THAILAND

### ▶▶ DRUK AIR (Airport Office)
Royal Bhutan Airlines
Room No Z 3 – 013 (3rd Floor)
Airlines Office Building
Suvarnabhumi International Airport
999/Moo 7, Racha Thewa,
Bang Phi, Samut Prakan 10540
Tel : +66 2 1343040/1343041
Fax : +66 2 1343042
Email : drukairbkk@drukair.com.bt

### ▶▶ DRUK AIR (City Office)
5th Floor, Suite No.141/4, Skulthai
Surawong Tower, Suriyawong Bangrak
Bangkok 10500, Thailand
Tel : +66 2 2379201-203
Fax : +66 2 2379200

## GSA

### ▶▶ S.S.TRAVEL SERVICE
10/12-13, S.S.Building, Convent Road,

Silom, Bangrak, Bangkok 10500
Thailand.
Tel     : +662 2334714/2350411/12
Fax     : +662 2367186
Email  : ss1lox1loxinfor.co.th

## BANGLADESH
▶▶ **DRUK AIR CORPORATION LTD.**
Zia International Airport,
Terminal 2, Second Floor, Room No.52
Dhaka, Bangladesh
Tel     : + 880 2 8911066/8917347
Fax     : +880 2 8913038
Email  : Ogyenpdorji@drukair.com.bt
           dhaka@drukair.com.bt

### GSA
▶▶ **MAMS AVIATION LTD.**
33, Gulshan North Avenue, Road 45,
Gulshan 2, Dhaka-1212, Bangladesh
PABX   : +880 2 9890802/
           8827969/8826896
Tel     : +880 2 9892862/9862243
Fax     : +880 2 8828439
Email  : mams@bdmail.net

### PSA
▶▶ **SKY BANGLA AVIATION LTD.**
Suite No. 6C (6th Floor)
Sonartori Tower, 12 Sonargaon Road,
Dhaka-1000, Bangladesh
Tel     : +880 2 8651270/8551271
Fax     : +880 2 9675624
Email  : ali@skybangla.com

▶▶ **BORAK TRAVELS (PVT) LTD.**
Unique Trade Centre, Level 5,
8 Panthapath, Kawran Bazaar,
Dhaka 1215, Bangladesh.
Tel     : +880 2 9137662/9129682/
           9146127/9118725
Fax     : +880 2 9131261/8823392
Email  : borak@cyberbangla.com

▶▶ **BORAK TRAVELS (PVT) LTD.**
51/B Kemal Ataturk Avenue,
Banani, Dhaka 1213, Bangladesh.

Tel     : +880 2 9885116-23
           Ext : 135/137/138
Fax     : +880 2 8823392
Email  : utt@bangla.net

## OFF LINE OFFICES
### HONG KONG
▶▶ GLOBAL UNION TRANSPORTATION LTD.
RM, 22-24, New Henry House
10 Ice Street, Central Hong Kong
Tel     : +852 28683231
Fax     : +852 28455078
Email  : josephlo@aeroglobal.com.hk

▶▶ **CHEUNG HUNG TOURIST SERVICES
CO. LTD.**
2/F1., Block-B, Carnarvon Mansion
12 Carnarvon Rd., T.S.T., Kowloon.
Tel     : +852 23695333
Fax     : +852 2739899
Email  : chts@netvigator.com

### KOREA
▶▶ **YALE SKY NET CO., LTD.**
1F/Hangang Building, 606-15 Mok 3
dong, Yangchun-Ku, Seoul, Korea
Tel     : +82 2 26523361
Fax     : +82 2 26439614
Email  : yiandres@hotmail.com
           gulee838@yahoo.co.kr

### SRI LANKA
▶▶ **HEMAS AIR SERVICES PVT. LTD.**
75 York Street, Colombo-1
Tel     : +94 1 243711
Fax     : +94 1 4731399
Email  : drukair@hemas.com

### TAIWAN
▶▶ **GLOBAL AVIATION SERVICES P. LTD.**
11F-2, 103, Nanking E. Road,
Sector 4, Taipei, Taiwan
Tel     : +886 2 87122113
Fax     : +886 2 87123151
Email  : pax@gastwn.com

# Medical facilities

Healthcare facility
in Bhutan

BASIC HEALTH UNIT AUTSHO

THE Jigme Dorji National Referral Hospital in Thimphu is the country's best medical facility, but as the name suggests is not equipped to handle serious illnesses or major injuries arising out of accidents. Towns such as Paro, Trongsa, Mongar and Trashigang that are district headquarters all have hospitals while many villages en route have primary health care clinics. There are almost no private physicians or clinics, so if you fall sick and need medical care you will have to visit the nearest hospital. You can expect reasonably prompt attention and your treatment will be free just as it is for the Bhutanese. Common antibiotics and medicines are available without the need of a prescription in the towns but specific drugs may or may not be available.

In case of an emergency you will have to make it to Paro from where you can fly to Delhi, Kolkata or Bangkok for treatment. In a nutshell, if you are not suffering from any serious ailment the medical set up will work fine for you. However, as a precaution do carry your own stock of medicines and cover yourself with medical insurance ■

# TRAVEL AND TOUR OPERATORS

A S of date there are close to two hundred recognised tour operators licensed by the Department of Tourism to operate in the country. Since all are certified, in theory they will provide the same minimum standard of service so even if you make a blind choice, you are unlikely to go very wrong. The advantage of a smaller operator is the personalised service – it would not be unusual for the owner or a partner to accompany you or at the very minimum oversee your visit from start to finish. On the other hand, the bigger operators have seasoned guides, some of whom speak foreign languages, and will take you through your paces effortlessly. However, size does matter while getting hotel bookings, particularly in season. Some of the leading tour operators in terms of volume of traffic are Bhutan Tourism Corporation Ltd. (BTCL), Etho Metho, International Treks and Tours, Yangphel Adventure Travel, Yu Druk Tours, Tashi Tours and Gangri Tours. A detailed list is provided as Appendix A ■

**On the way to Taktsang**

# Appendix A

## LIST OF TOUR OPERATORS

| NAME OF THE AGENT | PROPRIETOR & ADDRESS | E-MAIL & WEBSITE | PHONE/FAX |
|---|---|---|---|
| ▶▶ A H K E Adventure | Mr.Nyendra Wangchuk, Post Box: 1134, Thimphu | info@bhutanecoventure.com www.bhutanecoventure.com | +975 2 381010/ +975 2 1760 1482 +975 2 381010 (F) |
| ▶▶ A Himalayan Eco-Adventures | Pema P.O Box 812, Thimphu, Bhutan | ecotravel@druknet.bt | +975-2-332517, -17612017 332517 (F) |
| ▶▶ A Middle Path Karma to Bhutan | T. Rinchhen P.O. Box 177, Norzin Lam, Thimphu, Bhutan | middlepath2bhutan@druknet.bt | +975-2-325832 -322229 (F) |
| ▶▶ About Bhutan Tours & Treks | Dechen W. Penjor Post Box 666, Thimphu | aboutbhutan@druknet.bt www.aaboutbhutan.com | +975-2-323484 -323894 (F) |
| ▶▶ Access Bhutan Tours & Treks | Kinley Yangden P.O. box 993, Thimphu, Bhutan | accessbhutan@gmail.com www.accessbhutan.bt | +975-17110720, -17634525 |
| ▶▶ Aesthetic Bhutan Tours | Mr. Lhakpa Dorji / Thukten yeshi Post Box: 773 | aestheticbhutan@yahoo.com www.aestheticbhutan.com | +975 17600373 / 17600195 +975 2 322093 (F) |
| ▶▶ Aja Tours and Travels | Mr. Sonam Tobgay Post Box 468, Thimphu | kadotshering@hotmail.com | +975-2-326089 -326090 (F) |
| ▶▶ All Bhutan Connection | Choki Post Box 1176, Thimphu | bhutanconnection@druknet.bt www.abc.com.bt | +975-2-327012 326741 (F) |
| ▶▶ Alpine Bhutan Travel Service | Mrs. Gyelmo PO Box 1382, Thimphu | alpinebhutan@yahoo.com www.alpine-bhutan.com | +975-17612210 -334911 (F) |
| ▶▶ Amitabha Tours & Treks | Kelzang Rinchen, Post Box No: 1114 Thimphu. | info@amitabha-bhutan.com www.amitabha-bhutan.com | +975-2-337799 / -17117799 -337788 (F) |
| ▶▶ Ancient Bhutan Tours & Treks | Pema Gyelpo Post Box 1198, Thimphu | bhutanancient@druknet.bt www.bhutanancient.com.bt | +975-2-326677/- 17111474-332434 (F) |
| ▶▶ Bae Yul Excursion | Chimmi Tobgyel Post Box 437, Thimphu | baeyul@druknet.bt www.baeyul.com.bt | +975-2-324355 -323728 (F) |
| ▶▶ Barma Cultural Tours and Treks | Thinley Tobgay Post Box 988, Thimphu | barmatours@druknet.bt www.barmatours.com.bt | +975-2-365255/ -17110912-365014 |
| ▶▶ Bhutan "A" Vision | Pema Dorji Post Box 1040, Thimphu | management@bhutanavision.com | +975-2-326463 -327809 (F) |
| ▶▶ Bhutan Abbot Tours & Travels | Ugyen tenzin P.O.Box. 1411, Thimphu, Bhutan | youngzinkee@hotmail.com www.abbotbhutantours.com.bt | +975 2 335080, +975 17673072 -335158 (F) |
| ▶▶ Bhutan Adventure | Chimi Dorji Post Box 1320, Thimphu | eden@druknet.bt | +975-2-323459 -323460 (F) |
| ▶▶ Bhutan All Seasons Tours and Treks | Mr.Dawa Penjor PO Box- 625. Thimphu | bhutanallseasons@gmail.com www.bhutanallseasons.bt | +975 2 380090, +975 1760 1407 (M) +975 2 380121 (F) |
| ▶▶ Bhutan Aries Tours and Treks | Mr. B.L. Gurung PO Box: 238, Thimphu | bhutanaries@druknet.bt www.bhutanaries.bt | +975 2 327177, +975 17600369 |
| ▶▶ Bhutan Bigfoot Tours & Adventure | Karma Samten P.O Box 1155, Thimphu | bhutanbigfoot@druknet.bt info@bhutanbigfoot.com www.bhutanbigfoot.com | +975-2-328976/ -17604027 -334385 (F) |
| ▶▶ Bhutan Birding and Heritage Travels | Hishey Tshering Post Box 293, Thimphu | hishey@druknet.bt www.heritagetours.com.bt | +975-2-324407 326666 (F) |

| | | | |
|---|---|---|---|
| ▶▶ Bhutan Cultural Tours & Treks | Chhundu Tshering Post Box 615, Thimphu | | +975-2-323372 -323777 (F) |
| ▶▶ Bhutan Cypress Tours & Treks | Ugyen Wangmo & Chimi Lhaden Post Box, Thimphu | bhutancypress@druknet.bt www.bhutancypress.com.bt | +975-17611844/- 17600712 |
| ▶▶ Bhutan Dorji Holidays | Choden L. Dorji Post Box 550, Thimphu | dorji@druknet.bt | +975-2-322192 -325174 (F) |
| ▶▶ Bhutan Dragon Adventures | Mr.Karma Gyeltshen, PO Box- 304,Thimphu. | dragonadventures@druknet.bt www.go2bhutan.com | +975-2-333043, +975-17111318 (M) |
| ▶▶ Bhutan Eco-Expedition | Ugyen Lhendup Post Box 778, Thimphu | btt@druknet.bt www.bookbhutantours.com | 324589, 325926 (F) |
| ▶▶ Bhutan Eco- Tours & Adventure | Sangay Tshering Post Box 739, Thimphu | bhutanecotours@druknet.bt www.bhutanecoadventure.com | +975-2-323941 -323508 (F) |
| ▶▶ Bhutan Encounters | Tshering Wangchuk Post Box, Thimphu | | |
| ▶▶ Bhutan Enigma Tours and Treks | Kuenga Lekpa Dorji PO Box 368, Thimphu | Bhutanenigma@druknet.bt www.bhutanenigma.com.bt | +975-2-328983/ 17110789, 333593 (F) |
| ▶▶ Bhutan Evergreen Tours and Treks | Mr. Ratu Post Box # 980 | bhutanevergreen@druknet.bt www.bhutanevergreen.com | +975-2-335273, +975-17638481 +975-2-335274 (F) |
| ▶▶ Bhutan Expeditions | Tshewang Nidup Post Box 598, Thimphu | tsewangnidup@yahoo.com www.bhutan-expeditions.com | +975-2-326266 -326689 (F) |
| ▶▶ Bhutan Exploration | Lhundup Dorji Post Box, Thimphu | bhutanexploration@druknet.bt | +975-2-332302 321762 (F) |
| ▶▶ Bhutan Footprints Travel | Mr. Daza Jigme, Kelwang Building, P.B:732 Thimphu | info@tourbhutantravel.com www.tourbhutantravel.com | +975-2-334960, -327449, -334961 (F) +975-17608977(m) |
| ▶▶ Bhutan Gateway Travel | Mr. Tashi Tobgay, Thimphu. | gatewaytravel@druknet.bt www.bhutangateway.com | +975 1765 4623, +975 2 335617 +975 2 335583 (F) |
| ▶▶ Bhutan Highland Tours and Treks | Mr. D.D. Dhittal PO Box: 1303 Thimphu. | info@bhutanhtt.com www.bhutanhtt.com | +975 2 321514, +975 1760 0740 +975 2 321514 (F) |
| ▶▶ Bhutan Himalaya Tours and Treks | Dhendup Tshomo Post Box 1002, Thimphu | tshomo@druknet.bt | 323921 / 327987 323145 (F) |
| ▶▶ Bhutan Jambay Tours | Sonam Jambay Zam Post Box 547, Thimphu | | 17609001 |
| ▶▶ Bhutan Journeys | Sonam Chophel Post Box 473, Thimphu | info@bhutanjourneys.com www.bhutanjourneys.com | 328643 323370 (F) |
| ▶▶ Bhutan Karma Tours | Karma Dechog Post Box, Thimphu | | 380225/17613830 |
| ▶▶ Bhutan Kaze Tours and Treks | Singye Namgay Post Box 715, Thimphu | wings@druknet.bt | 323173 / 326623 326624 (F) |
| ▶▶ Bhutan Kiga Tours | Lexang Pem Dechey Post Box, Thimphu | | |
| ▶▶ Bhutan Kuenphen Tours and Treks | Dorji Tshering Post Box 1167, Paro | | +975-8-271 665 |
| ▶▶ Bhutan Lakhor Tours and Treks | Wangda Tobgyel, Paro. | Prayerwheel@druknet.bt www.bhutanprayerwheel.com | +975-8-272506, 17602474, 272504 (F) |
| ▶▶ Bhutan Lha Yul Tours and Treks | Tshering Pem Post Box 483, Thimphu | lhayul@druknet.bt www.lhayul.com | 325073 / 323744 325035 (F) |

# Appendix A

| | | | |
|---|---|---|---|
| Bhutan Lotus Tours & Travels | Rinzin Wangmo Post Box 847, Thimphu | rinzinwangmo2003@yahoo.com | 325561 / 17600051 327724 (F) |
| Bhutan Majestic Travel | Mr. Namgay Dorji GPO Box: 1148 Thimphu Bhutan | www.bhutanmajestictravel.com | 975-17111095 +975-2-334661 -334662 (F) |
| Bhutan Mandala Tours & Treks | Kesang Wangmo Post Box 397, Thimphu | mandala@druknet.bt www.bhutanmandala.com | 323676 / 324842 |
| Bhutan Men-Lha Adventures & Travelers | Contact: Tashi Gyeltshen Thimphu Bhutan GPO #1377 | menl-adventure@druknet.bt, tashiwangdrel@yahoo.com www.trekkingbhutan.com | +975-2-321555 /321559 -331730 (F) |
| Bhutan Mystical Tours & Adventure | Post Box-887 Thimphu, Kingdom of Bhutan | bmta@druknet.bt www.bhutanmystical.com | 326851   325468 |
| Bhutan Nature & Culture Adventure | Sangay Phurba Post Box 814, Thimphu | bnca@druknet.bt | 324778 328108 (F) |
| Bhutan Nature Expeditions | Sonam Tobgay / Kunzang W. Thaye / Lyonpo Dawa Tshering Post Box 318, Thimphu | bne@druknet.bt | 327784 327785 (F) |
| Bhutan Nomadic Tours | Mr. Tshewang Dorji, P.O.Box - 999 Thimphu. | nomadictours@druknet.bt www.bhutanomadictours.com | +975 2 334697 +975 2 324904 (F) |
| Bhutan Norphel Tours & Treks | Kinley Lemo Dorji Post Box 518, Thimphu | bnt@druknet.bt www.norphel.com.bt | 327506 327285 (F) |
| Bhutan Padma Osel Tours | Ashi Pema Lhaden Pem Pem Wangchuck Post Box, Thimphu | | |
| Bhutan Paradise Travels | Dasho Bap Yeshey Dorji Post Box, Thimphu | paradisebhutan@druknet.bt www.paradisebhutan.com | +975-2-326351 -332175 (F) |
| Bhutan Paragliding Tours | Karma Tshering Post Box 302, Thimphu Bhutan | bhutanparagliding@druknet.bt | +975-17604843 telefax: -323925 |
| Bhutan Peaceful Tours & Treks | Raman Rai Post Box 263, Thimphu | peaceful@druknet.bt www.bhutanpeacefultours.com | 327393 321578 (F) |
| Bhutan Pine Wood Tours & Treks | Lhendup Zangmo Post Box 916, Thimphu | pinewood@druknet.bt | 325924 325507 (F) |
| Bhutan Reisen | Sangay Khandu Post Box, Thimphu | | 333053 / 17600421 |
| Bhutan Scenic Tours | Tshering Dorji Post Box, Paro | chodex@druknet.bt www.bhutanscenictours.com.bt | +975-8-271634, +975-1711 8111 -271838 (F) |
| Bhutan Space Travel Agency | Kinley Yangzom Post Box, Thimphu | | |
| Bhutan Star Travel & Tours | Karma Lhamo P.O Box 1139, Thimphu | info@bhutanstartravel.com www.bhutanstartravel.com | 17600763 334597 (F) |
| Bhutan Sun Moon Tours | Zuri Tulku Rimpochey Post Box 420, Thimphu | | 325506 / 323212 325079 (F) |
| Bhutan Tantric Adventure | Jigme Tshultrim Post Box, Thimphu | tantric@druknet.bt | 322546 |
| Bhutan Tourism Corporation Ltd. | Post Box 159 Thimphu | btcl@druknet.bt www.kingdomofbhutan.com | 322647 / 324045 |
| Bhutan Tours & Travels Pvt. Ltd. | Kinley Chozom Post Box 224, Thimphu | bttpa@druknet.bt | 325770 / 325769 |

| Company | Contact / Address | Email / Website | Phone |
|---|---|---|---|
| ▶▶ Bhutan Travel Bureau | Samdrup Norbu/ Post Box 959, Thimphu | tours@btb.com.bt Tshering Tashi www.btb.com.bt | 321749   325100 (F) |
| ▶▶ Bhutan Travel Connection | Mr. Pelden Choeda, PO Box-481, Thimphu. | btconn@druknet.bt www.bhutantravelconnection.com | +975-2-321280 +975-17613637 (m) |
| ▶▶ Bhutan Travel Service | Karma Korko Post Box 919, Thimphu | btskoko@druknet.bt | 325785 325786 (F) |
| ▶▶ Bhutan Travelers | Karma Yangzom Post Box 1298, Thimphu | wladventures@druknet.bt www.bhutanadventure.com | 328868 328869 (F) |
| ▶▶ Bhutan Treks and Tours | Sonam Penjore Post Box, Thimphu | | |
| ▶▶ Bhutan Vacation Inc. | Karma Dupchu/Chhime Dorji Post Box 334, Thimphu | www.bhutanadventure.com btvac@druknet.bt | 326031 / 323990 326140 (F) |
| ▶▶ Bhutan Visit | Yeshey Dorji Post Box 1334, Lhaki Lam, Motithang, Thimphu, Bhutan | info@bhutanvisit.com www.bhutanvisit.com | +975 2-325811, -325817 -325811 (F) |
| ▶▶ Bhutan Wonderful Tours & Travels | Chungla Dorji Post Box 805, Thimphu | wonderfulbhutan@druknet.bt | 326707 |
| ▶▶ BhutanThuensum Tours and Treks | Post Box, Thimphu | | |
| ▶▶ Blue Heaven Tours | Tandin Namgyel Post Box 197, Thimphu | bhutantiger@druknet.bt | 17110666 322531 (F) |
| ▶▶ Blue Poppy Tours & Treks | Karma Wangdi, PO Box 1296, Thimphu | karma@bluepoppybhutan.com www.bluepoppybhutan.com | +975-2-333 540 +975-1760 4549 -333 541 (F) |
| ▶▶ Boonserm Tours & Treks | Tashi Dorji & Tashi Namgay Post Box 609, Thimphu | bonsem@druknet.bt www.explorebhutan.com | 322257 / 324725 323731 (F) |
| ▶▶ BTCL – Luxury Division BTCL | Post Box, Thimphu | | |
| ▶▶ Bumree Tours & Treks Post Box 649, Thimphu | Sonam Deki Tshering | bumree@druknet.bt | 361113 / 326496 321817 (F) |
| ▶▶ Changshe Norbu Tours & Treks | Thinley Lhendup Dorji Post Box 403, Thimphu | changshe@druknet.bt www.travelbhutan.org | 322740   324342 |
| ▶▶ Chhundu Tours & Travels | Khendum Dorji Post Box 149, Thimphu | chhundu@druknet.bt www.chhundu.com.bt | 322592 322645 (F) |
| ▶▶ Classic Bhutan Tours & Treks | Dorji Wangmo Post Box 1382, Thimphu | classic-bhutan@druknet.bt | 327984 326025 (F) |
| ▶▶ Clear Path Tours & Treks | Tshering Wangchuk Post Box , Thimphu | | |
| ▶▶ Clear Voyage Tours & Treks | Ugyen Lhamo Post Box, Thimphu | | |
| ▶▶ Dechen Cultural Tours & Trekking | Chencho Tshering Post Box 818, Thimphu | dechen@druknet.bt www.asiatours.net/bhutan | 321358 324408 (F) |
| ▶▶ Destination Bhutan Tours | Thinley Tshering Post Box 149, Thimphu | | 332271 / 998872 |
| ▶▶ Dewa Tours & Treks | Lobzang Choeda Lower Motithang Thimphu | dewatours@druknet.bt www.dewatours.com.bt | 975-2-333824 334682 (F) |
| ▶▶ Dharma Tours & Travels | Pema Yangzom Post Box 945, Thimphu | dharma@druknet.bt | 323524 / 351628 323524 (F) |
| ▶▶ Diethelm Travel Bhutan | Ms Dechen Wangmo Penjor P.O.Box 107, Thimphu | dwpenjor@druknet.bt www.diethelmtravel.com | 975-2-323484/321747 +975-2-323894 (F) |

| | | | |
|---|---|---|---|
| ▶ Discovery Bhutan | Ugyen Dorji | discovery@druknet.bt | 322457 |
| | Post Box 825, Thimphu | www.discoverybhutan.com | 322530 (F) |
| ▶ Dragon Tours & | Gembo Dorji | dragon@druknet.bt | 323599 |
| Trekkers | Post Box 452, Thimphu | www.bhutandragon.com | 323314 (F) |
| ▶ Druk Adventure | Kunzang Dorji | | 326409 |
| | Post Box, Thimphu | | 323669 (F) |
| ▶ Druk Himalayan | Ugyen Lham | drukhiml@druknet.bt | 327222 |
| Expeditions | Post Box 1167, Thimphu | | 321836 (F) |
| ▶ Druk Kuenchhaap | Rinchyan Dolmma & | www.drukkuenchhaaptours.com.bt | 332177, 328381 |
| Tours and Travels | Dolma Choso D | | 17600111, 17111727 |
| | Post box 479, Thimphu | | 332462 (F) |
| ▶ Drukgyel Tours & Treks | Tshering Dema | | 327619 |
| | Post Box, Thimphu | | 327457 (F) |
| ▶ Eagle Tours & Treks | Pema Wangchuk | eagle@druknet.bt | 327117 |
| | Post Box 458, Thimphu | | 326936 (F) |
| ▶ Eastern Himalaya | Tenzin Rigden | | |
| Adventure | Post Box, Thimphu | | |
| ▶ Eastern Horizons | Ram Kumar Pradhan (Oser) | oser@easternhorizons.com | +975 2 327775 |
| Adventure Travel | Thimphu. | www.easternhorizons.com | +975 17607174 |
| | | | +975 2 225105 (F) |
| ▶ Etho Metho | Dago Beda/Nim Gyaltshen/ | ethometho@druknet.bt | 323162 / 326113 |
| Tours & Treks | Jochu Dorji | www.ethometho.com | |
| | Post Box 360, Thimphu | | |
| ▶ Exotic Destination | Chencho Wangdi / | exotic@druknet.bt | 327405 / 327406 |
| Jigme Tshewang | Post Box 682, Thimphu | | 326171 (F) |
| ▶ Experience Bhutan | Tshering Tobgyal | info@experiencebhutan.com | 328961 |
| Travel | Post Box 975, Thimphu | | 328961 (F) |
| ▶ Gaden Tours & Treks | Dorji Wangdi | gaden@druknet.bt | 321066 |
| | Post Box 1346, Thimphu | www.gaden.com | 321066 (F) |
| ▶ Gagyel Lhundrup | Kunley | | |
| Tours & Trek | Post Box, Thimphu | | |
| ▶ Gangri Tours & | Kesang Namgyal / | gangri@druknet.bt | 323556 |
| Treks Co. | Kinley Gyaltshen/ | www.gangri.com | 323322 (F) |
| | Kipchu Dorji | | |
| | Post Box 607, Thimphu | | |
| ▶ Gangtey Palace | Chukie Om Dorji, | gangteypalace@druknet.bt | +975 2 322213 |
| Expeditions | P.O. Box: 382, Thimphu. | | +975 17111462 (m) |
| | | | +975 2 322040 (F) |
| ▶ Gems Tours & Travels | Norbu Tenzin | gem@druknet.bt | 328014 / 328015 |
| | Post box 382, Thimphu | | 328013 (F) |
| ▶ Geo-Cultural | Mr. Karma Tshering | geocultural@druknet.bt | 00975-2-332121 |
| Tours & Treks | Post Box 413, Thimphu | www.geobhutan.com | 00975-2-332122 (F) |
| ▶ Gyeldup Tours & Treks | Gasey Lhundup | gyeldup@druknet.bt | 325873 / 321440 |
| | Post Box 1082, Thimphu | | 325878 (F) |
| ▶ Happy Holidays | Tokey Dorji | tokey@druknet.bt | 322692, 326899 |
| | Post Box 522, Thimphu | www.happyholidays.com.bt | 323248 (F) |
| ▶ Himalayan Adventure | Kinley Tshering | t_dorji@druknet.bt | 328829 |
| | Post Box 1436, Thimphu | www.himalayan_adventures.com | 328830 (F) |
| ▶ Himalayan Adventure | Pema Choki | himalaya@druknet.bt | 351051 |
| - Bhutan | Post Box 258, Thimphu | www.bhutan.com | 351051 (F) |
| ▶ Himalayan Discovery | Yeshey Tshering | yeshup@druknet.bt | 326135 |
| | Post Box 705, Thimphu | | 324760 (F) |

| Company | Contact / Address | Email / Website | Phone |
|---|---|---|---|
| Himalayan Kingdom Tours | Phurba Wangmo/Pema Tashi<br>Post Box 213, Thimphu | hktours@druknet.bt<br>www.himalayankingdomtours.com | 326102<br>324449 (F) |
| Holiday Bhutan | Tshering Lhamo<br>Post Box,, Thimphu | | |
| Inner Bhutan Travel Services | Choden Wangmo Namgyel<br>Post Box 701, Thimphu | | |
| Insiders Bhutan Travel | Sonam Jatsho<br>Post Box 271, Thimphu | sjatso@yahoo.com<br>www.insidersbhutan.com | 321102 / 323961<br>324695 (F) |
| International Treks & Tours | Dechen Ongdi<br>Post Box 525, Thimphu | intrek@druknet.bt<br>www.intrektours.com | 326591 / 326848<br>324963 (F) |
| Jachung Tours & Treks | Genzin Zam/Ugyen Norzom<br>Post Box 789, Thimphu | jachung@druknet.bt | 322402<br>322741 (F) |
| Jamphel Tours & Travels | Dechen Jamyang<br>Post Box 289, Thimphu | jamphel@druknet.bt | 322204<br>324152 (F) |
| Jeroma Tours & Travels | Karma Tenzin<br>Post Box 645, Thimphu | jeroma@druknet.bt<br>www.bhutanguide.com | 327758<br>327757 (F) |
| Jigten Tours and Treks | Namgay Lhamo<br>Post Box, Thimphu | jigten@druknet.bt<br>www.jigten.com.bt | Te/fax : 322587 |
| JOJO's Adventure Bhutan | Tshering Tashi<br>Post Box 816,Thimphu | jojos@druknet.bt<br>www.jojos.com.bt | 328747, 17110305<br>332837 (F) |
| Kadakling Tours | P.O Box 832,<br>Thimphu, Bhutan | kadakling@druknet.bt<br>www.kadakling.com | +975-2-324362 |
| Kalachakra Tours & Treks | Phurba<br>Post Box 745, Thimphu | kalachakra-bhut@druknet.bt | 323304<br>325447 (F) |
| Karmic Tours & Treks | Karma Gayley<br>Post Box 1310, Thimphu | mail@karmictours.com<br>www.karmictours.com | 326836 |
| Keys to Bhutan | Gelay Jamtsho/<br>Anand Gurung<br>Post Box 604, Thimphu | mail@keystobhutan.com<br>www.keystobhutan.com | 327232<br>327233 (F) |
| Khamsa Tours & Treks | Karma Galay<br>Post Box 1371,<br>Changlam Plaza,Thimphu | khamsa@druknet.bt<br>www.bhutankhamsatravels.com | +975 2 323095/<br>+975 17111208<br>+975 2 324383 (F) |
| Khorlo Tours & Travel | Chhoten<br>Post Box 458, Thimphu | khorlotours@druknet.bt<br>www.khorlotours.com.bt | 328516<br>8272058 (F) |
| Kibou Tours & Treks | Tshering | | |
| Kingyal Tours | Kinley Wangmo<br>Post Box 826, Thimphu | | 326254 / 331706<br>328718 (F) |
| Kuzu Adventure | Ka Ka Tshering<br>Post Box, Thimphu | | |
| Laya Tours and Treks | Dorji Gyeltshen<br>Post Box, Thimphu | | |
| Lekzang Adventures | Ngawang Pem<br>Thimphu, Bhutan | lekzangadventures@druknet.bt | +975-17111664 |
| Lhomen Tours & Treks | Karchung Wangchuk /<br>Karma Dorji/<br>Yeshey Wangchuk<br>Post Box 341, Thimphu | lhomen@druknet.bt<br>www.lhomen.com.bt | 324148<br>323243 (F) |
| Lingkor Tours & Treks | Tashi Wangmo /<br>Tempa Choephel<br>Post Box 202, Thimphu | lingkor@druknet.bt<br>www.bhutan-tour.com | 323417 / 322624<br>323402 (F) |
| Lotus Adventure | Sonam Tobgay<br>Post Box 706, Thimphu | info@bhutanlotus.com | 322191 / 322419<br>325678 (F) |

| | | | |
|---|---|---|---|
| Luxury Division | Post Box, Thimphu | | |
| Mahakala Tours & Treks | Dechen Ongmo | dongmo@druknet.bt | +00975-2-327041, |
| | Post Box: 393 | | 334690, 17111262(M) |
| | | | +00975-2-334690 |
| Masagang Tours & Treks | Ugyen Wangdi | masagang@druknet.bt | 323206 |
| | Post Box 363, Thimphu | www.masagang.com | 323718 (F) |
| Menbar Travels | Mrs. kunzang W. Wangchuk | menbartravels@yahoo.com | +975 2 333777, |
| | | www.bhutanmenbartravels.com | 333999, 17110432(M). |
| Men-Lha Adventure | Tashi Gyeltshen | | |
| | Post Box, Thimphu | | |
| Middle Path | Rinzin Wangmo | | 272 481 |
| Adventure Travels | Post Box 932, Paro | | |
| Mystical Horizon | Tshering Penjor | | |
| Tours & Adventures | Post Box, Thimphu | | |
| Namgay Adventure | Namgay Tshering | namtshe@druknet.bt | 327587 |
| Travels | Post Box 545, Thimphu | | 323515 (F) |
| Namsay Adventure | Nima Selden Om | namsay@druknet.bt | 325616 / 326980 |
| | Post Box 549, Thimphu | | 324297 (F) |
| Nature Bhutan Tours | Ugyen Lhendup | | |
| | Post Box, Thimphu | | |
| Nature Tourism | Karma Jamtsho | nattouri@druknet.bt | 327355 / 321273 |
| | Post Box 673, Thimphu | www.naturetourism-bhutan.com | 327356 (F) |
| Nima Tours & Treks | Sherab Wangdi / | nimacomp@druknet.bt | 325299 |
| | Kinga Wangmo | www.bhutanmarathon.com | 322039 |
| | Post Box 180, Thimphu | | |
| Nirvana Expeditions | Sonam Dondup Dorjee | info@nirvanaexpeditons.com | 328875 |
| | Post Box 611, Thimphu | www.nirvanaexpeditions.com | 331781 (F) |
| Norda Expeditions | Karma Wangmo | norda@druknet.bt | 326818 / 325743 |
| | Post Box 1419, Thimphu | www.bhutannorda.com | 326818 (F) |
| Nor-Thrung | Sangay Tshoki | | |
| Tours & Travels | Post Box, Thimphu | | |
| Odiyan Discovery | Karma Temphel | odiyan@druknet.bt | 326835 |
| | Post Box 689, Thimphu | | 324926 (F) |
| Pacific Travel & Tours | Ugyen Tshering | | |
| | Post box, Thimphu | | |
| Passage to Himalayas | Leki Dorji | lekid@druknet.bt | 321726 / 325337 |
| | Post Box 1068, Thimphu | | 321727 (F) |
| Pegasus Adventure | Wangdi | pegasusadv@druknejt.bt | 332947 |
| | Post Box 737, Thimphu | | 332947 (F) |
| Peljor Dargay Tours | Nedup Dorji | | |
| | Post Box, Thimphu | | |
| Pema Tours & Travels | Dasho T. Yonten | | |
| | Post Box, Thimphu | | |
| Phuntshok Ling | Karma L. Dorjee | ptla@druknet.bt | 327044 |
| Adventure | Post Box 839, Thimphu | www.visitbhutan.com.bt | 327044 (F) |
| Pinnacle Tours & Treks | Wangchuk | pinnacle@druknet.bt | 327700 |
| | Post Box 775, Thimphu | | 327701 (F) |
| Prayer Flags | Sherub Zangmo | prayerflag@druknet.bt | 326423 / 17606935 |
| Tours & Adv. | Post Box 1457, Thimphu | | |
| Pristine Drukyul | Karma Letho | pristine@druknet.bt | 325455 |
| Tours & Treks | Post Box 346, Thimphu | www.bhutanpristine.com.bt | 325455 (F) |

| | | | |
|---|---|---|---|
| Proteus Tours & Travels | Khampa Dorji | proteustours@druknet.bt | 325333 / 325353 |
| | Post Box 222, Thimphu | | 325888 (F) |
| Rabsel Tours & Treks | Sangay Tenzin | rabsel@druknet.bt | 324165 / 325686 |
| | Post Box 488, Thimphu | | 324918 (F) |
| Rainbow Tours & Treks | Sonam Ongmo | rainbow@druknet.bt | 323270 |
| | Post Box 641, Thimphu | | 322960 (F) |
| Raven Tours & Treks | Deepak Tamang, | information@raventoursandtreks.com | |
| | P.O. Box:1299, Thimphu | www.raventoursandtreks.com | +975-2-326062, |
| | | | +975-17625294(m) |
| Rinchen Tours & Treks | Sangay Zam | dorji@druknet.bt | 324552 |
| | Post Box 550, Thimphu | | 323767 (F) |
| Rirab Tours & Treks | Tshering Wangmo | rirabtours@druknet.bt | 321623 |
| | Post Box 463, Thimphu | | 329230 (F) |
| Sacred Himalaya Travel | Tshetem Norbu, | tshetem@sacredhimalayatravel.com | |
| | PO Box: 830 Thimphu | www.sacredhimalayatravel.com | +975 2 325606 |
| | | +975 2 335163 (F) | |
| Sakten Tours & Treks Limited | Tshewang Rinzin | sakten@druknet.bt | 325567 / 324384 |
| | Post Box 532, Thimphu | www.bootan.com/sakten | 325574 (F) |
| Samden Adventures | Mr. Singye Dorji | mail@samdenadventures.com | +975 2 333975, |
| | Post Box: 610 | www.samdenadventures.com | +975 17110867 |
| | | | +975 2 334771 (F) |
| Seewang Tours & Adventure | Madan Kumar | | |
| | Post Box, Thimphu | | |
| Shangrila Bhutan Tours & Treks | Mr. Duptho Rinzin | shangrila@druknet.bt | +975 2 321189, |
| | Post Box 541, Thimphu | www.bhutan.bz | +975 1711 1011 |
| | | | +975 2 324410 (F) |
| Silver Dragon Tours & Treks | Pelden Tshewang | silverdragon@druknet.bt | 328122 |
| | Post Box 227, Thimphu | | 328121 (F) |
| Sky Kingdom Adventures | Kinley Wangchuk | info@skykingdomadventures.com | 325029 / 323496 (F) |
| | Post Box 309, Thimphu | www.skykingdomadventures.com | |
| Sky Travels | Tshering Jamtsho | sky@druknet.bt | 326944 / 323651 (F) |
| | Post Box 1052, Thimphu | www.bhutansky.com | |
| Snow Leopard Trekking Co. | Singye Dorji | snowlprd@druknet.bt | 321822 |
| | Post Box 953, Thimphu | | 325684 (F) |
| Snow Lion Adventure Travels | Sangay Khandu | skarmtt@druknet.bt | +975-2-323511 |
| | Post Box: 796, Thimphu | www.snowlion.com.bt | -322481 (F) |
| Snow White Treks & Tours | Kencho Wangmo Dorji | snowwhite@druknet.bt | 323028, 17111161 |
| | Post Box 112, Thimphu | kenchod@yahoo.com | 321696 (F) |
| | | www.snowwhitetours.com.bt | |
| Sophun Tours & Treks | Kesang Dema Namgyel | sophun@druknet.bt | 328557 |
| | Post Box 317, Thimphu | www.sophuntravels.com.bt | 321319 (F) |
| Taktsang Tours & Travels | Dorji Tshering | taktsang@druknet.bt | 322102 / 326719 |
| | Post Box 199, Thimphu | www.bhutantaktsang.com.bt | 323284 (F) |
| Tara Tours & Travels | Yeshey Wangmo | tt_tours@druknet.bt | 325157 |
| | Post Box 314, Thimphu | | 324619 (F) |
| Tashi Tours & Travels | Dasho U. Dorji | tasitour@druknet.bt | 323027 / 323361 |
| | Post Box 423, Thimphu | | 323666 (F) |
| Thimphu Tours & Treks | Kezang Choejoe | ttt@druknet.bt | 321093 / 325469 |
| | Post Box 866, Thimphu | | 321346 (F) |
| Thoesam Tours & Treks | Lhatu Tshering | thoesam@druknet.bt | 324857 |
| | Post Box 629, Thimphu | www.thoesamtours.com | 323593 (F) |

# Appendix A

| Company | Contact / Address | Email / Website | Phone / Fax |
|---|---|---|---|
| Thunder Dragon Treks & Tours | Wangchuk Wangdi Post Box 303, Thimphu | thunder@druknet.bt | 321999 / 321963 321999 (F) |
| Trans Himalaya Tours & Trekking | Kunzang Lhamo Khorko Post Box, Thimphu | | 324451 323592 (F) |
| Tsachog Tours & Treks | Chenda Dorji Post Box, Thimphu | | |
| Tsende Tours & Travels | Sonam Dorji Post Box, Thimphu | | 326977 |
| Tsenden Travel Service | Ganesh Ghimiray Post Box 1042 Thimphu | bhutantsendentravel@druknet.bt www.bhutantsendentravel.com | 321059 328084 (F) |
| TTT Tshering Tours & Treks | Tshering Wangdi Post Box, Thimphu | office@ttt-bhutan.net | |
| Vajra Guru Spiritual Travel | Dr. Karma Wangchuk P.O. Box:1094, Thimphu, Bhutan | vajraguru@druknet.bt bhutanspiritual.com | +975-2-335588, +975-17636588 +975-2-339988 (F) |
| Wangchuk Tours & Treks | Chencho Tshering Post Box 507, Thimphu | wchuktt@druknet.bt www.wangchuktt.com.bt | 326233 326232 (F) |
| White Lotus Tours & Travels | KRP Namgyel Post Box 480, Thimphu | whitelotus@druknet.bt www.whitelotustours.com | 324499 326070 (F) |
| White Tara Tours & Treks | Sonam Choden Dorji Post Box 467, Thimphu | wtara@druknet.bt | 322585 324152 (F) |
| Wind Horse Tours & Treks | Ugen Tenzin Post Box 1021, Thimphu | windhor@druknet.bt www.bhutanholiday.com | 326026 326025 |
| Yak Adventure Travel | Tandin Tshewang Post Box 1136, Thimphu | yaktravel@druknet.com www.visit2bhutan.com | 333040 333043 (F) |
| YANA Expeditions Inc. | Tashi Tobgay Post Box 319, Thimphu | yana@druknet.bt www.discoverbhutan.biz | 332329 331583 (F) |
| Yangphel Adventure Travel | Ugen Rinzin Post Box 236, Thimphu | md@yangphel.com www.aboutbhutan.com | 323293 / 321873 322897 (F) |
| Yarkay Tours & Treks | Phub Zam Post Box 107, Thimphu | yarkay@druknet.bt www.aaboutbhutan.com | +975-2-322628/ 323894 (F) |
| Yod Sel Tours & Treks | Daw Penjor Post Box 547, Thimphu | dawa@druknet.bt www.bhutanyodsel.com | 323912 323589 (F) |
| Yu Druk Tours & Travels | Sonam Wangmo / Rinzin O. Wangchuk Post Box 140, Thimphu | yudruk@druknet.bt www.yudruk.com | 323461 / 321905 322116 |
| Yungtoed Tours & Treks | Yungtoed Meser Threndel Post Box 1420, Thimphu | yungtoed@druknet.bt www.yungtoed.com.bt | 328544 328545 (F) |
| Zamling Tours & Travels | Dipendra Giri Post Box 961, Thimphu | zamling@druknet.bt | 323177 323177 (F) |
| Zanah Tours & Treks | Sonam Yangden Post Box, Thimphu | wangdens@hotmail.com | 324302 331484 (F) |
| Zhidey Tours & Treks | Jurmey Tshewang Post Box 841, Thimphu | zhidey@hotmail.com | 328324 327511 (F) |
| Zigkor Tours & Travels | Rebcca Gurung Post Box 797, Thimphu | | 328800 329111 (F) |

# APPENDIX B

## LIST OF HOTELS

### BUMTHANG

| NAME OF HOTEL | TELEPHONE | ROOMS | | RATE : NU/RS | |
|---|---|---|---|---|---|
| Mountain Lodge mtnlodge@druknet.bt | 631255 T 631275 F | 27 | Single 2 Double 21 Deluxe 4 | 1500 1500 2500 | 1700 |
| Jakar Village Lodge gyeldup@druknet.bt | 631242 T 631377 F | 22 | Double 20 Deluxe 2 | 1350 2000 | 1500 |
| Swiss Guest House swissguesthouse@druknet.bt | 631145 T 631918 F | 10 | Double 10 | 1300 | 1500 |
| Gongkhar Guest House | 631288 T / 631345 F | 18 | Double 18 | 1350 | 1500 |
| Yangphel G/ House | 631191 T | 10 | Double 10 | 1300 | 1800 |
| Wangdicholing Resort wangdicholingresort@druknet.bt | 631452 T / 631278 F | 38 | Single 6 Double 30 Suite 2 | 1450 1450 2500 | 1550 |
| River Lodge pemadawa@druknet.bt | 631287 T | 35 | Single 5 Double 20 Deluxe 5 Suite 1 | 1400 1400 2000 4950 | 1500 |
| Leki Guest House lekilodge@druknet.bt | 631231 T 631845 F | 20 | Double 20 | 600 | 2000 |
| Kaila Guest House | 631219 T / 631247 F | 18 | Double 18 | 1300 | 1500 |
| Udee Guest House udee@druknet.bt | 631139 T 631309 F | 10 | Double 10 | 1200 | 1300 |
| Mepham G/ House | 631738 T / 631329 F | 18 | Double 18 | 1200 | 1300 |
| Rinchenling Lodge jampel@druknet.bt | 631147 T 631103 F | 18 | Single 2 Double 16 | 1500 | 1750 |
| Hotel Home | 631666 T/ 7612962 (M) | 16 | Double 16 | 1450 | 1550 |

### MONGAR

| NAME OF HOTEL | TELEPHONE | ROOMS | | RATE : NU/RS | |
|---|---|---|---|---|---|
| Shongkhar Guest House | 641107 T | 9 | Single 1 Double 7 Suite 1 | 500 1400 | 800 |
| Druk Zhongkhar Lodge drukzhongkhar@druknet.bt | 641587 T 641590 F | 18 | Single 2 Double 12 Deluxe 1 Suite 3 | 1800 2000 2200 2500 | |

### PARO

| NAME OF HOTEL | TELEPHONE | ROOMS | | RATE : NU/RS | |
|---|---|---|---|---|---|
| Namsey Hotel namseyresort@druknet.bt | 240620 T | 42 | Single 2 Double 28 Deluxe 12 | 1700 1950 2250 | 1900 2500 |
| Kichu Resort kresort@druknet.bt intkichu@druknet.bt | 271647 T | 53 | Single 10 Double 17 Deluxe 24 Suite 2 | 1800 2400 3000 5000 | |
| Tiger Nest Resort | 271310 T / 271640 F | 15 | Double 15 | 1300 | 1500 |
| Hotel Olathang ohotel@druknet.bt | 271305 T 271454 F | 59 | Double 41 Deluxe 12 | 1625 3500 | 2000 |

# Appendix B

| | | | | | |
|---|---|---|---|---|---|
| Dechen Hill Resort<br>dchncot@druknet.bt | 271392 T | 17 | Double 17 | 1300 | 1600 |
| Hotel Peljorling | 271365 T<br>272462 F | 4 | Single 1<br>Double 3 | 450 | 650 |
| Hotel Pegyel | 271472 T<br>271965 F | 17 | Single 4<br>Double13 | 1500<br>1800 | |
| Pelrig Cottages | 272472 T | 25 | Single 4<br>Double 17<br>Cottages 4 | 1800<br><br>3500 | 2000 |
| Hotel Gangtey Palace<br>hganteyp@druknet.bt | 271301 T<br>271452 F | 23 | Deluxe 3<br>Standard 16<br>Cottages 4<br>Suite | 2500<br>2000<br>1200<br>3500 | 3000<br>2200<br>1500 |
| Mandala Resort<br>mandala@druknet.bt | 272478 T<br>272478 F | 12 | Double 12 | 1200 | 1500 |
| Samdencholing Eco Resort<br>samden_choling@druknet.bt | 271509 T<br>271826 F | 17 | Single 1<br>Double 16 | 1200<br>1400 | |
| Hotel Jor - Yang<br>joryangz@druknet.bt | 271747/272498 T<br>271557 F | 21 | Single 2<br>Double 12<br>Deluxe 6<br>Suite 1 | 1400<br>1800<br>2000<br>3500 | |
| Hotel Holiday Home<br>hhh@druknet.bt | 272101 T<br>272103 F | 9 | Double 7<br>Suite 2 | 1500<br>2500 | 1800 |
| Rinchenling Lodge<br>nawangd@druknet.bt | 240394 T<br>240396 F | 18 | Single<br>Double 18<br>Deluxe | 1600<br>1800<br>2000 | 1800<br>2000<br>2300 |
| Hotel Zhiwaling<br>reservation@zhiwaling.com | 271277 T<br>271456 F | 45 | Double 40<br>Deluxe 4<br>Suite 1 | 10215<br>20205<br>42750 | 14175 |
| Amankora Resort<br>amankora@amanresorts.com | 272623 T<br>272999 F | 24 | Suite 24 | 37125 | 40500 |
| Uhma Resort | 271597 T<br>271513 F | 29 | Single 9<br>Villas 9<br>Deluxe 9<br>Suite 2 | 12,600<br><br>20250<br>25875 | 40500 |
| Hotel Valley View | 240107/ 272541 T<br>240109 F | 20 | Double 15<br>Deluxe 5 | 1700<br>2000 | 2000<br>2500 |

## PHUNTSHOLING

| | | | | | |
|---|---|---|---|---|---|
| Central Hotel | 252172 T<br>252173/252022 F | 21 | Single 6<br>Double 6<br>Deluxe 6<br>Suite 3 | 450<br><br>675<br>1000 | 550 |
| Namgay Hotel<br>hotel_namgay@yahoo.com<br>hotelnamgay@druknet.bt | 252374 / 253947 T<br>254147 F | 18 | Double 4<br>Deluxe 4<br>Suite 10 | 1100<br>1500<br>1950 | 1300 |
| Hotel Druk | 252426 T<br>252929 F | 29 | Double 26<br>Suite 3 | 1500<br>5500 | 2000 |
| Peljorling Hotel | 252883 T | 9 | Single 2<br>Double 4<br>Deluxe 2<br>Suite 1 | 275<br><br>400<br>600 | 350 |
| Hotel Sinchula<br>hotelsinchula@yahoo.com | 252589 T<br>252772 F | 14 | Single 3<br>Double 5<br>Deluxe 7 | 450<br>650<br>1000 | |

| Property | Phone | Rooms | Room type | Rate | Rate |
|---|---|---|---|---|---|
| Lhaki Hotel<br>lhakihotel@druknet.bt | 257111 T<br>257222 T<br>251185 F | 30 | Single 2<br>Double 11<br>Deluxe 11<br>Suite 6 | 1800<br><br>2400<br>4500 | <br>2300 |

## PUNAKHA

| Property | Phone | Rooms | Room type | Rate | Rate |
|---|---|---|---|---|---|
| Hotel Zangdo Pelri<br>hotzang@druknet.bt | 584125 / 584321 T<br>584203 F<br>17606619 M | 45 | Single 1<br>Double 23<br>Deluxe 20<br>Suite 1 | 1700<br>2100<br>2100<br>5000 | |
| Meri Phuensum Resort | 584195 / 584237 T<br>584236 F | 24 | Single 2<br>Double 17<br>Deluxe 5 | 1500<br>1700<br>1700 | <br><br>1850 |
| Damchen Resort | 584354 T<br>584449 F | 5 | Double 4<br>Deluxe 1 | 1250<br>1400 | 1400 |
| Amankora Resort<br>amankora@amanresorts.com | 584222 T<br>584555 F | 8 | Suite 8 | 37125 | 40500 |
| Hotel Y.T<br>hotelyt@druknet.bt<br>hotelyt@yahoo.com | 376014 R<br>376012 H<br>376029 F | 17 | Single 3<br>Double 13<br>Deluxe 1 | 1450<br>1700<br>2200 | |

## SAMDRUP JONGKHAR

| Property | Phone | Rooms | Room type | Rate | Rate |
|---|---|---|---|---|---|
| Tashi Longched Trokhang Hotel | 251470 T | 19 | Double 14<br>Deluxe 5 | 350<br>450 | |
| Hotel Peljorling | 251094 T<br>251308/251318 F | 13 | Double 13 | 700 | 1000 |
| Hotel Friends | 251545 T | 9 | Double 9 | 200 | 300 |

## THIMPHU

| Property | Phone | Rooms | Room type | Rate | Rate |
|---|---|---|---|---|---|
| Hotel River View<br>riverview@druknet.bt | 325029 T<br>323496 F | 51 | Single 20<br>Deluxe 18<br>Suite 11<br>Deluxe Suite | 1500<br>2000<br>4000<br>26000 | <br>2400 |
| Druk Hotel<br>drukhotel@druknet.bt<br>www.drukhotels.com | 322966 T<br>322677 F | 53 | Standard (reg 16)<br>Deluxe<br>Suite<br>Deluxe(Exe 37)<br>Suite<br>Extra Bed | 2700<br>3500<br>6000<br>4000<br>7000<br>500 | 3000<br>4000 |
| Motithang Hotel | 322435 T<br>328058 F | 15 | Single 1<br>Double 13<br>Deluxe 1<br>Suite 1 | 1500<br>1700<br>2500<br>3500 | |
| Hotel Pedling<br>pedling@druknet.bt | 325714 / 328988 T<br>323592  F | 39 | Double 32<br>Deluxe 4<br>Suite 3 | 1450<br>2000<br>3000 | 1800<br>2500<br>3500 |
| Hotel Jomolhari<br>hoteljumolhari@druknet.bt<br>www.jomolhari.com | 322747 T<br>324412 F | 26 | Double 17<br>Deluxe 3<br>Suite 6 | 2500<br>3200<br>4500 | 2900<br>3600<br>5500 |
| Jambayang Resort<br>jamyangs@druknet.bt | 322349 T<br>323669 F | 18 | Single 10<br>Double 5<br>Deluxe<br>Suite 3 | 1200<br>1800<br>1800<br>2500 | |

| Hotel | Phone | Rooms | Room Type | Rate | Rate |
|---|---|---|---|---|---|
| Hotel Wangchuk<br>htlwchuk@druknet.bt<br>www.wangchuck.com | 323532 T<br>323222/326232 F | 20 | Double 8<br>Deluxe 12 | 1550<br>1800 | 1950<br>2200 |
| Druk Sherig G/ House<br>travel@druknet.bt | 322598 T<br>322714 F | 12 | Single 2<br>Double 6<br>Suite 4 | 1400<br>2400<br>2800 | |
| Yeezin G/ House<br>yeedzin@druknet.bt | 332119 T<br>324995 F | 20 | Single 4<br>Double 7<br>Deluxe 5<br>Suite 4 | 700<br>1000<br>1200<br>1100 | |
| Hotel Galingkha | 328126 T, 325296 F | 10 | Double 10 | 1000 | 1500 |
| Nor- trung Hotel<br>nor-trung@druknet.bt | 332944 T<br>333818 F | 10 | Double 8<br>Suite 2 | 1500<br>1900 | |
| Hotel Dragon Roots<br>droots@druknet.bt | 332820 T<br>332823 F | 30 | Single 8<br>Double 19<br>Suite 3 | 1800<br>2200<br>3000 | 4000 |
| Amankora Resort<br>amankora@amanresorts.com | 334224 T<br>331999 F | 16 | Suite 16 | 37,125 | |
| Chuniding Resort<br>kesangchoedon@hotmail.com | 351493 T, 17612929 M<br>351643 F | 10 | Double 8<br>Deluxe 2 | 1000<br>2000 | 1500 |
| Wangchuk Resort<br>htlwchuk@druknet.bt<br>www.wangchuck.com | 365262 T<br>326232 F | 24 | Deluxe 17<br>Suite 7 | 2200 | 2800 |
| Hotel Phuntsho Pelri | 334971 T<br>334974 F | 46 | Single 1<br>Double 38<br>Deluxe 5<br>Suite 2 | 1700<br>2000<br>2500<br>2500 | 3000<br>3500 |
| **TRASHIGANG** | | | | | |
| Druk Doetjung Hotel | 521214 T / 521269 F | 12 | Double 12 | 650 | 850 |
| Kelling Guest House | 521145 T | 10 | Double 8<br>Deluxe 2 | 750<br>1500 | |
| **TRONGSA** | | | | | |
| Hotel Norling | 521171 T / 521178 F | 10 | Double 10 | 1050 | 1200 |
| Phuenzhi G/ House<br>puenzhi@druknet.bt | 521197 T<br>521356 F | 32 | Single 4<br>Double 28 | 1200<br>1200 | 1500 |
| Yangkhil Resort<br>yangkhilresort@druknet.bt | 521417 T<br>521420 F | 21 | Single 4<br>Double 16<br>Deluxe 1 | 1600<br>1600<br>2300 | 1800 |
| **WANGDUEPHODRANG** | | | | | |
| Dragon Nest Resort<br>nest@druknet.bt | 480521/480522 T<br>480503 F | 17 | Double 17<br>Deluxe 2 | 1000/1600<br>1100/1900 | 1300/1900<br>1400/2100 |
| Thegchen Phodrang G/ H | 490025 T | 8 | Double 7<br>Deluxe 1 | 700<br>1200 | 1000 |
| Kichu Resort | 481359 T<br>481360 F | 26 | Double 22<br>Deluxe 3<br>Suite 1 | 1650<br>2400<br>4400 | 2400 |
| Hotel Dewachen | 490007 T | 16 | Double 16 | 1500 | 1800 |
| Amankora Resort<br>amankora@amanresorts.com | 490049 T<br>490050 F | 8 | Suite 8 | 37125 | 40500 |

# INDEX

# INDEX

# Notes

# Discount Coupons

## 20% OFF
on food

**DAGMAR RESTAURANT**

Paro

A good option
for a wholesome meal

## 20% OFF
on food

 **Olathang Hotel**

Paro

For the most sumptous
buffet meal in town

## 20% OFF
on food

**CHHARO RESTAURANT**

Paro

This is the place for
great local cuisine

## 20% OFF
on food

 *zhiwa Ling* Hotel

Paro

Savour the multi cuisine
fare on offer here

To entail the discount offered you need to present the book with the relevant coupon intact. Since this is a new concept, we suggest you do so at the onset, before ordering, just in case staff needs to confirm with the management.

The author and publisher are not responsible for any establishment reneging on their commitment of a discount. However, we would greatly appreciate your feedback on this discount offer and welcome suggestions to improve it.

Email us at: drivingholidays@yahoo.co.in

To entail the discount offered you need to present the book with the relevant coupon intact. Since this is a new concept, we suggest you do so at the onset, before ordering, just in case staff needs to confirm with the management.

The author and publisher are not responsible for any establishment reneging on their commitment of a discount. However, we would greatly appreciate your feedback on this discount offer and welcome suggestions to improve it.

Email us at: drivingholidays@yahoo.co.in

To entail the discount offered you need to present the book with the relevant coupon intact. Since this is a new concept, we suggest you do so at the onset, before ordering, just in case staff needs to confirm with the management.

The author and publisher are not responsible for any establishment reneging on their commitment of a discount. However, we would greatly appreciate your feedback on this discount offer and welcome suggestions to improve it.

Email us at: drivingholidays@yahoo.co.in

# Discount Coupons

**20%**
OFF
on food

**Red Rice Restaurant**

Paro

Cosy ambience with
great fusion food

**20%**
OFF
on food & room

*Hotel Pedling*

Thimphu

A great Indian buffet meal
cooked to perfection

**20%**
OFF
on food

 **Hotel Druk**

Phuentsholing

Offers Indian and
Chinese Cuisine

**20%**
OFF
on food

 **Hotel Druk**

Thimphu

The best tandoori cuisine
in town

To entail the discount offered you need
to present the book with the relevant
coupon intact. Since this is a new concept,
we suggest you do so at the onset, before
ordering, just in case staff needs to confirm
with the management.
The author and publisher are not responsible
for any establishment reneging on their
commitment of a discount. However, we
would greatly appreciate your feedback on
this discount offer and welcome suggestions
to improve it.
Email us at: drivingholidays@yahoo.co.in

To entail the discount offered you need
to present the book with the relevant
coupon intact. Since this is a new concept,
we suggest you do so at the onset, before
ordering, just in case staff needs to confirm
with the management.
The author and publisher are not responsible
for any establishment reneging on their
commitment of a discount. However, we
would greatly appreciate your feedback on
this discount offer and welcome suggestions
to improve it.
Email us at: drivingholidays@yahoo.co.in

To entail the discount offered you need
to present the book with the relevant
coupon intact. Since this is a new concept,
we suggest you do so at the onset, before
ordering, just in case staff needs to confirm
with the management.
The author and publisher are not responsible
for any establishment reneging on their
commitment of a discount. However, we
would greatly appreciate your feedback on
this discount offer and welcome suggestions
to improve it.
Email us at: drivingholidays@yahoo.co.in

To entail the discount offered you need
to present the book with the relevant
coupon intact. Since this is a new concept,
we suggest you do so at the onset, before
ordering, just in case staff needs to confirm
with the management.
The author and publisher are not responsible
for any establishment reneging on their
commitment of a discount. However, we
would greatly appreciate your feedback on
this discount offer and welcome suggestions
to improve it.
Email us at: drivingholidays@yahoo.co.in

# Discount coupons

**Thai Cuisine Restaurant**

Thimphu

The only Thai food in town with authentic flavours

Thimphu

A classy restaurant with delicately flavoured multi cuisine

## 20% OFF
on food

**Wangchuk Hotel**

Thimphu

Good wholesome food at economical prices

## 20% OFF
on food

**Plums Café**

Thimphu

A happening place with the very best traditional cuisine

To entail the discount offered you need to present the book with the relevant coupon intact. Since this is a new concept, we suggest you do so at the onset, before ordering, just in case staff needs to confirm with the management.
The author and publisher are not responsible for any establishment reneging on their commitment of a discount. However, we would greatly appreciate your feedback on this discount offer and welcome suggestions to improve it.
Email us at: drivingholidays@yahoo.co.in

To entail the discount offered you need to present the book with the relevant coupon intact. Since this is a new concept, we suggest you do so at the onset, before ordering, just in case staff needs to confirm with the management.
The author and publisher are not responsible for any establishment reneging on their commitment of a discount. However, we would greatly appreciate your feedback on this discount offer and welcome suggestions to improve it.
Email us at: drivingholidays@yahoo.co.in

To entail the discount offered you need to present the book with the relevant coupon intact. Since this is a new concept, we suggest you do so at the onset, before ordering, just in case staff needs to confirm with the management.
The author and publisher are not responsible for any establishment reneging on their commitment of a discount. However, we would greatly appreciate your feedback on this discount offer and welcome suggestions to improve it.
Email us at: drivingholidays@yahoo.co.in

To entail the discount offered you need to present the book with the relevant coupon intact. Since this is a new concept, we suggest you do so at the onset, before ordering, just in case staff needs to confirm with the management.
The author and publisher are not responsible for any establishment reneging on their commitment of a discount. However, we would greatly appreciate your feedback on this discount offer and welcome suggestions to improve it.
Email us at: drivingholidays@yahoo.co.in

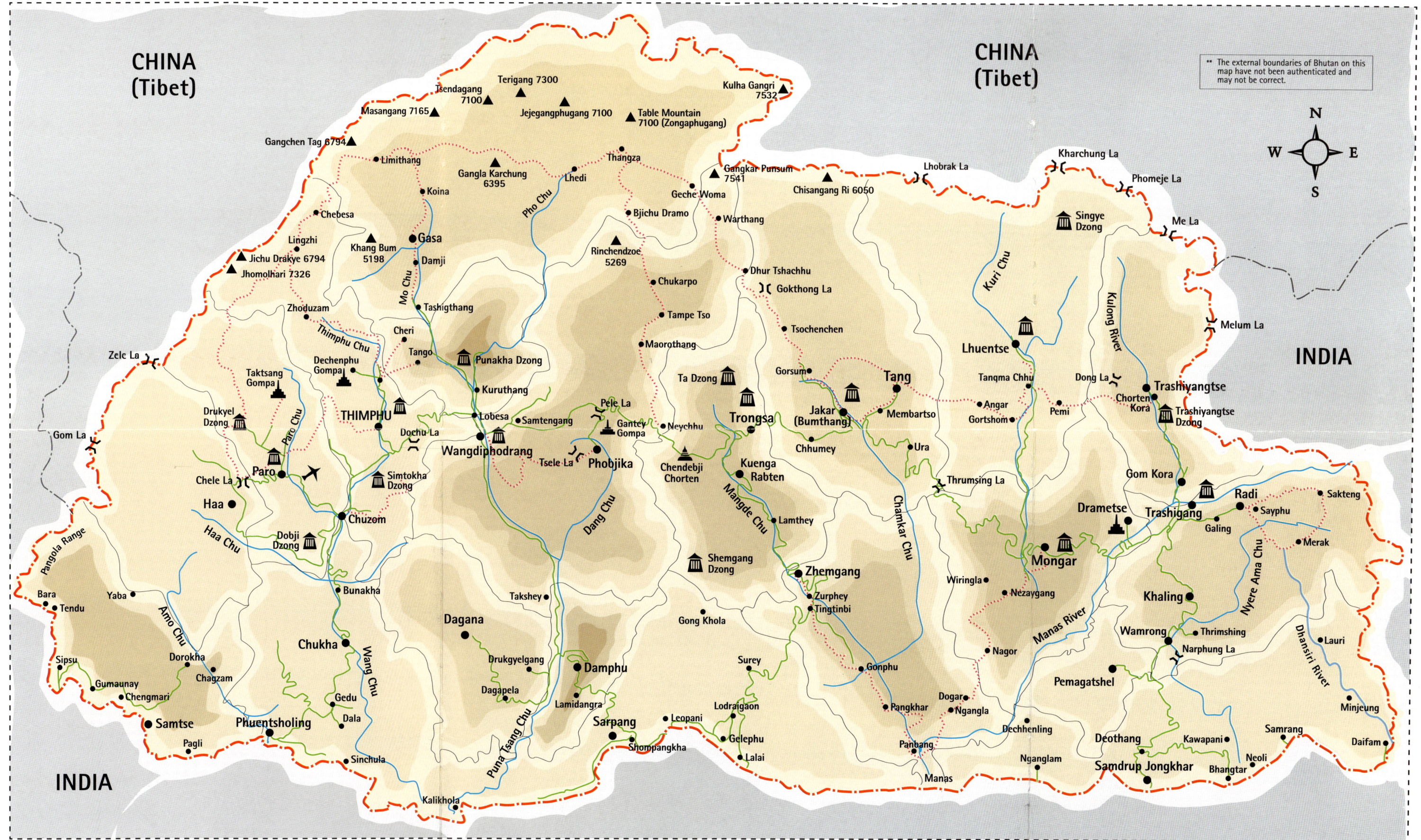